ATS-10   ADMISSION TEST SERIES

This is your
PASSBOOK for...

GRE

Graduate Record Examination - General (Aptitude) Test

Test Preparation Study Guide
Questions & Answers

NATIONAL LEARNING CORPORATION®

COPYRIGHT NOTICE

This book is SOLELY intended for, is sold ONLY to, and its use is RESTRICTED to individual, bona fide applicants or candidates who qualify by virtue of having seriously filed applications for appropriate license, certificate, professional and/or promotional advancement, higher school matriculation, scholarship, or other legitimate requirements of education and/or governmental authorities.

This book is NOT intended for use, class instruction, tutoring, training, duplication, copying, reprinting, excerption, or adaptation, etc., by:

1) Other publishers
2) Proprietors and/or Instructors of "Coaching" and/or Preparatory Courses
3) Personnel and/or Training Divisions of commercial, industrial, and governmental organizations
4) Schools, colleges, or universities and/or their departments and staffs, including teachers and other personnel
5) Testing Agencies or Bureaus
6) Study groups which seek by the purchase of a single volume to copy and/or duplicate and/or adapt this material for use by the group as a whole without having purchased individual volumes for each of the members of the group
7) Et al.

Such persons would be in violation of appropriate Federal and State statutes.

PROVISION OF LICENSING AGREEMENTS – Recognized educational, commercial, industrial, and governmental institutions and organizations, and others legitimately engaged in educational pursuits, including training, testing, and measurement activities, may address request for a licensing agreement to the copyright owners, who will determine whether, and under what conditions, including fees and charges, the materials in this book may be used them. In other words, a licensing facility exists for the legitimate use of the material in this book on other than an individual basis. However, it is asseverated and affirmed here that the material in this book CANNOT be used without the receipt of the express permission of such a licensing agreement from the Publishers. Inquiries re licensing should be addressed to the company, attention rights and permissions department.

All rights reserved, including the right of reproduction in whole or in part, in any form or by any means, electronic or mechanical, including photocopying, recording, or by any information storage and retrieval system, without permission in writing from the Publisher.

Copyright © 2025 by
National Learning Corporation

212 Michael Drive, Syosset, NY 11791
(516) 921-8888 • www.passbooks.com
E-mail: info@passbooks.com

PASSBOOK® SERIES

THE *PASSBOOK® SERIES* has been created to prepare applicants and candidates for the ultimate academic battlefield – the examination room.

At some time in our lives, each and every one of us may be required to take an examination – for validation, matriculation, admission, qualification, registration, certification, or licensure.

Based on the assumption that every applicant or candidate has met the basic formal educational standards, has taken the required number of courses, and read the necessary texts, the *PASSBOOK® SERIES* furnishes the one special preparation which may assure passing with confidence, instead of failing with insecurity. Examination questions – together with answers – are furnished as the basic vehicle for study so that the mysteries of the examination and its compounding difficulties may be eliminated or diminished by a sure method.

This book is meant to help you pass your examination provided that you qualify and are serious in your objective.

The entire field is reviewed through the huge store of content information which is succinctly presented through a provocative and challenging approach – the question-and-answer method.

A climate of success is established by furnishing the correct answers at the end of each test.

You soon learn to recognize types of questions, forms of questions, and patterns of questioning. You may even begin to anticipate expected outcomes.

You perceive that many questions are repeated or adapted so that you can gain acute insights, which may enable you to score many sure points.

You learn how to confront new questions, or types of questions, and to attack them confidently and work out the correct answers.

You note objectives and emphases, and recognize pitfalls and dangers, so that you may make positive educational adjustments.

Moreover, you are kept fully informed in relation to new concepts, methods, practices, and directions in the field.

You discover that you are actually taking the examination all the time: you are preparing for the examination by "taking" an examination, not by reading extraneous and/or supererogatory textbooks.

In short, this PASSBOOK®, used directedly, should be an important factor in helping you to pass your test.

GRADUATE RECORD EXAMINATION
GENERAL (APTITUDE) TEST

Topics Tested: Reading
                      Grammar
                      Vocabulary

Question Types: Sentence Completions
                      Analogies
                      Reading Comprehension
                      Antonyms

There is one scored verbal section with approximately 7 sentence completions, 7 analogies, 8 antonyms, and 8 reading comprehension questions. If the experimental section is also verbal, you will see two sections, but only one will be scored.

Sentence Completions
Sentence completion questions test how well you can determine the logic of a sentence. You are always shown a sentence with either one or two words missing. Your job is to pick the answer choice with the word, or words, that best fill the blank(s). You won't need any outside knowledge to answer these questions. In fact, bringing outside content knowledge to bear will probably only cause problems for you. All the information you need will be right there in the sentence itself.

Analogies
Analogies test your vocabulary and your understanding of word relationships. You will see a pair of words in capital letters that are related in some way. For instance: AIRPLANE: HANGAR. These are referred to as the "stem words." There are five answer choices, each consisting of another word pair. Your task is to identify the answer choice with the word pair that is related in the same way as the stem words.

Think carefully about the stem words and establish the relationship between them before looking at the answer choices. It helps to devise a word or phrase that relates the two words in a meaningful way. For instance, an AIRPLANE is stored or kept in a HANGAR. Likewise, money is stored or kept in a vault.

So this would be the correct answer. A choice like propeller: flight would not be correct, since the relationship of the two words is different—even though the two words are related to the general subject of planes and flying.

Antonyms
Antonyms present you with a single word followed by five answer choices containing words or short phrases. Your task is to find the answer choice that's most nearly opposite in meaning to the original word. These questions obviously test vocabulary. So if yours could use some work, spend time improving it.

Reading Comprehension
Reading Comprehension is a staple of standardized tests, so you've probably seen this type of question before on the SAT. Expect GRE passages to be tougher and more dense, and often kind of dull. These passages are taken from three broad areas: social sciences, natural sciences, and humanities. Essentially, Reading Comprehension is meant to test your ability to grasp the content of written material and make some quick conclusions about it. You'll see questions about the main idea of a passage, its inferences, arguments, tone, or about specific details in the passage. Don't make the mistake of poring over a passage trying to memorize details. Instead, read through a passage briskly, actively, and strategically. Pay attention to the topic and scope of the passage as you read.

Analytical Writing Section

Topics Tested:
- Grammar
- Writing Ability
- Persuasive Argument

Question Types:
- Analysis of an Issue
- Analysis of an Argument

The goal of the GRE's Analytical Writing Section is to gauge how well you can provide cogent written responses to complex ideas and issues. It tests the kind of high-level thinking and writing skills that are generally viewed as essential for success in most graduate school programs.

Structure
The Analytical Writing Section consists of two analytical writing tasks.

A 45-minute "Present Your Perspective on an Issue" task. The "issue" task states an opinion on an issue of broad interest and asks test takers to address the issue from any perspective.

A 30-minute "Analyze an Argument" task. The "argument" task requires test takers to critique an argument by discussing how well reasoned they find it.

Each essay in the AWM will be scored from 0-6, though students will only receive a single score for both essays; individual essay scores will not be reported.

Quantitative Section

Topics Tested:
- Basic Math
- Mathematical Concepts
- Quantitative Reasoning

Question Types:
- Problem Solving
- Quantitative Comparisons

There is one scored math section consisting of 14 quantitative comparisons and 14 problem solving questions, of which 3 or 4 will be graph questions. If your experimental section is also quantitative, you will have two quantitative sections, only one of which will be scored.

Quantitative Comparisons
Quantitative Comparisons do not require you to solve for a particular value; rather they ask you to compare two quantities and try to determine which, if either, is larger. Each quantitative comparison displays two mathematical expressions in boxes—one in Column A and one in Column B. Sometimes additional information is provided. It's usually centered right above the two quantities.

Problem Solving
Problem solving questions test various math concepts, including percentages, simultaneous equations, symbolism, special triangles, multiple and odd-ball figures, mean, median, mode, range, and probability Several problem solving questions test your ability to read graphs, interpret data, and solve math proble When working with graphs, first look carefully at the data and understand how it's presented. Read the titles and check the scales to see how the information is measured and watch for any accompanying notes.

HOW TO TAKE A TEST

I. YOU MUST PASS AN EXAMINATION

A. WHAT EVERY CANDIDATE SHOULD KNOW

Examination applicants often ask us for help in preparing for the written test. What can I study in advance? What kinds of questions will be asked? How will the test be given? How will the papers be graded?

As an applicant for a civil service examination, you may be wondering about some of these things. Our purpose here is to suggest effective methods of advance study and to describe civil service examinations.

Your chances for success on this examination can be increased if you know how to prepare. Those "pre-examination jitters" can be reduced if you know what to expect. You can even experience an adventure in good citizenship if you know why civil service exams are given.

B. WHY ARE CIVIL SERVICE EXAMINATIONS GIVEN?

Civil service examinations are important to you in two ways. As a citizen, you want public jobs filled by employees who know how to do their work. As a job seeker, you want a fair chance to compete for that job on an equal footing with other candidates. The best-known means of accomplishing this two-fold goal is the competitive examination.

Exams are widely publicized throughout the nation. They may be administered for jobs in federal, state, city, municipal, town or village governments or agencies.

Any citizen may apply, with some limitations, such as the age or residence of applicants. Your experience and education may be reviewed to see whether you meet the requirements for the particular examination. When these requirements exist, they are reasonable and applied consistently to all applicants. Thus, a competitive examination may cause you some uneasiness now, but it is your privilege and safeguard.

C. HOW ARE CIVIL SERVICE EXAMS DEVELOPED?

Examinations are carefully written by trained technicians who are specialists in the field known as "psychological measurement," in consultation with recognized authorities in the field of work that the test will cover. These experts recommend the subject matter areas or skills to be tested; only those knowledges or skills important to your success on the job are included. The most reliable books and source materials available are used as references. Together, the experts and technicians judge the difficulty level of the questions.

Test technicians know how to phrase questions so that the problem is clearly stated. Their ethics do not permit "trick" or "catch" questions. Questions may have been tried out on sample groups, or subjected to statistical analysis, to determine their usefulness.

Written tests are often used in combination with performance tests, ratings of training and experience, and oral interviews. All of these measures combine to form the best-known means of finding the right person for the right job.

II. HOW TO PASS THE WRITTEN TEST

A. NATURE OF THE EXAMINATION

To prepare intelligently for civil service examinations, you should know how they differ from school examinations you have taken. In school you were assigned certain definite pages to read or subjects to cover. The examination questions were quite detailed and usually emphasized memory. Civil service exams, on the other hand, try to discover your present ability to perform the duties of a position, plus your potentiality to learn these duties. In other words, a civil service exam attempts to predict how successful you will be. Questions cover such a broad area that they cannot be as minute and detailed as school exam questions.

In the public service similar kinds of work, or positions, are grouped together in one "class." This process is known as *position-classification*. All the positions in a class are paid according to the salary range for that class. One class title covers all of these positions, and they are all tested by the same examination.

B. FOUR BASIC STEPS

1) Study the announcement

How, then, can you know what subjects to study? Our best answer is: "Learn as much as possible about the class of positions for which you've applied." The exam will test the knowledge, skills and abilities needed to do the work.

Your most valuable source of information about the position you want is the official exam announcement. This announcement lists the training and experience qualifications. Check these standards and apply only if you come reasonably close to meeting them.

The brief description of the position in the examination announcement offers some clues to the subjects which will be tested. Think about the job itself. Review the duties in your mind. Can you perform them, or are there some in which you are rusty? Fill in the blank spots in your preparation.

Many jurisdictions preview the written test in the exam announcement by including a section called "Knowledge and Abilities Required," "Scope of the Examination," or some similar heading. Here you will find out specifically what fields will be tested.

2) Review your own background

Once you learn in general what the position is all about, and what you need to know to do the work, ask yourself which subjects you already know fairly well and which need improvement. You may wonder whether to concentrate on improving your strong areas or on building some background in your fields of weakness. When the announcement has specified "some knowledge" or "considerable knowledge," or has used adjectives like "beginning principles of…" or "advanced … methods," you can get a clue as to the number and difficulty of questions to be asked in any given field. More questions, and hence broader coverage, would be included for those subjects which are more important in the work. Now weigh your strengths and weaknesses against the job requirements and prepare accordingly.

3) Determine the level of the position

Another way to tell how intensively you should prepare is to understand the level of the job for which you are applying. Is it the entering level? In other words, is this the position in which beginners in a field of work are hired? Or is it an intermediate or advanced level? Sometimes this is indicated by such words as "Junior" or "Senior" in the class title. Other jurisdictions use Roman numerals to designate the level – Clerk I, Clerk II, for example. The word "Supervisor" sometimes appears in the title. If the level is not indicated by the title, check the description of duties. Will you be working under very close supervision, or will you have responsibility for independent decisions in this work?

4) Choose appropriate study materials

Now that you know the subjects to be examined and the relative amount of each subject to be covered, you can choose suitable study materials. For beginning level jobs, or even advanced ones, if you have a pronounced weakness in some aspect of your training, read a modern, standard textbook in that field. Be sure it is up to date and has general coverage. Such books are normally available at your library, and the librarian will be glad to help you locate one. For entry-level positions, questions of appropriate difficulty are chosen – neither highly advanced questions, nor those too simple. Such questions require careful thought but not advanced training.

If the position for which you are applying is technical or advanced, you will read more advanced, specialized material. If you are already familiar with the basic principles of your field, elementary textbooks would waste your time. Concentrate on advanced textbooks and technical periodicals. Think through the concepts and review difficult problems in your field.

These are all general sources. You can get more ideas on your own initiative, following these leads. For example, training manuals and publications of the government agency which employs workers in your field can be useful, particularly for technical and professional positions. A letter or visit to the government department involved may result in more specific study suggestions, and certainly will provide you with a more definite idea of the exact nature of the position you are seeking.

III. KINDS OF TESTS

Tests are used for purposes other than measuring knowledge and ability to perform specified duties. For some positions, it is equally important to test ability to make adjustments to new situations or to profit from training. In others, basic mental abilities not dependent on information are essential. Questions which test these things may not appear as pertinent to the duties of the position as those which test for knowledge and information. Yet they are often highly important parts of a fair examination. For very general questions, it is almost impossible to help you direct your study efforts. What we can do is to point out some of the more common of these general abilities needed in public service positions and describe some typical questions.

1) General information

Broad, general information has been found useful for predicting job success in some kinds of work. This is tested in a variety of ways, from vocabulary lists to questions about current events. Basic background in some field of work, such as sociology or economics, may be sampled in a group of questions. Often these are principles which have become familiar to most persons through exposure rather than through formal training. It is difficult to advise you how to study for these questions; being alert to the world around you is our best suggestion.

2) Verbal ability

An example of an ability needed in many positions is verbal or language ability. Verbal ability is, in brief, the ability to use and understand words. Vocabulary and grammar tests are typical measures of this ability. Reading comprehension or paragraph interpretation questions are common in many kinds of civil service tests. You are given a paragraph of written material and asked to find its central meaning.

3) Numerical ability

Number skills can be tested by the familiar arithmetic problem, by checking paired lists of numbers to see which are alike and which are different, or by interpreting charts and graphs. In the latter test, a graph may be printed in the test booklet which you are asked to use as the basis for answering questions.

4) Observation

A popular test for law-enforcement positions is the observation test. A picture is shown to you for several minutes, then taken away. Questions about the picture test your ability to observe both details and larger elements.

5) Following directions

In many positions in the public service, the employee must be able to carry out written instructions dependably and accurately. You may be given a chart with several columns, each column listing a variety of information. The questions require you to carry out directions involving the information given in the chart.

6) Skills and aptitudes

Performance tests effectively measure some manual skills and aptitudes. When the skill is one in which you are trained, such as typing or shorthand, you can practice. These tests are often very much like those given in business school or high school courses. For many of the other skills and aptitudes, however, no short-time preparation can be made. Skills and abilities natural to you or that you have developed throughout your lifetime are being tested.

Many of the general questions just described provide all the data needed to answer the questions and ask you to use your reasoning ability to find the answers. Your best preparation for these tests, as well as for tests of facts and ideas, is to be at your physical and mental best. You, no doubt, have your own methods of getting into an exam-taking mood and keeping "in shape." The next section lists some ideas on this subject.

IV. KINDS OF QUESTIONS

Only rarely is the "essay" question, which you answer in narrative form, used in civil service tests. Civil service tests are usually of the short-answer type. Full instructions for answering these questions will be given to you at the examination. But in case this is your first experience with short-answer questions and separate answer sheets, here is what you need to know:

1) Multiple-choice Questions

Most popular of the short-answer questions is the "multiple choice" or "best answer" question. It can be used, for example, to test for factual knowledge, ability to solve problems or judgment in meeting situations found at work.

A multiple-choice question is normally one of three types—
- It can begin with an incomplete statement followed by several possible endings. You are to find the one ending which *best* completes the statement, although some of the others may not be entirely wrong.
- It can also be a complete statement in the form of a question which is answered by choosing one of the statements listed.

- It can be in the form of a problem – again you select the best answer.

Here is an example of a multiple-choice question with a discussion which should give you some clues as to the method for choosing the right answer:

When an employee has a complaint about his assignment, the action which will *best* help him overcome his difficulty is to
   A. discuss his difficulty with his coworkers
   B. take the problem to the head of the organization
   C. take the problem to the person who gave him the assignment
   D. say nothing to anyone about his complaint

In answering this question, you should study each of the choices to find which is best. Consider choice "A" – Certainly an employee may discuss his complaint with fellow employees, but no change or improvement can result, and the complaint remains unresolved. Choice "B" is a poor choice since the head of the organization probably does not know what assignment you have been given, and taking your problem to him is known as "going over the head" of the supervisor. The supervisor, or person who made the assignment, is the person who can clarify it or correct any injustice. Choice "C" is, therefore, correct. To say nothing, as in choice "D," is unwise. Supervisors have and interest in knowing the problems employees are facing, and the employee is seeking a solution to his problem.

2) True/False Questions

The "true/false" or "right/wrong" form of question is sometimes used. Here a complete statement is given. Your job is to decide whether the statement is right or wrong.

SAMPLE: A roaming cell-phone call to a nearby city costs less than a non-roaming call to a distant city.

This statement is wrong, or false, since roaming calls are more expensive.

This is not a complete list of all possible question forms, although most of the others are variations of these common types. You will always get complete directions for answering questions. Be sure you understand *how* to mark your answers – ask questions until you do.

V. RECORDING YOUR ANSWERS

Computer terminals are used more and more today for many different kinds of exams.
For an examination with very few applicants, you may be told to record your answers in the test booklet itself. Separate answer sheets are much more common. If this separate answer sheet is to be scored by machine – and this is often the case – it is highly important that you mark your answers correctly in order to get credit.

An electronic scoring machine is often used in civil service offices because of the speed with which papers can be scored. Machine-scored answer sheets must be marked with a pencil, which will be given to you. This pencil has a high graphite content which responds to the electronic scoring machine. As a matter of fact, stray dots may register as answers, so do not let your pencil rest on the answer sheet while you are pondering the correct answer. Also, if your pencil lead breaks or is otherwise defective, ask for another.

Since the answer sheet will be dropped in a slot in the scoring machine, be careful not to bend the corners or get the paper crumpled.

The answer sheet normally has five vertical columns of numbers, with 30 numbers to a column. These numbers correspond to the question numbers in your test booklet. After each number, going across the page are four or five pairs of dotted lines. These short dotted lines have small letters or numbers above them. The first two pairs may also have a "T" or "F" above the letters. This indicates that the first two pairs only are to be used if the questions are of the true-false type. If the questions are multiple choice, disregard the "T" and "F" and pay attention only to the small letters or numbers.

Answer your questions in the manner of the sample that follows:

32. The largest city in the United States is
    A. Washington, D.C.
    B. New York City
    C. Chicago
    D. Detroit
    E. San Francisco

1) Choose the answer you think is best. (New York City is the largest, so "B" is correct.)
2) Find the row of dotted lines numbered the same as the question you are answering. (Find row number 32)
3) Find the pair of dotted lines corresponding to the answer. (Find the pair of lines under the mark "B.")
4) Make a solid black mark between the dotted lines.

VI. BEFORE THE TEST

Common sense will help you find procedures to follow to get ready for an examination. Too many of us, however, overlook these sensible measures. Indeed, nervousness and fatigue have been found to be the most serious reasons why applicants fail to do their best on civil service tests. Here is a list of reminders:

- Begin your preparation early – Don't wait until the last minute to go scurrying around for books and materials or to find out what the position is all about.
- Prepare continuously – An hour a night for a week is better than an all-night cram session. This has been definitely established. What is more, a night a week for a month will return better dividends than crowding your study into a shorter period of time.
- Locate the place of the exam – You have been sent a notice telling you when and where to report for the examination. If the location is in a different town or otherwise unfamiliar to you, it would be well to inquire the best route and learn something about the building.
- Relax the night before the test – Allow your mind to rest. Do not study at all that night. Plan some mild recreation or diversion; then go to bed early and get a good night's sleep.
- Get up early enough to make a leisurely trip to the place for the test – This way unforeseen events, traffic snarls, unfamiliar buildings, etc. will not upset you.
- Dress comfortably – A written test is not a fashion show. You will be known by number and not by name, so wear something comfortable.

- Leave excess paraphernalia at home – Shopping bags and odd bundles will get in your way. You need bring only the items mentioned in the official notice you received; usually everything you need is provided. Do not bring reference books to the exam. They will only confuse those last minutes and be taken away from you when in the test room.
- Arrive somewhat ahead of time – If because of transportation schedules you must get there very early, bring a newspaper or magazine to take your mind off yourself while waiting.
- Locate the examination room – When you have found the proper room, you will be directed to the seat or part of the room where you will sit. Sometimes you are given a sheet of instructions to read while you are waiting. Do not fill out any forms until you are told to do so; just read them and be prepared.
- Relax and prepare to listen to the instructions
- If you have any physical problem that may keep you from doing your best, be sure to tell the test administrator. If you are sick or in poor health, you really cannot do your best on the exam. You can come back and take the test some other time.

VII. AT THE TEST

The day of the test is here and you have the test booklet in your hand. The temptation to get going is very strong. Caution! There is more to success than knowing the right answers. You must know how to identify your papers and understand variations in the type of short-answer question used in this particular examination. Follow these suggestions for maximum results from your efforts:

1) Cooperate with the monitor

The test administrator has a duty to create a situation in which you can be as much at ease as possible. He will give instructions, tell you when to begin, check to see that you are marking your answer sheet correctly, and so on. He is not there to guard you, although he will see that your competitors do not take unfair advantage. He wants to help you do your best.

2) Listen to all instructions

Don't jump the gun! Wait until you understand all directions. In most civil service tests you get more time than you need to answer the questions. So don't be in a hurry. Read each word of instructions until you clearly understand the meaning. Study the examples, listen to all announcements and follow directions. Ask questions if you do not understand what to do.

3) Identify your papers

Civil service exams are usually identified by number only. You will be assigned a number; you must not put your name on your test papers. Be sure to copy your number correctly. Since more than one exam may be given, copy your exact examination title.

4) Plan your time

Unless you are told that a test is a "speed" or "rate of work" test, speed itself is usually not important. Time enough to answer all the questions will be provided, but this does not mean that you have all day. An overall time limit has been set. Divide the total time (in minutes) by the number of questions to determine the approximate time you have for each question.

5) Do not linger over difficult questions

If you come across a difficult question, mark it with a paper clip (useful to have along) and come back to it when you have been through the booklet. One caution if you do this – be sure to skip a number on your answer sheet as well. Check often to be sure that you have not lost your place and that you are marking in the row numbered the same as the question you are answering.

6) Read the questions

Be sure you know what the question asks! Many capable people are unsuccessful because they failed to *read* the questions correctly.

7) Answer all questions

Unless you have been instructed that a penalty will be deducted for incorrect answers, it is better to guess than to omit a question.

8) Speed tests

It is often better NOT to guess on speed tests. It has been found that on timed tests people are tempted to spend the last few seconds before time is called in marking answers at random – without even reading them – in the hope of picking up a few extra points. To discourage this practice, the instructions may warn you that your score will be "corrected" for guessing. That is, a penalty will be applied. The incorrect answers will be deducted from the correct ones, or some other penalty formula will be used.

9) Review your answers

If you finish before time is called, go back to the questions you guessed or omitted to give them further thought. Review other answers if you have time.

10) Return your test materials

If you are ready to leave before others have finished or time is called, take ALL your materials to the monitor and leave quietly. Never take any test material with you. The monitor can discover whose papers are not complete, and taking a test booklet may be grounds for disqualification.

VIII. EXAMINATION TECHNIQUES

1) Read the general instructions carefully. These are usually printed on the first page of the exam booklet. As a rule, these instructions refer to the timing of the examination; the fact that you should not start work until the signal and must stop work at a signal, etc. If there are any *special* instructions, such as a choice of questions to be answered, make sure that you note this instruction carefully.

2) When you are ready to start work on the examination, that is as soon as the signal has been given, read the instructions to each question booklet, underline any key words or phrases, such as *least, best, outline, describe* and the like. In this way you will tend to answer as requested rather than discover on reviewing your paper that you *listed without describing*, that you selected the *worst* choice rather than the *best* choice, etc.

3) If the examination is of the objective or multiple-choice type – that is, each question will also give a series of possible answers: A, B, C or D, and you are called upon to select the best answer and write the letter next to that answer on your answer paper – it is advisable to start answering each question in turn. There may be anywhere from 50 to 100 such questions in the three or four hours allotted and you can see how much time would be taken if you read through all the questions before beginning to answer any. Furthermore, if you come across a question or group of questions which you know would be difficult to answer, it would undoubtedly affect your handling of all the other questions.

4) If the examination is of the essay type and contains but a few questions, it is a moot point as to whether you should read all the questions before starting to answer any one. Of course, if you are given a choice – say five out of seven and the like – then it is essential to read all the questions so you can eliminate the two that are most difficult. If, however, you are asked to answer all the questions, there may be danger in trying to answer the easiest one first because you may find that you will spend too much time on it. The best technique is to answer the first question, then proceed to the second, etc.

5) Time your answers. Before the exam begins, write down the time it started, then add the time allowed for the examination and write down the time it must be completed, then divide the time available somewhat as follows:
   - If 3-1/2 hours are allowed, that would be 210 minutes. If you have 80 objective-type questions, that would be an average of 2-1/2 minutes per question. Allow yourself no more than 2 minutes per question, or a total of 160 minutes, which will permit about 50 minutes to review.
   - If for the time allotment of 210 minutes there are 7 essay questions to answer, that would average about 30 minutes a question. Give yourself only 25 minutes per question so that you have about 35 minutes to review.

6) The most important instruction is to *read each question* and make sure you know what is wanted. The second most important instruction is to *time yourself properly* so that you answer every question. The third most important instruction is to *answer every question*. Guess if you have to but include something for each question. Remember that you will receive no credit for a blank and will probably receive some credit if you write something in answer to an essay question. If you guess a letter – say "B" for a multiple-choice question – you may have guessed right. If you leave a blank as an answer to a multiple-choice question, the examiners may respect your feelings but it will not add a point to your score. Some exams may penalize you for wrong answers, so in such cases *only*, you may not want to guess unless you have some basis for your answer.

7) Suggestions
   a. Objective-type questions
      1. Examine the question booklet for proper sequence of pages and questions
      2. Read all instructions carefully
      3. Skip any question which seems too difficult; return to it after all other questions have been answered
      4. Apportion your time properly; do not spend too much time on any single question or group of questions

5. Note and underline key words – *all, most, fewest, least, best, worst, same, opposite,* etc.
6. Pay particular attention to negatives
7. Note unusual option, e.g., unduly long, short, complex, different or similar in content to the body of the question
8. Observe the use of "hedging" words – *probably, may, most likely,* etc.
9. Make sure that your answer is put next to the same number as the question
10. Do not second-guess unless you have good reason to believe the second answer is definitely more correct
11. Cross out original answer if you decide another answer is more accurate; do not erase until you are ready to hand your paper in
12. Answer all questions; guess unless instructed otherwise
13. Leave time for review

b. Essay questions
   1. Read each question carefully
   2. Determine exactly what is wanted. Underline key words or phrases.
   3. Decide on outline or paragraph answer
   4. Include many different points and elements unless asked to develop any one or two points or elements
   5. Show impartiality by giving pros and cons unless directed to select one side only
   6. Make and write down any assumptions you find necessary to answer the questions
   7. Watch your English, grammar, punctuation and choice of words
   8. Time your answers; don't crowd material

8) Answering the essay question

Most essay questions can be answered by framing the specific response around several key words or ideas. Here are a few such key words or ideas:

M's: manpower, materials, methods, money, management
P's: purpose, program, policy, plan, procedure, practice, problems, pitfalls, personnel, public relations

   a. Six basic steps in handling problems:
      1. Preliminary plan and background development
      2. Collect information, data and facts
      3. Analyze and interpret information, data and facts
      4. Analyze and develop solutions as well as make recommendations
      5. Prepare report and sell recommendations
      6. Install recommendations and follow up effectiveness

   b. Pitfalls to avoid
      1. *Taking things for granted* – A statement of the situation does not necessarily imply that each of the elements is necessarily true; for example, a complaint may be invalid and biased so that all that can be taken for granted is that a complaint has been registered

2. *Considering only one side of a situation* – Wherever possible, indicate several alternatives and then point out the reasons you selected the best one
3. *Failing to indicate follow up* – Whenever your answer indicates action on your part, make certain that you will take proper follow-up action to see how successful your recommendations, procedures or actions turn out to be
4. *Taking too long in answering any single question* – Remember to time your answers properly

IX. AFTER THE TEST

Scoring procedures differ in detail among civil service jurisdictions although the general principles are the same. Whether the papers are hand-scored or graded by machine we have described, they are nearly always graded by number. That is, the person who marks the paper knows only the number – never the name – of the applicant. Not until all the papers have been graded will they be matched with names. If other tests, such as training and experience or oral interview ratings have been given, scores will be combined. Different parts of the examination usually have different weights. For example, the written test might count 60 percent of the final grade, and a rating of training and experience 40 percent. In many jurisdictions, veterans will have a certain number of points added to their grades.

After the final grade has been determined, the names are placed in grade order and an eligible list is established. There are various methods for resolving ties between those who get the same final grade – probably the most common is to place first the name of the person whose application was received first. Job offers are made from the eligible list in the order the names appear on it. You will be notified of your grade and your rank as soon as all these computations have been made. This will be done as rapidly as possible.

People who are found to meet the requirements in the announcement are called "eligibles." Their names are put on a list of eligible candidates. An eligible's chances of getting a job depend on how high he stands on this list and how fast agencies are filling jobs from the list.

When a job is to be filled from a list of eligibles, the agency asks for the names of people on the list of eligibles for that job. When the civil service commission receives this request, it sends to the agency the names of the three people highest on this list. Or, if the job to be filled has specialized requirements, the office sends the agency the names of the top three persons who meet these requirements from the general list.

The appointing officer makes a choice from among the three people whose names were sent to him. If the selected person accepts the appointment, the names of the others are put back on the list to be considered for future openings.

That is the rule in hiring from all kinds of eligible lists, whether they are for typist, carpenter, chemist, or something else. For every vacancy, the appointing officer has his choice of any one of the top three eligibles on the list. This explains why the person whose name is on top of the list sometimes does not get an appointment when some of the persons lower on the list do. If the appointing officer chooses the second or third eligible, the No. 1 eligible does not get a job at once, but stays on the list until he is appointed or the list is terminated.

X. HOW TO PASS THE INTERVIEW TEST

The examination for which you applied requires an oral interview test. You have already taken the written test and you are now being called for the interview test – the final part of the formal examination.

You may think that it is not possible to prepare for an interview test and that there are no procedures to follow during an interview. Our purpose is to point out some things you can do in advance that will help you and some good rules to follow and pitfalls to avoid while you are being interviewed.

What is an interview supposed to test?

The written examination is designed to test the technical knowledge and competence of the candidate; the oral is designed to evaluate intangible qualities, not readily measured otherwise, and to establish a list showing the relative fitness of each candidate – as measured against his competitors – for the position sought. Scoring is not on the basis of "right" and "wrong," but on a sliding scale of values ranging from "not passable" to "outstanding." As a matter of fact, it is possible to achieve a relatively low score without a single "incorrect" answer because of evident weakness in the qualities being measured.

Occasionally, an examination may consist entirely of an oral test – either an individual or a group oral. In such cases, information is sought concerning the technical knowledges and abilities of the candidate, since there has been no written examination for this purpose. More commonly, however, an oral test is used to supplement a written examination.

Who conducts interviews?

The composition of oral boards varies among different jurisdictions. In nearly all, a representative of the personnel department serves as chairman. One of the members of the board may be a representative of the department in which the candidate would work. In some cases, "outside experts" are used, and, frequently, a businessman or some other representative of the general public is asked to serve. Labor and management or other special groups may be represented. The aim is to secure the services of experts in the appropriate field.

However the board is composed, it is a good idea (and not at all improper or unethical) to ascertain in advance of the interview who the members are and what groups they represent. When you are introduced to them, you will have some idea of their backgrounds and interests, and at least you will not stutter and stammer over their names.

What should be done before the interview?

While knowledge about the board members is useful and takes some of the surprise element out of the interview, there is other preparation which is more substantive. It *is* possible to prepare for an oral interview – in several ways:

1) Keep a copy of your application and review it carefully before the interview

This may be the only document before the oral board, and the starting point of the interview. Know what education and experience you have listed there, and the sequence and dates of all of it. Sometimes the board will ask you to review the highlights of your experience for them; you should not have to hem and haw doing it.

2) Study the class specification and the examination announcement

Usually, the oral board has one or both of these to guide them. The qualities, characteristics or knowledges required by the position sought are stated in these documents. They offer valuable clues as to the nature of the oral interview. For example, if the job involves supervisory responsibilities, the announcement will usually indicate that knowledge of modern supervisory methods and the qualifications of the candidate as a supervisor will be tested. If so, you can expect such questions, frequently in the form of a hypothetical situation which you are expected to solve. NEVER go into an oral without knowledge of the duties and responsibilities of the job you seek.

3) Think through each qualification required

Try to visualize the kind of questions you would ask if you were a board member. How well could you answer them? Try especially to appraise your own knowledge and background in each area, *measured against the job sought*, and identify any areas in which you are weak. Be critical and realistic – do not flatter yourself.

4) Do some general reading in areas in which you feel you may be weak

For example, if the job involves supervision and your past experience has NOT, some general reading in supervisory methods and practices, particularly in the field of human relations, might be useful. Do NOT study agency procedures or detailed manuals. The oral board will be testing your understanding and capacity, not your memory.

5) Get a good night's sleep and watch your general health and mental attitude

You will want a clear head at the interview. Take care of a cold or any other minor ailment, and of course, no hangovers.

What should be done on the day of the interview?

Now comes the day of the interview itself. Give yourself plenty of time to get there. Plan to arrive somewhat ahead of the scheduled time, particularly if your appointment is in the fore part of the day. If a previous candidate fails to appear, the board might be ready for you a bit early. By early afternoon an oral board is almost invariably behind schedule if there are many candidates, and you may have to wait. Take along a book or magazine to read, or your application to review, but leave any extraneous material in the waiting room when you go in for your interview. In any event, relax and compose yourself.

The matter of dress is important. The board is forming impressions about you – from your experience, your manners, your attitude, and your appearance. Give your personal appearance careful attention. Dress your best, but not your flashiest. Choose conservative, appropriate clothing, and be sure it is immaculate. This is a business interview, and your appearance should indicate that you regard it as such. Besides, being well groomed and properly dressed will help boost your confidence.

Sooner or later, someone will call your name and escort you into the interview room. *This is it.* From here on you are on your own. It is too late for any more preparation. But remember, you asked for this opportunity to prove your fitness, and you are here because your request was granted.

What happens when you go in?

The usual sequence of events will be as follows: The clerk (who is often the board stenographer) will introduce you to the chairman of the oral board, who will introduce you to the other members of the board. Acknowledge the introductions before you sit down. Do not be surprised if you find a microphone facing you or a stenotypist sitting by. Oral interviews are usually recorded in the event of an appeal or other review.

Usually the chairman of the board will open the interview by reviewing the highlights of your education and work experience from your application – primarily for the benefit of the other members of the board, as well as to get the material into the record. Do not interrupt or comment unless there is an error or significant misinterpretation; if that is the case, do not hesitate. But do not quibble about insignificant matters. Also, he will usually ask you some question about your education, experience or your present job – partly to get you to start talking and to establish the interviewing "rapport." He may start the actual questioning, or turn it over to one of the other members. Frequently, each member undertakes the questioning on a particular area, one in which he is perhaps most competent, so you can expect each member to participate in the examination. Because time is limited, you may also expect some rather abrupt switches in the direction the questioning takes, so do not be upset by it. Normally, a board member will not pursue a single line of questioning unless he discovers a particular strength or weakness.

After each member has participated, the chairman will usually ask whether any member has any further questions, then will ask you if you have anything you wish to add. Unless you are expecting this question, it may floor you. Worse, it may start you off on an extended, extemporaneous speech. The board is not usually seeking more information. The question is principally to offer you a last opportunity to present further qualifications or to indicate that you have nothing to add. So, if you feel that a significant qualification or characteristic has been overlooked, it is proper to point it out in a sentence or so. Do not compliment the board on the thoroughness of their examination – they have been sketchy, and you know it. If you wish, merely say, "No thank you, I have nothing further to add." This is a point where you can "talk yourself out" of a good impression or fail to present an important bit of information. Remember, *you close the interview yourself*.

The chairman will then say, "That is all, Mr. _____, thank you." Do not be startled; the interview is over, and quicker than you think. Thank him, gather your belongings and take your leave. Save your sigh of relief for the other side of the door.

How to put your best foot forward

Throughout this entire process, you may feel that the board individually and collectively is trying to pierce your defenses, seek out your hidden weaknesses and embarrass and confuse you. Actually, this is not true. They are obliged to make an appraisal of your qualifications for the job you are seeking, and they want to see you in your best light. Remember, they must interview all candidates and a non-cooperative candidate may become a failure in spite of their best efforts to bring out his qualifications. Here are 15 suggestions that will help you:

1) Be natural – Keep your attitude confident, not cocky

If you are not confident that you can do the job, do not expect the board to be. Do not apologize for your weaknesses, try to bring out your strong points. The board is interested in a positive, not negative, presentation. Cockiness will antagonize any board member and make him wonder if you are covering up a weakness by a false show of strength.

2) Get comfortable, but don't lounge or sprawl

Sit erectly but not stiffly. A careless posture may lead the board to conclude that you are careless in other things, or at least that you are not impressed by the importance of the occasion. Either conclusion is natural, even if incorrect. Do not fuss with your clothing, a pencil or an ashtray. Your hands may occasionally be useful to emphasize a point; do not let them become a point of distraction.

3) Do not wisecrack or make small talk

This is a serious situation, and your attitude should show that you consider it as such. Further, the time of the board is limited – they do not want to waste it, and neither should you.

4) Do not exaggerate your experience or abilities

In the first place, from information in the application or other interviews and sources, the board may know more about you than you think. Secondly, you probably will not get away with it. An experienced board is rather adept at spotting such a situation, so do not take the chance.

5) If you know a board member, do not make a point of it, yet do not hide it

Certainly you are not fooling him, and probably not the other members of the board. Do not try to take advantage of your acquaintanceship – it will probably do you little good.

6) Do not dominate the interview

Let the board do that. They will give you the clues – do not assume that you have to do all the talking. Realize that the board has a number of questions to ask you, and do not try to take up all the interview time by showing off your extensive knowledge of the answer to the first one.

7) Be attentive

You only have 20 minutes or so, and you should keep your attention at its sharpest throughout. When a member is addressing a problem or question to you, give him your undivided attention. Address your reply principally to him, but do not exclude the other board members.

8) Do not interrupt

A board member may be stating a problem for you to analyze. He will ask you a question when the time comes. Let him state the problem, and wait for the question.

9) Make sure you understand the question

Do not try to answer until you are sure what the question is. If it is not clear, restate it in your own words or ask the board member to clarify it for you. However, do not haggle about minor elements.

10) Reply promptly but not hastily

A common entry on oral board rating sheets is "candidate responded readily," or "candidate hesitated in replies." Respond as promptly and quickly as you can, but do not jump to a hasty, ill-considered answer.

11) Do not be peremptory in your answers

A brief answer is proper – but do not fire your answer back. That is a losing game from your point of view. The board member can probably ask questions much faster than you can answer them.

12) Do not try to create the answer you think the board member wants

He is interested in what kind of mind you have and how it works – not in playing games. Furthermore, he can usually spot this practice and will actually grade you down on it.

13) Do not switch sides in your reply merely to agree with a board member

Frequently, a member will take a contrary position merely to draw you out and to see if you are willing and able to defend your point of view. Do not start a debate, yet do not surrender a good position. If a position is worth taking, it is worth defending.

14) Do not be afraid to admit an error in judgment if you are shown to be wrong

The board knows that you are forced to reply without any opportunity for careful consideration. Your answer may be demonstrably wrong. If so, admit it and get on with the interview.

15) Do not dwell at length on your present job

The opening question may relate to your present assignment. Answer the question but do not go into an extended discussion. You are being examined for a *new* job, not your present one. As a matter of fact, try to phrase ALL your answers in terms of the job for which you are being examined.

Basis of Rating

Probably you will forget most of these "do's" and "don'ts" when you walk into the oral interview room. Even remembering them all will not ensure you a passing grade. Perhaps you did not have the qualifications in the first place. But remembering them will help you to put your best foot forward, without treading on the toes of the board members.

Rumor and popular opinion to the contrary notwithstanding, an oral board wants you to make the best appearance possible. They know you are under pressure – but they also want to see how you respond to it as a guide to what your reaction would be under the pressures of the job you seek. They will be influenced by the degree of poise you display, the personal traits you show and the manner in which you respond.

ABOUT THIS BOOK

This book contains tests divided into Examination Sections. Go through each test, answering every question in the margin. We have also attached a sample answer sheet at the back of the book that can be removed and used. At the end of each test look at the answer key and check your answers. On the ones you got wrong, look at the right answer choice and learn. Do not fill in the answers first. Do not memorize the questions and answers, but understand the answer and principles involved. On your test, the questions will likely be different from the samples. Questions are changed and new ones added. If you understand these past questions you should have success with any changes that arise. Tests may consist of several types of questions. We have additional books on each subject should more study be advisable or necessary for you. Finally, the more you study, the better prepared you will be. This book is intended to be the last thing you study before you walk into the examination room. Prior study of relevant texts is also recommended. NLC publishes some of these in our Fundamental Series. Knowledge and good sense are important factors in passing your exam. Good luck also helps. So now study this Passbook, absorb the material contained within and take that knowledge into the examination. Then do your best to pass that exam.

EXAMINATION SECTION

VERBAL ANALOGIES

The verbal-analogy type question is now a staple component of tests of general and mental ability, scholastic aptitude, professional qualification, and civil service examinations. This question-type is also being used for achievement testing.

The verbal analogy is considered an excellent measure for evaluating the ability of the student to reason with and in words. It is not, primarily, a test of vocabulary *per se,* for very rarely are the words that are used in this type of question difficult or abstruse in meaning (as they are, for example, in the same-opposite or sentence-completion type). Rather, they are everyday terms and phrases descriptive of materials and actions familiar to all of us.

The verbal analogy is a test of *word relationships* and *idea relationships,* involving a neat and algebraic-like arrangement in ratio (proportion) form not of numbers but of words. Some testers see in this type of question the development on the verbal (linguistic or qualitative) side of the same logical reasoning as occurs on the mathematical (numerical or quantitative) side in number problems. This type of question is ranked just after the reading-comprehension type in difficulty. However, it constitutes by far the most fascinating and challenging area in aptitude testing.

In general, three levels of ability are involved in answering the verbal analogy question.

First, and easiest in this connection, is the ability to understand the meanings of the words used in the question (understanding).

Second, and more difficult, is the ability to comprehend the relationship between the subject-, or question-, pair of words (the process of logical reasoning).

Third, and most difficult of all, is the ability to select from the five (pairs of) choices given, that choice which bears the same relationship to (within) itself as the subject words bear to one another. This involves analysis, comparison, and judgment (the process of evaluation).

In the verbal-analogy type of question, two important symbols are employed, which must be thoroughly understood beforehand. These are the colon(:), which is to be translated into words, when reading the question, in the same way as its mathematical equivalent, that is, "is to"; and the double colon (::), which is to be translated as "in the same way as." Thus, the analogy, BURGLAR: PRISON :: juvenile delinquent : reformatory, is to be read, <u>A burglar is to a prison in the same way as a juvenile delinquent isto a reformatory.</u> Or, reading for meaning, we could say instead, "A burglar is punished by being sent to a prison in the same way as a juvenile delinquent is punished by being sent to a reformatory."

SAMPLE QUESTIONS AND EXPLANATIONS

DIRECTIONS: Each question in this part consists of a pair of words in capital letters, which-have a certain relationship to each other, followed *either* by a third word in capital letters and five lettered words in small letters (1 blank missing) OR by five lettered pairs of words in small letters (2 blanks missing). Choose *either* the letter of the word that is related to the third word in capital letters OR of the pair of words that are related to each other in the same way as the first two capitalized words are related to each other, and mark the appropriate space on your answer sheet.

1. EROSION : ROCKS :: DISSIPATION : _____ 1._____
    A. character B. temperance C. penance D. influence
    E. sincerity

2. MUNDANE : SPIRITUAL :: SECULAR :

   A. scientist   B. clerical   C. pecuniary   D. municipal
   E. teacher

3. ANARCHY : LAWLESSNESS : : _____ : _____

   A. autocracy : peace   B. disturbance : safety
   C. government : order   D. confusion : law
   E. democracy : dictatorship

4. UMBRELLA : RAIN : : _____ : _____

   A. roof : snow   B. screen : insects
   C. sewer : water   D. body : disease
   E. gong : dinner

EXPLANATION OF QUESTION 1

Item A, character, is correct.

Erosion is a geological development that wears away Rocks. This is an example of a cause-effect relationship -- a concrete relationship.

Dissipation wears away character (Item A) in the same way -- however, this is an abstract relationship.

But the comparison is apt and appropriate. This is a usual, general type of analogy whose difficulty is compounded by the fact that a concrete relationship is compared with an abstract one.

Item B, temperance (moderation), is merely one aspect of character.

Item C, penance (repentance), bears no relationship to dissipation in the sense of the subject words.

Item D, influence, and Item E, sincerity, may or may not be affected by dissipation.

This question is an example of a one-blank analogy, that is, only one word is to be supplied in the answer (a subject pair and a third subject word being given in the question itself).

EXPLANATION OF QUESTION 2

Item B, clerical, is correct.

Mundane means worldly, earthly. The opposite of this word is spiritual -- unworldly, devout, eternal. This is a relationship of opposites.

Secular means worldly, earthly, temporal. It is a synonym for mundane. What is needed as the answer is an opposite equal in meaning to spiritual

   A. A scientist may or may not be worldly or spiritual. At any rate, an adjective is needed as an answer, and scientist is a noun.
   B. Clerical ("pertaining to the clergy") denotes, usually, apiritual or religious qualities. It is an adjective. This is the correct answer.
   C. Pecuniary refers to money, and may, therefore, be regarded as a synonym for secular.
   D. Municipal refers to municipalities or cities, and has no standing here as an answer.
   E. A teacher may or may not be worldly or spiritual. At any rate, just as for A. scientist, it is a noun and not an adjective, which is needed as an answer here.

EXPLANATION OF QUESTION 3

Item C, government : order, is correct.

Anarchy, or no government, is characterized by lawlessness while a government is characterized by order. This is an example of an object situation) : characteristic relationship.

Item A, autocracy : peace, is incorrect since very often autocracy (absolute monarchy or rule by an individual) is characterized by war.

Item B, disturbance : safety, is manifestly untrue.

Item D, confusion : law, is likewise untrue.

Item E, democracy : dictatorship, bears no relationship to the meaning conveyed by the subject pair.

This is an example of a two-blank analogy, that is, a pair of words is to be supplied. This is the more difficult type of analogy, and the one most frequently encountered on advanced-level examinations.

EXPLANATION OF QUESTION 4

Item B, screen : insects, is correct.

By means of an umbrella, one keeps the rain off his person just as a screen keeps insects out of the house. This is an example of an object: assists relationship.

Item A, roof : snow, is not correct since a roof keeps out many other things as well, e.g., light, heat, rain, insects, etc.

Item C, sewer : water, is incorrect since a sewer keeps water in or water flows through and in a sewer.

Item D, body : disease, is incorrect since often disease enters and destroys the body.

Item E, gong : dinner, is incorrect since the gong merely summons to dinner but does not keep anyone away.

As can be discerned from the examples above, there are many possible relationships on which word analogies may be formed. Some of these will be listed and illustrated below. However, the important point is not to ponder over labels and attempt to peg the relationships thereby. This is as unnecessary as it is time-consuming. The real object, or the real method, is to examine and to fully comprehend the relationship expressed in the subject pair and *then* to select as the correct answer that item which *most approximately* is in greatest consonance with all or most of the aspects of the given relationship.

TYPES AND FORMS OF ANALOGY QUESTIONS

Some or all of the following types of analogies or relationships are to be encountered on examinations.

1. PART : WHOLE
    Example: LEG : BODY :: wheel : car

2. CAUSE : EFFECT
    Example: RAIN : FLOOD :: disease : epidemic

3. CONCRETE : ABSTRACT
    Example: ROAD : VEHICLE :: life : person

4. WORD : SYNONYM
    Example: VACUOUS : EMPTY :: seemly : fit

5. **WORD : ANTONYM**
    Example: SLAVE : FREEMAN :: desolate : joyous

6. **OBJECT : MATERIAL**
    Example: COAT : WOOL :: dress : cotton

7. **OBJECT : DEFINITION**
    Example: ASSEVERATE : AFFIRM :: segregate : separate

8. **OBJECT : SEX**
    Example: COLT : MARE :: buck : doe

9. **TIME : TIME**
    Example: DAY : NIGHT :: sunrise : sunset

10. **DEGREE : DEGREE**
    Example: HAPPY : ECSTATIC :: warm : hot

11. **OBJECT : TOOL**
    Example: STENCIL : TYPEWRITER :: thread : needle

12. **USER : TOOL**
    Example: FARMER : HOE :: dentist : drill

13. **CREATOR : CREATION**
    Example: ARTIST : PICTURE :: poet : poem

14. **CATEGORY : TYPE**
    Example: RODENT : SQUIRREL :: fish : flounder

15. **PERSON (ANIMAL,ETC.) : CHARACTERISTIC**
    Example: MONSTER : FEROCITY :: baby : helplessness

16. **OBJECT : CHARACTERISTIC**
    Example: PICKLE : SOUR :: sugar : sweet

17. **PERSON : FUNCTION**
    Example: TEACHER : EDUCATION :: doctor : health

18. **INSTRUMENT : FUNCTION**
    Example: CAMERA : PHOTOGRAPHY :: ruler : measurement

19. **WORD : GRAMMATICAL FORM**
    Example: WE : I :: they : he

20. **SYMBOL : ATTITUDE**
    Example: SALUTE : PATRIOTISM :: prayer : religion

21. **REWARD : ACTION**
    Example: MEDAL : BRAVERY :: trophy : championship

22. **OBJECT : ASSISTS**
    Example: WATER : THIRST :: food : hunger

23. OBJECT : HINDERS
    Example: NOISE : STUDY :: rut : car
24. PERSON : RELATIONSHIP
    Example: FATHER : SON :: uncle : nephew
25. OBJECT : LOCALE
    Example: SHIP : WATER :: airplane : air
26. OBJECT : METHOD
    Example: DOOR : KEY :: safe : combination
27. QUALITY : PROFUSION
    Example: WIND : TORNADO :: water : flood
28. QUALITY : ABSENCE
    Example: FORTITUDE : COWARDICE :: carefully : casually
29. SIZE : SIZE
    Example: BOAT : SHIP :: lake : sea
30. GENUS : SPECIES
    Example: RODENT : RAT :: canine : wolf

There are other relationships, but these will suffice to show some of those more frequently occurring.

SUGGESTIONS FOR ANSWERING THE VERBAL ANALOGY QUESTION (APTITUDE)

1. Always keep in mind that a verbal analogy is a relationship of likeness between two things, consisting in the resemblances not, usually, of the things themselves but of two or more of their attributes, functions, circumstances, or effects. Therefore, in the one-blank or two-blank questions, you are not looking so much for similarity in structure (although this may prove to be a factor, too), as you are for a relationship in the functioning of the subject words.
2. How do we proceed to answer the verbal-analogy type question? *First,* discover for yourself in a meaningful way the exact relationship existing between the subject words. Whether you are able to label or tag this relationship is not so important (as we have said before) as to understand the relationship that exists. The logical *second* and *final* step is to examine the possible answers given and to ascertain which of these possibilities, on the basis of *meaning, order,* and *form,* bears a similar relationship to the subject pair.
3. For the analogy in question, the subject words (i.e., the question words given in the first part of the analogy) need not be of the same class, type, order, or species as the object words (i.e., the answer-words or fill-ins). For example, in the analogy, BUCCANEER:SAILOR :: fungus : plant, the subject words (in capital letters) are types of people, the object words (in small letters) refer to types of things. However, the analogy that exists is on the basis of a descriptive relationship between these two different sets of words. (The first word in each pair constitutes the depredatory or despoiling form of the second, which is the general category name.) Thus, it is actually the total effect of the *first pair* on each other that is being compared with the total effect of the *second pair* on each other: *this is what really counts,* and not the individual components of each pair.

4. The order of the object words must be in the same sequence as the order of the subject words. For example, the analogy, INAUGURATION : PRESIDENT :: ordination : priest, is correct. But, INAUGURATION : PRESIDENT :: priest : ordination, would be incorrect. Watch for this <u>reversal</u> of order in word sequence; it is a common source of entrapment for the uninitiated.
5. Likewise, it is necessary to check to see that the parts of speech used in the analogy are the same, and occur in the same sequence. For example, if the subject pair contains a noun and an adjective in that order, the object pair <u>must</u> contain a noun and an adjective in *that* order. Thus, MOTHER : GOOD :: murderer : bad, is correct. But, MOTHER : GOOD :: murderer : badly, is incorrect.
6. The best way to answer the analogy question -- one-blank or two-blanks -- is to study intensively the relationship contained in the given pair. Having fully comprehended this relationship and, perhaps, having "labeled" it, proceed to scan the possible answers, choosing the most likely one. This will save time, and avoid needless trial and error.

VERBAL ANALOGIES
EXAMINATION SECTION
TEST 1

DIRECTIONS: Each question consists of two capitalized words which have a certain relationship to each other, followed by five lettered pairs of words in small letters. Choose the letter of the pair of words which are related to each other in the SAME way as the words of the capitalized pair are related to each other. *PRINT THE LETTER OF THE CORRECT ANSWER IN THE SPACE AT THE RIGHT.*

1. DISEASE : IMMUNITY :: _____ : _____ 1.____
   A. crime : pardon B. custom : practice C. debt : bankruptcy
   D. tax : exemption E. travel : deduction

2. RESPONSIBILITY : RELEASE :: _____ : _____ 2.____
   A. duty : refrain B. promise : renege C. debt : honor
   D. blame : vindicate E. position : retract

3. PENDULUM : SWING :: _____ : _____ 3.____
   A. pulley : ladder B. hand : clock C. lever : crowbar
   D. balance : seesaw E. weight : fulcrum

4. NADIR : ZENITH :: _____ : _____ 4.____
   A. depression : recovery
   B. perigee : apogamy
   C. earth : sky
   D. appanage : station
   E. threshold : lintel

5. ROB : CONFISCATE :: _____ : _____ 5.____
   A. punish : revenge B. walk : trespass C. insult : offend
   D. murder : execute E. take : accept

6. WORKER : UNEMPLOYED :: _____ : _____ 6.____
   A. crop : barren
   B. property : useless
   C. purchase : unnecessary
   D. visitor : unwelcome
   E. field : fallow

7. PROFUSION : AUSTERITY :: _____ : _____ 7.____
   A. capitalism : socialism
   B. erudition : reprise
   C. logic : irrationality
   D. affluence : frugality
   E. effluence : confluence

8. REPERTOIRE : OPERA :: _____ : _____ 8.____
   A. suits : closet B. team : baseball C. melody : harmony
   D. wardrobe : costume E. chest : drawers

2 (#1)

9. DISDAIN : AFFRONT :: _____ : _____
   A. perjury : boos
   B. pleasure : pain
   C. approval : applause
   D. age : wrinkle
   E. grimace : awry

   9.____

10. SALES : ADVERTISING :: _____ : _____
    A. votes : campaigning
    B. savings : banking
    C. liquor : drinking
    D. troops : leading
    E. weakness : strength

    10.____

11. ATTACK : MURDER :: _____ : _____
    A. filial : fraternal
    B. mind : body
    C. paroxysm : parricide
    D. sudden : poison
    E. diseased : dead

    11.____

12. BALTIC : INDIAN :: _____ : _____
    A. Mediterranean : Pacific
    B. Atlantic : Caribbean
    C. Arctic : Gulf of Mexico
    D. Black Sea : Persian Gulf
    E. Antarctic : Andaman Sea

    12.____

13. PROFESSION : STRUGGLE :: _____ : _____
    A. strong : weak
    B. métier : melee
    C. mixed : confusion
    D. vocation : trade
    E. expert : novice

    13.____

14. ALLOYS : ATMOSPHERE :: _____ : _____
    A. weight : measure
    B. metallurgy : meteorology
    C. technology : science
    D. archaic : present

    14.____

15. GRAM : KILOGRAM :: _____ : _____
    A. millimeter : centimeter
    B. dekameter : decimeter
    C. mile : kilometer
    D. micron : microbe
    E. Centigrade : Fahrenheit

    15.____

16. PRESIDENT : FRANCE :: _____ : _____
    A. Queen Elizabeth : England
    B. king : Belgium
    C. president : United States
    D. governor : state
    E. king : Italy

    16.____

17. HAND : DIAL :: _____ : _____
    A. time : number
    B. light : lamp
    C. ticking : talking
    D. clock : radio
    E. time : space

    17.____

18. ANNEX : BUILDING :: _____ : _____
    A. pin : clasp
    B. stone : setting
    C. cell : prison
    D. branch : tree
    E. island : mainland

    18.____

19. FLOOR : PARQUET :: _____ : _____
    A. elevator : escalator
    B. functional : ornamental
    C. filigree : scroll
    D. wreath : nosegay
    E. head : hair

    19.____

20. DEVIL : DRUGGIST :: _____ : _____   20._____
    A. demon : farmer   B. demonology : pharmacology
    C. medieval : primitive   D. dispensed : compounded
    E. Faustian : Freudian

21. ELECTRICITY : GAS :: _____ : _____   21._____
    A. lighter : match   B. current : flow   C. fire : flame
    D. conductor : ignition   E. train : automobile

22. - : HYPHEN :: _____ : _____   22._____
    A. x : division   B. $: pound   C. symbol : word
    D. y : geometry   E. & : sum

23. WILD : DOMESTICATED :: _____ : _____   23._____
    A. jungle : forest   B. atavistic : masochistic
    C. cave : dwelling   D. animal : man
    E. primitive : civilized

24. INEPT : TACTLESS :: _____ : _____   24._____
    A. right : left   B. evil : sinful   C. clever : stupid
    D. depraved : foolish   E. maladroit : gauche

25. INTERVENE : INTERCEDE :: _____ : _____   25._____
    A. interfere : impute B. interpose : intrude   C. arbitrate : argue
    D. meditate : mediate E. space : species

KEY (CORRECT ANSWERS)

1.	D	11.	C
2.	D	12.	A
3.	C	13.	B
4.	E	14.	B
5.	D	15.	A
6.	E	16.	C
7.	D	17.	D
8.	D	18.	D
9.	C	19.	B
10.	A	20.	B

21.	B
22.	C
23.	E
24.	E
25.	B

TEST 2

DIRECTIONS: Each question consists of two capitalized words which have a certain relationship to each other, followed by five lettered pairs of words in small letters. Choose the letter of the pair of words which are related to each other in the SAME way as the words of the capitalized pair are related to each other. *PRINT THE LETTER OF THE CORRECT ANSWER IN THE SPACE AT THE RIGHT.*

1. PITHY : BOMBASTIC :: _____ : _____
   A. verbose : taciturn
   B. garrulous : pompous
   C. meagre : replete
   D. laconic : grandiloquent
   E. concise : precise

2. MANAGER : TEAM :: _____ : _____
   A. President : Congress
   B. Speaker : Senate
   C. captain : crew
   D. minister : hierarchy
   E. principal : P.T.A.

3. STEEPLE : LEDGE :: _____ : _____
   A. citadel : tower
   B. spire : dungeon
   C. warp : woof
   D. peak : summit
   E. cone : roof

4. CREDULOUS : UNCTUOUS :: _____ : _____
   A. ingenious : artful
   B. ingenuous : urbane
   C. naïve : provincial
   D. benign : benignant
   E. cantankerous : peevish

5. PHILIPPIC : ABUSE :: _____ : _____
   A. eulogy : mirth
   B. tirade : tears
   C. sycophancy : music
   D. encomium : praise
   E. intrepidity : fear

6. CUMULATIVE : ACCRETIVE :: _____ : _____
   A. indigenous : spontaneous
   B. reticence : verbosity
   C. philately : numismatics
   D. indigence : poverty
   E. culvert : bridge

7. UNCONSTRAINED : IMPROVISED :: _____ : _____
   A. unrehearsed : prepared
   B. simultaneous : pithy
   C. premeditated : unpremeditated
   D. extemporaneous : contemporaneous
   E. spontaneous : impromptu

8. INORDINACY : EXCESSIVE :: _____ : _____
   A. applause : approval
   B. anomaly : irregular
   C. remuneration : payable
   D. provocation : irritate
   E. emulation : insidious

2 (#2)

9. PLEBEIAN : PATRICIAN :: _____ : _____
   A. Democrat : Republican
   B. Communist : Conservative
   C. serf : fief
   D. vassal : lord
   E. common man : elite

9._____

10. FLEETING : EPHEMERAL :: _____ : _____
    A. permanent : temporary
    B. casual : persistent
    C. transient : evanescent
    D. temporary : permanent
    E. passing : perceptible

10._____

11. INSTRUMENTALIST : ORGANIST :: _____ : _____
    A. harmonist : contrapuntist
    B. quartet : counterpoint
    C. lute : lutenist
    D. singer : composition
    E. cello : violoncello

11._____

12. ADULTERATE : COMPOUND :: _____ : _____
    A. fusión : blend
    B. commingle : miscellany
    C. interpretation : commingling
    D. interpolate : amalgamate
    E. mix : potpourri

12._____

13. QUIESCENCE : INDOLENCE :: _____ : _____
    A. lurk : abeyance
    B. concealed : potential
    C. latency : dormancy
    D. escape : observation
    E. suppress : inertia

13._____

14. BROGUE : JARGONIST :: _____ : _____
    A. patois : neologist
    B. empathy : psychiatrist
    C. dialect : Anglicism
    D. country : patriot
    E. gazette : journalist

14._____

15. DENIAL : DISCLAIMER :: _____ : _____
    A. veto : ignore
    B. contradiction : convention
    C. cancel : canker
    D. disavowal : negation
    E. gainsay : contradict

15._____

16. FATE : PREDESTINATION :: _____ : _____
    A. doom : destiny
    B. appointed : office
    C. elect : fated
    D. exigency : inevitability
    E. lot : choice

16._____

17. LETHARGY : EXHAUSTION :: _____ : _____
    A. laziness : weariness
    B. continence : ennui
    C. enfeebled : haggard
    D. exertion : tiredness
    E. lassitude : fatigue

17._____

18. QUALM : IRRESOLUTION :: _____ : _____
    A. fear : diffidence
    B. fright : stampede
    C. awe : trust
    D. sanguine : apprehensive
    E. nightmare : alarm

18._____

3 (#2)

19. WAR : SURRENDER :: _____ : _____
    A. victor : accede   B. grant : scholarship   C. election : concede
    D. state : cede   E. prison : confess

20. BALD EAGLE : GROUSE :: _____ : _____
    A. termite : cockroach B. chanticleer : rooster   C. falcon : pheasant
    D. peacock : hen   E. vulture : hawk

21. ORANGUTAN : BRONCHO :: _____ : _____
    A. antelope : trotter   B. Wales : United States
    C. caribou : marmoset   D. ewe : ram
    E. steeplechaser : pacer

22. UNITED STATES : FRANCE :: _____ : _____
    A. official : citizen   B. policeman : gendarme
    C. officer : attendant   D. New York : Louisiana
    E. west : east

23. SEOUL : SOUTH KOREA :: _____ : _____
    A. Estopil : Portugal   B. Pnom Penh : Laos   C. Barcelona : Spain
    C. London : England   E. Venezuela : Caracas

24. PERSECUTION : PARANOIA :: _____ : _____
    A. altruism : megalomania   B. neurosis : psychosis
    C. dichotomy : schizophrenia   D. extraversion : claustrophobia
    E. disease : symptom

25. ONE : TWO :: _____ : _____
    A. century : millennium   B. planet : astronomy
    C. year : twenty   D. month : year
    E. decade : score

KEY (CORRECT ANSWERS)

1.	D		11.	A
2.	C		12.	D
3.	C		13.	C
4.	B		14.	A
5.	D		15.	D
6.	D		16.	A
7.	E		17.	E
8.	B		18.	A
9.	E		19.	C
10.	C		20.	C

21. A
22. B
23. D
24. C
25. E

TEST 3

DIRECTIONS: Each question consists of two capitalized words which have a certain relationship to each other, followed by five lettered pairs of words in small letters. Choose the letter of the pair of words which are related to each other in the SAME way as the words of the capitalized pair are related to each other. *PRINT THE LETTER OF THE CORRECT ANSWER IN THE SPACE AT THE RIGHT.*

1. CHAFFER : BARGAIN :: _____ : _____   1.____
   A. scarify : cleanse
   B. hector : befriend
   C. propitiate : placate
   D. improvise : intercalate
   E. decollate : decode

2. SPANIEL : FAWNING PERSON :: _____ : _____   2.____
   A. cameo : miniature   B. nonage : minority   C. pediment : obstacle
   D. flacon : flag   E. marasca : wine

3. SEMINAL : ORIGINATIVE :: _____ : _____   3.____
   A. sullied : inflamed
   B. beleaguered : besieged
   C. viable : moribund
   D. amorphous : remanent
   E. quintan : fourth

4. SLAKE : ALLAY :: _____ : _____   4.____
   A. comport : frolic   B. beset : assail   C. parry : join
   D. revet : review   E. remonstrate : concur

5. SALAAM : OBEISANCE :: _____ : _____   5.____
   A. jape : hiatus
   B. ethos : fundamental spirit of a culture
   C. gravamen : greeting
   D. chanticleer : fox
   E. ablation : inhalation

6. SLATTERNLY : SLOVENLY :: _____ : _____   6.____
   A. complaisant : priggish
   B. myopic : farsighted
   C. awry : convex
   D. oblate : flattened at the poles
   E. slavish : sleazy

7. PREEN : SLEEK :: _____ : _____   7.____
   A. extrapolate : disengage
   B. discountenance : disconcert
   C. bandy : banter
   D. cense : ascribe
   E. cite : proscribe

8. SATRAP : EXECUTE :: _____ : _____   8.____
   A. rigmarole : prolix talk
   B. apostasy : denunciation
   C. apogee : perigee
   D. allotrophy : allusion
   E. chaldron : chalice

2 (#3)

9. INCHOATE : NASCENT :: _____ : _____
   A. extirpative : invective
   B. contumacious : headstrong
   C. disinterested : prejudiced
   D. veracious : mendacious
   E. abandoned : manumitted

10. RAIL : REVILE :: _____ : _____
    A. abjure : appeal to
    B. vouchsafe : contemplate
    C. execrate : curse
    D. exorcise : criticize
    E. ablactate : abominate

11. ANTONYM : OPPOSITE :: _____ : _____
    A. antonym : unlike
    B. metaphor : poetry
    C. triangle : pyramid
    D. synonym : sme
    E. metonymy : versification

12. READER : PUNCTUATION :: _____ : _____
    A. telegraph operator : Morse
    B. vocabulary : alphabet
    C. English : pronunciation
    D. bicyclist : roadblock
    E. motorist : road sign

13. OCEAN : ROAD :: _____ : _____
    A. ship : hurricane
    B. canal : road
    C. storm : accident
    D. buoy : detour
    E. warning : signal

14. MATTER : ESSENCE :: _____ : _____
    A. play : outcome
    B. matter : particle
    C. molecule : atom
    D. paragraph : gist
    E. epitome : paraphrase

15. PENURIOUS : SLUM :: _____ : _____
    A. captive : jail
    B. parched : desert
    C. withered : plant
    D. inundated : flood
    E. glum : outlook

16. DEMEANOR : CHARACTER :: _____ : _____
    A. personality : qualities
    B. aspect : appearance
    C. vestibule : apartment
    D. facade : building
    E. front : affront

17. HAIR : TRIM :: _____ : _____
    A. beard : shave
    B. lawn : mow
    C. wool : shear
    D. shrub : prune
    E. scissors : cut

18. WORK : PUTTER :: _____ : _____
    A. bum : thief
    B. late : laggard
    C. regress : ingress
    D. diligent : tardy
    E. wait : loiter

19. EXILE : SANCTUARY :: _____ : _____
    A. child : bed
    B. refugee : haven
    C. berth : stowaway
    D. fish : bowl
    E. prisoner : dungeon

20. CAR : HORN :: _____ : _____
    A. air raid : siren   B. swimmer : bell buoy   C. singer : tune
    D. train : whistle   E. ship : anchor

21. SETTING : DIAMOND :: _____ : _____
    A. sash : window   B. frame : picture   C. shell : egg
    D. painting : canvas   E. border : exile

22. AFFECTION : PASSION :: _____ : _____
    A. storm : sea   B. contraction : dilation
    C. atmospheric pressure : clear day   D. breeze : gale
    E. wind : gale

23. TEAR : CUT :: _____ : _____
    A. wrinkle : fold   B. paper : refuse   C. wrinkle : smooth
    D. steal : lose   E. sprinkle : rub

24. FIGHTER : BELL :: _____ : _____
    A. butterfly hunter : net   B. fencer : sword
    C. writer : pen   D. dog : whistle
    E. sprinter : gun

25. PLANT : FUNGUS :: _____ : _____
    A. transient : permanent   B. mate : captain
    C. sailor : pirate   D. police : thief
    E. wolf : prey

KEY (CORRECT ANSWERS)

1.	C	11.	D
2.	B	12.	E
3.	B	13.	D
4.	B	14.	D
5.	B	15.	B
6.	D	16.	D
7.	B	17.	D
8.	A	18.	E
9.	B	19.	B
10.	C	20.	D

21.	B
22.	E
23.	A
24.	E
25.	C

TEST 4

DIRECTIONS: Each question consists of two capitalized words which have a certain relationship to each other, followed by five lettered pairs of words in small letters. Choose the letter of the pair of words which are related to each other in the SAME way as the words of the capitalized pair are related to each other. *PRINT THE LETTER OF THE CORRECT ANSWER IN THE SPACE AT THE RIGHT.*

1. EVENING : MORNING :: _____ : _____
   A. coming : going   B. ten : five   C. sunset : sunrise
   D. spring : autumn   E. despair : hope
1.____

2. RUNG : RING :: _____ : _____
   A. arisen : arise   B. drunk : drink   C. stroke : strike
   D. sang : sing   E. clang : cling
2.____

3. ENTHUSIASTIC : APPROVING :: _____ : _____
   A. disliking : liking   B. pink : red
   C. frigid : cool   D. bitter : sour
   E. apathetic : disapproving
3.____

4. MOLECULE : ATOM :: _____ : _____
   A. kennel : dog   B. shelf : book   C. sea : fish
   D. regiment : soldier   E. star : galaxy
4.____

5. ACT : PLAY :: _____ : _____
   A. notes : staff   B. harmony : counterpoint
   C. melody : harmony   D. key : piano
   E. movement : symphony
5.____

6. APIARY : BEES :: _____ : _____
   A. dog : kennel   B. fish : aquarium   C. mortuary : people
   D. corral : cattle   E. breviary : priest
6.____

7. STRANDS : ROPE :: _____ : _____
   A. sugar : cane   B. warp : woof   C. links : chain
   D. train : cars   E. rivers : ocean
7.____

8. BODY : SKIN :: _____ : _____
   A. window : door   B. ink : crayon   C. book : cover
   D. write : compose   E. spelling : grammar
8.____

9. PENCIL : LEAD :: _____ : _____
   A. lighter : fluid   B. keys : typewriter   C. cup : coffee
   D. book : page   E. razor : blade
9.____

2 (#4)

10. AIRPLANE : LOCOMOTION :: _____ : _____   10.____
    A. statement : contention   B. canoe : paddle
    C. hero : worship   D. spectacles : vision
    E. hay : horse

11. STREAM : RIVER :: _____ : _____   11.____
    A. land : water   B. village : suburb   C. cape : continent
    D. sea : ocean   E. city : country

12. RECTANGLE : SQUARE :: _____ : _____   12.____
    A. line : perimeter   B. triangle : square   C. square : diamond
    D. circle : square   E. oval : circle

13. EMOLUMENT : INCENTIVE :: _____ : _____   13.____
    A. deed : crime   B. play : plot   C. criminal : reward
    D. dance : movement   E. reward : capture

14. WOLF : PROWL :: _____ : _____   14.____
    A. rat : gnaw   B. monkey : mimic   C. reader : browse
    D. trooper : lurk   E. gang : highjack

15. FOND : INFATUATION :: _____ : _____   15.____
    A. affectionate : adumbration   B. calm : listless
    C. eager : sentimentality   D. glib : fluency
    E. enthusiastic : fervor

16. CONCORD : DISCORD :: _____ : _____   16.____
    A. alliance : organization   B. treaty : covenant
    C. conciliation : revolution   D. entreaty : parity
    E. pact : feud

17. EXTENUATE : CRIME :: _____ : _____   17.____
    A. condone : error   B. placate : pardon   C. expiate : sin
    D. moderate : tone   E. reprisal : retaliation

18. APPENDIX : PREFACE :: _____ : _____   18.____
    A. glossary : index   B. preface : table of contents
    C. progeny : proletariat   D. footnote : emendation
    E. epilogue : prologue

19. SUBSEQUENT : COINCIDENTAL :: _____ : _____   19.____
    A. posthumous : following   B. now : there
    C. consecutive : ensuing   D. posterior : simultaneous
    E. prolonged : before

20. MUNDANE : SPIRITUAL :: _____ : _____   20.____
    A. scientist : missionary   B. secular : altruistic
    C. municipal : ecclesiastical   D. pecuniary : musical
    E. student : teacher

21. UNSCRUPULOUS : QUALMS :: _____ : _____
    A. remorseless : compassion
    B. intrepid : rashness
    C. opportunist : opportunity
    D. querulous : lamentation
    E. impenitent : sin

22. SOPHISTRY : LOGIC :: _____ : _____
    A. discretion : improvidence
    B. spirit : spiritualism
    C. reason : rationalization
    D. feeling : intuition
    E. wisdom : sophistication

23. TRESPASSER : BARK :: _____ : _____
    A. snake : hiss
    B. burglar : alarm
    C. crossing : bell
    D. air raid : siren
    E. ship : buoy

24. RESEARCH : FELLOWSHIP :: _____ : _____
    A. honor : medal
    B. merit : scholarship
    C. student : bonus
    D. matrimony : dowry
    E. study : grant

25. IMPEND : DEMISE :: _____ : _____
    A. loom : disaster
    B. question : puzzle
    C. imminent : eminent
    D. howl : storm
    E. hurt : penalty

KEY (CORRECT ANSWERS)

1.	C	11.	D
2.	B	12.	E
3.	D	13.	E
4.	E	14.	E
5.	E	15.	E
6.	D	16.	E
7.	C	17.	A
8.	C	18.	E
9.	E	19.	D
10.	D	20.	B

21.	A
22.	D
23.	B
24.	E
25.	A

TEST 5

DIRECTIONS: Each question consists of two capitalized words which have a certain relationship to each other, followed by five lettered pairs of words in small letters. Choose the letter of the pair of words which are related to each other in the SAME way as the words of the capitalized pair are related to each other. *PRINT THE LETTER OF THE CORRECT ANSWER IN THE SPACE AT THE RIGHT.*

1. DEATH : DEMISE :: _____ : _____
   A. frightful : horrid   B. resistance : invasion
   C. asylum : insane   D. life : breath
   E. might : right
1._____

2. DRAGON : DINOSAUR :: _____ : _____
   A. descendant : ancestor   B. medieval : prehistoric
   C. fabulous : real   D. creditable : veritable
   E. amphibian : reptile
2._____

3. SHIP : NAVIGATION :: _____ : _____
   A. promoter : event   B. victory : leader
   C. conduct : conscience   D. state : army
   E. nation : patriotism
3._____

4. GUFFAW : LAUGH :: _____ : _____
   A. lament : cry   B. wail : whimper   C. face : mouth
   D. chuckle : snicker   E. smirk : simper
4._____

5. ANARCHY : CHAOS :: _____ : _____
   A. government : order   B. beast : beauty   C. government : law
   D. rule : order   E. totalitarian : mob
5._____

6. INFINITE : FINITE :: _____ : _____
   A. second : minute   B. hour : minute   C. era : decade
   D. month : day   E. immortality : mortality
6._____

7. WATER : BOAT :: _____ : _____
   A. locomotive : steam   B. wagon : horse   C. air : dirigible
   D. lion : tiger   E. gasoline : taxi
7._____

8. INAUGURATION : PRESIDENT :: _____ : _____
   A. promulgation : list   B. matriculation : student
   C. election : candidate   D. promotion : officer
   E. ordination : priest
8._____

9. OMNIPOTENT : VASSAL :: _____ : _____
   A. soldier : civilian   B. policeman : prisoner
   C. master : slave   D. captain : tar
   E. native : alien
9._____

10. SAME : SYNONYM :: _____ : _____ 10.____
    A. bell : bellows   B. false : pseudonym   C. same : homonym
    D. botanist : biologist E. opposite : antonym

KEY (CORRECT ANSWERS)

1.	A	6.	E
2.	C	7.	C
3.	C	8.	E
4.	B	9.	C
5.	A	10.	E

VERBAL ANALOGIES – 2 BLANKS
EXAMINATION SECTION
TEST 1

DIRECTIONS: Each question in this part consists of two capitalized words which have a certain relationship to each other, followed by five lettered pairs of words in small letters. Choose the letter of the pair of words which are related to each other in the SAME way as the words of the capitalized pair are related to each other. *PRINT THE LETTER OF THE CORRECT ANSWER IN THE SPACE AT THE RIGHT.*

1. RETINA : EYE : : _____ . _____　　　　　　　　　　　　　　　　　　　　　　1.____
   - A. pupil : film
   - B. light : aperture
   - C. lens : camera
   - D. telescope : battleship
   - E. speed : focus

2. MOTIVATION : AGENDA : : _____ : _____　　　　　　　　　　　　　　　　　　2.____
   - A. eye : blink
   - B. reflex : reaction
   - C. tears : crying
   - D. involuntary : voluntary
   - E. thought : speech

3. FINITE : INTERMINABLE :: _____ : _____　　　　　　　　　　　　　　　　　　3.____
   - A. close : far
   - B. horizon : skyline
   - C. limit : infinity
   - D. boundless : determinate
   - E. time : space

4. SIDE BY SIDE : UP AND DOWN : : _____ : _____　　　　　　　　　　　　　　4.____
   - A. across : horizontal
   - B. angle : sphere
   - C. floor : wall
   - D. juxtaposition : vertical
   - E. right angle : rectangle

5. CONCISE : TRANSPOSED :: _____ : _____　　　　　　　　　　　　　　　　　5.____
   - A. remark : game
   - B. pithy : lengthy
   - C. epithet : repetition
   - D. epigram : anagram
   - E. letter : word

6. HAND : GRASP :: _____ : _____　　　　　　　　　　　　　　　　　　　　　　6.____
   - A. ladder : rung
   - B. hearing : ears
   - C. object : touch
   - D. foot : stand
   - E. walk : run

7. WADING : SWIMMING : : _____ : _____　　　　　　　　　　　　　　　　　　7.____
   - A. telegraph : code
   - B. word : sentence
   - C. racing : diving
   - D. parachute : aeroplane
   - E. letter : cable

8. SHIP : VAULT :: _____ : _____　　　　　　　　　　　　　　　　　　　　　　8.____
   - A. escape : prison
   - B. riot : convicts
   - C. guns : soldiers
   - D. door : lock
   - E. radar : alarm

9. COMPETITION : INDUSTRY : : _____ : _____　　　　　　　　　　　　　　　　9.____
   - A. soldier : battle
   - B. passive : active
   - C. company : merger
   - D. hostility : war
   - E. power : president

25

10. EPITHET : INSULTING :: _____ : _____
    A. epigram : metaphor
    B. epitaph : mourning
    C. clever : laughable
    D. joke : jibe
    E. witticism : amusing

11. NULLIFICATION : NARRATION :: _____ : _____
    A. account : remedy
    B. action : counteraction
    C. antidote : anecdote
    D. medicinal : mercurial
    E. enmity : affection

12. SKIS : POLES :: _____ : _____
    A. ship : rope
    B. horse : bridle
    C. escalator : stairs
    D. paddle : canoe
    E. scooter : motor

13. MUMMER : FESTIVITY :: _____ : _____
    A. playwright : theater
    B. humor : arena
    C. midget : giant
    D. drama : actor
    E. clown : circus

14. WALL : POSTER :: _____ : _____
    A. placard : notice
    B. magazine : advertisement
    C. title : book jacket
    D. leaflet : sentence
    E. reading : selling

15. BALLOON : ASCENSION :: _____ : _____
    A. globe : axis
    B. planet : satellite
    C. earth : rotation
    D. sphere : circumference
    E. ladder : descend

16. EXECUTIVE : COMPANY :: _____ : _____
    A. president : military
    B. factory : foreman
    C. general : army
    D. laborer : field
    E. equestrian : cavalry

17. PREFIX : SUFFIX :: _____ : _____
    A. Latin : Greek
    B. process : behavior
    C. ex : ism
    D. act : from
    E. past : present

18. BADMINTON : SHUTTLECOCK :: _____ : _____
    A. racket : tennis
    B. mineral : game
    C. golf : iron
    D. hockey : ice
    E. jai alai : mallet

19. ART : COLLAGE :: _____ : _____
    A. music : orchestra
    B. literature : publisher
    C. dance : ballet
    D. creativity : inspiration
    E. painting : ainter

20. HERITAGE : UNION :: _____ : _____
    A. patriarchy : matriarchy
    B. father : mother
    C. thriftiness : marriage
    D. patrimony : matrimony
    E. acrimony : conjunction

21. PILGRIMAGE : SHRINE : : _____ : _____   21._____
    A. voyage : vessel   B. safari : animal
    C. automobile : race   D. hounds : hunt
    E. excursion : trip

22. SCHOLAR : DUNCE : : _____ : _____   22._____
    A. dolt : seer   B. save : spend   C. savant : simpleton
    D. detailed : disarranged   E. thinking : impulsive-
                                     ness

23. SERUM : SYRINGE : : _____ : _____   23._____
    A. file : cabinet   B. drop : eye
    C. piece : mosaic   D. solvent : substance
    E. toothpa'ste : tube

24. WAX : CANDLE : : _____ : _____   24._____
    A. door : knov   B. engine : propulsion   C. sand : desert
    D. tape : magnetic   E. photograph ; image

25. BATHOS : PATHOS : : _____ : _____   25._____
    A. anti-climax : letdown
    B. elevated : commonplace
    C. sentimentalism : compassion
    D. insincere : old fashioned
    E. understated : overstated

KEY (CORRECT ANSWERS)

1.	C	11.	C
2.	B	12.	B
3.	C	13.	E
4.	D	14.	B
5.	D	15.	C
6.	D	16.	C
7.	E	17.	C
8.	E	18.	C
9.	D	19.	C
10.	E	20.	D

21. B
22. C
23. E
24. C
25. C

———

TEST 2

DIRECTIONS: Each question in this part consists of two capitalized words which have a certain relationship to each other, followed by five lettered pairs of words in small letters. Choose the letter of the pair of words which are related to each other in the SAME way as the words of the capitalized pair are related to each other. *PRINT THE LETTER OF THE CORRECT ANSWER IN THE SPACE AT THE RIGHT.*

1. ACCUSED : ALIBI :: _____ : _____   1.____
   - A. pedestal : speech
   - B. witness : testimony
   - C. graph : lie detector
   - D. interpreter : translation
   - E. swallow : summer

2. ACCUSE : CONDEMN :: _____ : _____   2.____
   - A. evidence : indication
   - B. indict : convict
   - C. penalize : blame
   - D. absolve : punish
   - E. volunteer : draft

3. PLAGUE : POPULACE :: _____ : _____   3.____
   - A. illness : hospital
   - B. slum : city
   - C. ulcer : cancer
   - D. island : ocean
   - E. poverty : impoverished

4. DRILL : DENTIST :: _____ : _____   4.____
   - A. cavalry : horses
   - B. soldier : sword
   - C. weapon : felon
   - D. whistle : dog
   - E. writer : pen

5. MILE : FOOT :: _____ : _____   5.____
   - A. decade : generation
   - B. years : score
   - C. hunjdred : hundreds
   - D. aeon : century
   - E. ounce : pound

6. PERIMETER : CIRCUMFERENCE :: _____ : _____   6.____
   - A. planet : sun
   - B. periphery : circle
   - C. hypotenuse : angle
   - D. earth : satellite
   - E. solar system : plant

7. SPACE : TIME :: _____ : _____   7.____
   - A. gravity : speed
   - B. millesecond : light
   - C. force : pull
   - D. time : depth
   - E. displacement : hour

8. PLOT : CONSPIRACY :: _____ : _____   8.____
   - A. scheme : idea
   - B. factory : store
   - C. salesman : customer
   - D. plan : blueprint
   - E. cave : rock

9. DISTANCE : METER :: _____ : _____   9.____
   - A. size : fit
   - B. dimension : shape
   - C. depth : ocean
   - D. length : measure
   - E. weight : ounce

10. ARKOW : BOW :: _____ : _____   10.____
    - A. chamber : rifle
    - B. rapier : blade
    - C. shoot : cannon

D. bullet : pistol E. stone : throw

11. MAGAZINE : CARTRIDGE :: _____ : _____
    A. article : column   B. cart : wheel   C. newspaper : journal
    D. periodical : story   E. quarterly : book

12. TEL AVIV : SICILY :: _____ : _____
    A. Lisbon : Monte Carlo   B. Gibraltar : Tangier
    C. Pound : Lira   D. Guatemala : South Africa
    E. Denmark : Haiti

13. RHINOPLASTY : SURGERY :: _____ : _____
    A. tomato : vegetable   B. snake : animal
    C. rhinestone : diamond   D. paleography : extinct species
    E. rhinoceros : mammal

14. BRICK : CEMENTED :: _____ : _____
    A. wood. : saw   B. eraser : erasure   C. applique : applied
    D. wheel : spin   E. book : read

15. FATUOUS : DULLARD :: _____ : _____
    A. mendicant suppliant   B. inane : witless
    C. destitute solicitor   D. obsequious : beggar
    E. penurious spendthrift

16. ANNOTATION : ADVOCATE :: _____ : _____
    A. pistil : plant   B. apostil : apostle   C. footnote : following
    D. deception : disciple   E. atheist : theologist

17. ICE : WATER :: _____ : _____
    A. rain : snow   B. plane : safety belt   C. sky : clouds
    D. calendar : date   E. wood : sap

18. BURDEN : GRATUITY :: _____ : _____
    A. harbinger : spring   B. debt : debtor
    C. obstacle : clearing   D. onus : lagniappe
    E. omen : guilt

19. RECTANGULAR : BOOK :: _____ : _____
    A. adhesive : tape   B. hexagonal : pentagon
    C. square : circle   D. oval : egg
    E. circumference : globe

20. DIAPHANOUSNESS : CELLOPHANE :: _____ : _____
    A. pellucidity : cloud   B. opacity : wall
    C. hyaline : muscle   D. perspicacity : lucidity
    E. draperies : window

21. WELD : JOINT :: _____ : _____

    A. separation : boring
    B. piercing : knife
    C. perforate : hole
    D. union : merger
    E. deteriorate : process

22. SYSTEMATIC : METHODICAL :: _____ : _____

    A. sequacious : sequential
    B. subservient : slave
    C. following : event
    D. legal : process
    E. alienate : organize

23. POSTPONE : PREVENT :: _____ : _____

    A. delaying : disposal
    B. procrastinate : obviate
    C. lazy : forestall
    D. afraid : obstacle
    E. trifling : erasing

24. ANTHRACITE : COAL :: _____ : _____

    A. charcoal : coal
    B. mercury : quicksilver
    C. combustible : substance
    D. air : pressure
    E. graphite : carbon

25. MONOLOGUE : CALUMNY :: _____ : _____

    A. Hamlet : deprecatory
    B. language : defamatory
    C. loneliness : contrariness
    D. soliloquy : obloquy
    E. actor : politician

KEY (CORRECT ANSWERS)

1.	B	11.	D
2.	B	12.	C
3.	B	13.	E
4.	C	14.	C
5.	D	15.	D
6.	B	16.	B
7.	E	17.	E
8.	D	18.	D
9.	E	19.	D
10.	D	20.	B

21. C
22. A
23. B
24. E
25. D

TEST 3

DIRECTIONS: Each question in this part consists of two capitalized words which have a certain relationship to each other, followed by five lettered pairs of words in small letters. Choose the letter of the pair of words which are related to each other in the SAME way as the words of the capitalized pair are related to each other. *PRINT THE LETTER OF THE CORRECT ANSWER IN THE SPACE AT THE RIGHT.*

1. METRONOME : PENDULUM :: _____ : _____   1.___
   - A. man : invention
   - B. track : parallel
   - C. horizontal : vertical
   - D. wheel : axle
   - E. compartment : train

2. BOVINE : COW :: _____ : _____   2.___
   - A. supine : man
   - B. asinine : donkey
   - C. domesticated : wild
   - D. feline : cat
   - E. anthropoid : anthropology

3. CONNECTED : SURROUNDED :: _____ : _____   3.___
   - A. mountainous : flat
   - B. state : city
   - C. peninsula : island
   - D. populated : isolated
   - E. channel : isthmus

4. VERB : NOUN :: _____ : _____   4.___
   - A. forms : language
   - B. adverb : pronoun
   - C. type : kind
   - D. conjugation : declension
   - E. transitive : intransitive

5. HOSPITALITY : HOST :: _____ : _____   5.___
   - A. expatriate : exile
   - B. asylum : country
   - C. prisoner : prison
   - D. board : parole
   - E. inmate : institution

6. MINED : MANUFACTURED :: _____ : _____   6.___
   - A. paddle : canoe
   - B. stick : hockey
   - C. mallet : croquet
   - D. ore : boat
   - E. mineral : vegetable

7. KEROSENE : ELECTRIC :: _____ : _____   7.___
   - A. predecessor : forerunner
   - B. prince : king
   - C. helicopter : jet
   - D. precursor : successor
   - E. prophecy : event

8. HOUSE : BOAT :: _____ : _____   8.___
   - A. hatch : cabin
   - B. door : starboard
   - C. sailor : navy
   - D. window : porthole
   - E. submarine : telescope

9. COINS : NUMISMATIST :: _____ : _____   9.___
   - A. actor : audience
   - B. drama : review
   - C. race : parlay
   - D. ballet : dancer
   - E. dance : balletomane

32

2 (#3)

10. NET : ACROBAT :: _____ : _____   10._____
    A. siren : air raid   B. aeroplane : parachute
    C. fire escape : tenant   D. scream : child
    E. web : spider

11. ELECTION : POPULAR :: _____ : _____   11._____
    A. issue : obscurfe   B. plebiscite : plebeian
    C. vote : citizen   D. quorum : representatives
    E. plague : populace

12. SUBLIMINAL : JOY : : _____ : _____   12._____
    A. sympathetic : displacement   B. participating : feeling
    C. substitutional : gratification   D. vicarious : pleasure
    E. fantasy : pain

13. INK : PEN :: _____ : _____   13._____
    A. umbrella : rain   B. air : vacuum   C. gas : automobile
    D. mercury : thermometer E. parachute : jumper

14. OMISSION : EMISSION :: _____ : _____   14._____
    A. whisper : vowel   B. resonant : vocal   C. break : sustain
    D. hiatus : sound   E. memory : lapse

15. SIGNAL : STUDENT :: _____ : _____   15._____
    A. sophistication : absurdity
    B. sophist : casuist
    C. casuistry : reasoning
    D. semaphoric : sophomoric
    E. process : specious

16. FORECAST : PROPHECY :: _____ : _____   16._____
    A. weather : oracle
    B. climate : air
    C. meteorologist : clairvoyant
    D. practical : phenomenal
    E. table : crystal ball

17. VERBOSITY : VOLUBILITY :: _____ : _____   17._____
    A. prattle : talkative   B. loquacity : garrulity
    C. idle : gossip   D. speech : eloquence
    E. prolific : proliferation

18. TRICKERY : TWOFOLD :: _____ : _____   18._____
    A. pretend : decay   B. credulity : complex
    C. delude : duple   D. swindle : victimize
    E. dupery : duplex

19. MELODIOUS : INSTRUMENT :: _____ : _____   19._____
    A. quiet : organ   B. song : paean   C. dulcet : dulcimer

33

D. surcease : bagpipe   E. modulate : choir

20. TEMPLE : BOAT : : _____ : _____
    A. pagoda : gondola   B. Italy : India   C. water : land
    D. boattower   E. vessel : building

21. ATTENDANT EXHIBITION :: _____ : _____
    A. leaf book   B. errand: palace   C. words : folio
    D. page pageant   E. table : tableau

22. COPY : ORIGINAL :: _____ : _____
    A. several : one   B. telegraph : transmission
    C. image : photograph   D. photostat : document
    E. device : photography

23. PHYTOLOGY : PLANT : : _____ : _____
    A. philology : philosophy   B. zoology : animal
    C. penology : penalty   D. training : lion
    E. phrenology : head

24. MOUSE : CAT : : _____ : _____
    A. horses : chase   B. fox : hound   C. detectives : thieves
    D. jaguar : ocelot   E. fire engine : fire

25. SPORT : SWIMMING : : _____ : _____
    A. hiking : walking   B. game : chess
    C. crossword : puzzle   D. gambling : cards
    E. chance : skill

KEY (CORRECT ANSWERS)

1. D
2. D
3. C
4. D
5. B

6. D
7. D
8. D
9. E
10. C

11. B
12. D
13. D
14. D
15. D

16. C
17. B
18. E
19. C
20. A

21. D
22. D
23. B
24. B
25. B

TEST 4

DIRECTIONS: Each question in this part consists of two capitalized words which have a certain relationship to each other, followed by five lettered pairs of words in small letters. Choose the letter of the pair of words which are related to each other in the SAME way as the words of the capitalized pair are related to each other. *PRINT THE LETTER OF THE CORRECT ANSWER IN THE SPACE AT THE RIGHT.*

1. WALK : RIDE : : _____ : _____   1.___

    A. horse : rider
    B. person : sculptor
    C. pedestrian : equestrian
    D. citizen : knight
    E. bridle path : sidewalk

2. CHARM : STATUE : : _____ : _____   2.___

    A. man : God
    B. magic : religion
    C. priest : sorcerer
    D. natural : supernatural
    E. experience : manifestation

3. CONTRABAND : NEUTRAL : : _____ : _____   3.___

    A. pirate : high seas
    B. illegal : market
    C. narcotics : smuggler
    D. stolen : property
    E. goods : illegal

4. PEKING : VENICE :: _____ : _____   4.___

    A. south : north
    B. car : rickshaw
    C. west : east
    D. oriental : occidental
    E. nationality : country

5. FREIGHTER : CARGO :: _____ : _____   5.___

    A. tourist : class
    B. fleet : navy
    C. trawler : tug
    D. whaler : vessel
    E. liner : passenger

6. FAN : BELT : : _____ : _____   6.___

    A. nut : bolt
    B. electricity : fan
    C. propeller : helicopter
    D. carriage : wheel
    E. hammer : nail

7. TEMPER : EMBELLISH :: _____ : _____   7.___

    A. iambic pentameter: blank verse
    B. exaggeration : understatement
    C. moderation : hyperbole
    D. dearth : sparsity
    E. dissonance : cacophony

8. NUMBER : SUM : : _____ : _____   8.___

    A. add : divide
    B. totality : universe
    C. segment : complex
    D. decimal : fraction
    E. multiply : equate

36

2 (#4)

9. CUPIDITY : PROFUSION :: _____ : _____ 9.____
   A. extravagance : waste   B. parsimony : prodigality
   C. lavish : starve   D. avarice : stinginess
   E. dissipate : begrudge

10. WALLPAPER : WALL :: _____ : _____ 10.____
    A. canvas : paint   B. advertisement : billboard
    C. pen : ink   D. wood : mineral
    E. picture : frame

11. BLACK : RED :: _____ : _____ 11.____
    A. deterioration : improvement   B. debt : debit
    C. enter : ledger   D. profit : loss
    E. debit : credit

12. WHITE : TRUCE :: _____ : _____ 12.____
    A. yellow : fever   B. red : stop   C. black : death
    D. red : green   E. blue : sky

13. SQUARE ROD : AREA :: _____ : _____ 13.____
    A. gram : time   B. pound : ounce   C. measure : surface
    D. space : league   E. ocean : depth

14. ABYSS : PROJECTION :: _____ : _____ 14.____
    A. extension : prominence   B. mountain : canyon
    C. river : ditch   D. pit : protuberance
    E. depth : length

15. LUNG : MAN :: _____ : _____ 15.____
    A. beak : bird   B. arm : octopus   C. gill : fish
    D. stinger : bee   E. claw : cat

16. GAS : ASPHYXIATION :: _____ : _____ 16.____
    A. guillotine : executioner   B. rope : hanging
    C. air : suffocation   D. epidemic : holocaust
    E. burning : fire

17. MAGNETISM : ATTRACTION :: _____ : _____ 17.____
    A. magician : rabbit   B. hypnotic : hagiologic
    C. mesmerism : induction   D. psychic : phenomenon
    E. conduction : electricity

18. RESTAURANT : DINNER :: _____ : _____ 18.____
    A. calendar : date   B. business : letter   C. tailor : mend
    D. post office : stamp   E. delivery : mail

19. CADGE : PLUNDER :: _____ : _____ 19.____
    A. mendicant : marauder   B. beggar : masquerader
    C. raider : parasite   D. poor : rich
    E. settle : roam

20. SOUND : DISPUTE :: _____ : _____
    A. refutation : principle   B. phonetician : polemicist
    C. aggressive : controversy   D. interpreter : anarchist
    E. friendly : hostile

21. HUMANITARIANISM : LITERATURE :: _____ : _____
    A. philanthropy : philology   B. legend: linguistics
    C. culture : altruism   D. patriot : anglophile
    E. speech : welfare

22. MANKIND : WOMEN :: _____ : _____
    A. miserliness : polygamy   B. female : male
    C. egotism : cynicism   D. hatred : incivility
    E. misanthropy : misogny

23. BODY : MIME :: _____ : _____
    A. music : instrument   B. singer : speaker   C. voice : song
    D. symphony : concert   E. athlete : running

24. SPHERE : CIRCUIT :: _____ : _____
    A. concentric : roundabout   B. turn : circumflection
    C. coil : spiral   D. circumnavigation : world
    E. radius : center

25. FANTASY : PHENOMENON :: _____ : _____
    A. illusion : actuality   B. delusion : desert
    C. vision : mental image   D. chimera : mirage
    E. fact : fancy

KEY (CORRECT ANSWERS)

1. C
2. B
3. C
4. D
5. E

6. C
7. C
8. C
9. B
10. B

11. D
12. B
13. C
14. D
15. C

16. B
17. C
18. D
19. A
20. B

21. A
22. E
23. C
24. A
25. D

TEST 5

DIRECTIONS: Each question in this part consists of two capitalized words which have a certain relationship to each other, followed by five lettered pairs of words in small letters. Choose the letter of the pair of words which are related to each other in the SAME way as the words of the capitalized pair are related to each other. *PRINT THE LETTER OF THE CORRECT ANSWER IN THE SPACE AT THE RIGHT.*

1. SKATERS : RINK :: _____ : _____ 1.__
   A. tires : automobiles
   B. traffic : street
   C. sidewalk : pedestrian
   D. path : horse
   E. signal : policeman

2. FEE : ATTORNEY : : _____ : _____ 2.__
   A. percentage : part
   B. remuneration : reward
   C. expense : income
   D. commission : agent
   E. salary : recompense

3. CITY : MAYOR :: _____ : _____ 3.__
   A. taxpayer : citizen
   B. senator : state
   C. state : governor
   D. president : country
   E. Assembly Chamber : Speaker

4. FLAGRANT : BEHAVIOR : : _____ : _____ 4.__
   A. evil : doer
   B. heinous : villainous
   C. crime : wrong
   D. nefarious : deed
   E. iniquitous : atrocious

5. DOCTRINAIRE : CONTRADICTION :: _____ : _____ . 5.__
   A. true : false
   B. familiar : strange
   C. orthodox : paradox
   D. reason : unreason
   E. usual : exceptional

6. PRUDENCE : SAGACITY :: _____ : _____ 6.__
   A. man : judge
   B. fool : seer
   C. wise : rash
   D. discreet : judicious
   E. discriminate : indiscriminate

7. VALVE : TANK : : _____ : _____ 7.__
   A. pipe : water
   B. spray : hose
   C. hose : garden
   D. faucet : tank
   E. liquid : solid

8. SYNTHETIC : GENUINE : : _____ : _____ 8.__
   A. tin : aluminum
   B. raincoat : handbag
   C. cotton : wool
   D. plastic : leather
   E. nylon : orlon

9. WINTER : SUMMER : : _____ : _____ 9.__
   A. ice : fire
   B. refrigeration : cooking
   C. insulation : prefabrication
   D. heating : air conditioning
   E. degree : temperature

40

10. CORRESPONDENT : JOURNALIST :: _____ : _____ 10. ____

    A. foreign : intrigue
    B. agent : emissary
    C. welfare : social worker
    D. CIA : intelligence
    E. briefing : member

KEY (CORRECT ANSWERS)

1. B
2. D
3. C
4. D
5. C

6. D
7. D
8. D
9. D
10. B

VERBAL ANALOGIES – 2 BLANKS
EXAMINATION SECTION
TEST 1

DIRECTIONS: Each question in this part consists of two capitalized words which have a certain relationship to each other, followed by five lettered pairs of words in small letters. Choose the letter of the pair of words which are related to each other in the SAME way as the words of the capitalized pair are related to each other. *PRINT THE LETTER OF THE CORRECT ANSWER IN THE SPACE AT THE RIGHT.*

1. PRESS : NATION :: _____ : _____
    A. village : reputation
    B. gossip : hamlet
    C. gossip : newspaper
    D. truth : story
    E. chapter : book

2. INK : BLOTTER :: _____ : _____
    A. spore : sponge
    B. water : sponge
    C. water : wet
    D. pen : pencil
    E. margin : hole

3. DEMOCRACY : AUTOCRACY :: _____ : _____
    A. leisure class : aristocracy
    B. freedom : tyranny
    C. tyranny : nobility
    D. mob : despot
    E. poverty : wealth

4. GESTATION : BIRTH :: _____ : _____
    A. seedling : towering oak
    B. ponder : puzzle
    C. hypothesis : premise
    D. solution : crystallization
    E. answer : question

5. KNOWLEDGE : RUDIMENTS :: _____ : _____
    A. sophistication : ingenuity
    B. virtuoso : tyro
    C. end : beginning
    D. complexity : elementary
    E. bellicosity : ingenuousness

6. UNSHACKLE : FETTERS :: _____ : _____
    A. pardon : prisoner
    B. slake : thirst
    C. devour : food
    D. loose : tight
    E. vent : ire

7. INDOLENCE : CURSORILY :: _____ : _____
    A. determination : flatteringly
    B. error : not thoroughly
    C. ardor : elusively
    D. perfunctory : diligently
    E. zeal : assiduously

8. ANCIENT : OLD :: _____ : _____
   A. demented : vexed
   B. peremptory : positive
   C. ineluctable : indefeasible
   D. celibate : without relatives
   E. generosity : parsimony

9. RECUPERATION : VACATION :: _____ : _____
   A. refugee : homeland
   B. redress : lawsuit
   C. bail : sentence
   D. cajole : jailor
   E. joy : sorrow

10. WATER : JUG :: _____ : _____
    A. disillusionment : life
    B. acid : carboy
    C. destructiveness : railway
    D. solution : mineral
    E. discipline : army

11. DOCK : SHIP :: _____ : _____
    A. lair : fox
    B. home : parent
    C. station : train
    D. whistle : cab
    E. haven : refugee

12. POEM : EPIC :: _____ : _____
    A. scenery : play
    B. mustache : face
    C. drape : window
    D. setting : ring
    E. art : cubism

13. DAWN : DAY :: _____ : _____
    A. fight : might
    B. telegram : event
    C. harbinger : spring
    D. tail : comet
    E. spring : winter

14. CULMINATE : TERMINATE :: _____ : _____
    A. start : finish
    B. pinnacle : climax
    C. maturity : homestretch
    D. baptism : birth
    E. meridian : setting

15. RAFTERS : ROOF :: _____ : _____
    A. ribs : umbrella
    B. roof : rafters
    C. garret : house
    D. spokes : hub
    E. skeleton : frame

16. UNCLE : NIECE :: _____ : _____
    A. aunt : nephew
    B. father : daughter
    C. nephew : niece
    D. mother : daughter-in-law
    E. minor : adult

17. FINS : FEET :: _____ : _____
    A. water : air
    B. gills : lungs
    C. mouth : ears
    D. tail : feathers
    E. wings : arms

18. SAND : POWDER :: _____ : _____   18._____
    A. sawdust : flour   B. bread : wood
    C. table : chair   D. sky : water
    E. rain : snow

19. CAKE : COOKIES :: _____ : _____   19._____
    A. pie : dessert   B. salad : dressing
    C. steak : lamb chops   D. chicken : egg
    E. bread : biscuit

20. PENCIL : PEN :: _____ : _____   20._____
    A. baseball bat : baseball   B. pencil : eraser
    C. wall : brick   D. broom : mop
    E. water : wash

21. BEAT : MEASURE :: _____ : _____   21._____
    A. pedometer : hydrometer   B. daylight saving : standard time
    C. chronometer : calendar   D. sun-dial : candle power
    E. chronicle : anachronism

22. PROLOGUE : EPILOGUE :: _____ : _____   22._____
    A. coda : prelude   B. elephant : tail
    C. glossary : appendix   D. alpha : omega
    E. plot : denouement

23. DECADE : YEAR :: _____ : _____   23._____
    A. year : month   B. month : day
    C. minute : second   D. hour : minute
    E. millennium : century

24. COOL : FRIGID :: _____ : _____   24._____
    A. turgid : horrid   B. tepid : torrid
    C. livid : lurid   D. pool : placid
    E. tumid : turbid

25. SPLASH : INUNDATE :: _____ : _____   25._____
    A. crawl : creep   B. freeze : jell
    C. freshen : clean   D. drizzle : drench
    E. drift : swim

KEY (CORRECT ANSWERS)

1. B
2. B
3. B
4. D
5. B

6. E
7. E
8. B
9. B
10. B

11. C
12. E
13. C
14. E
15. A

16. B
17. B
18. A
19. E
20. D

21. C
22. D
23. E
24. B
25. D

TEST 2

DIRECTIONS: Each question in this part consists of two capitalized words which have a certain relationship to each other, followed by five lettered pairs of words in small letters. Choose the letter of the pair of words which are related to each other in the SAME way as the words of the capitalized pair are related to each other. *PRINT THE LETTER OF THE CORRECT ANSWER IN THE SPACE AT THE RIGHT.*

1. ACKNOWLEDGMENT : RUMOR :: _____ : _____ 1._____
   A. affirmation : report
   B. testify : certify
   C. probably : possible
   D. reputation : gossip
   E. servility : dependability

2. SAGACITY : EXPERIENCE :: _____ : _____ 2._____
   A. failure : timorousness
   B. study : mastery
   C. heredity : wisdom
   D. smarting : ointment
   E. experiment : hypothesis

3. CRISIS : DISEASE :: _____ : _____ 3._____
   A. prelude : interlude
   B. emergency : decision
   C. coup d'état : revolution
   D. apex : flight
   E. climax : battle

4. CAPRICIOUS : VAGARY :: _____ : _____ 4._____
   A. unstable : stability
   B. aberrant : constancy
   C. variable : wind
   D. inconstant : vacillation
   E. vacillating : steadfastness

5. MIND : PREJUDICE :: _____ : _____ 5._____
   A. crime : sex
   B. sun : shade
   C. sky : cloud
   D. ugly : thought
   E. knowledge : obtuse

6. SLIM : OBESE :: _____ : _____ 6._____
   A. cow : pig
   B. state : nation
   C. mountain : sea
   D. tremendous : prodigious
   E. terse : turgid

7. WHEEL : HUB :: _____ : _____ 7._____
   A. earth : axis
   B. state : nation
   C. mountain : sea
   D. earth : sun
   E. orbit : firmament

8. IMPURITIES : FILTER :: _____ : _____ 8._____
   A. water : faucet
   B. failures : examination
   C. remedies : petition
   D. quality : denier
   E. wheat : chaff

47

2 (#2)

9. MEDICINE : DOSE :: _____ : _____ 9._____
   A. vegetables : portion
   B. oatmeal : spoon
   C. bread : loaf
   D. water : glass
   E. fish : vitamins

10. PITCH : ROOF :: _____ : _____ 10._____
    A. altitude : hill
    B. grade : mountain
    C. shingles : roof
    D. depth – valley
    E. height : hill

11. REPETITION : MONOTONY :: _____ : _____ 11._____
    A. callowness : inexperience
    B. attempt : achievement
    C. dissipation : depravity
    D. familiarity : recognition
    E. interest : boredom

12. CALAMITY : DISTRESS :: _____ : _____ 12._____
    A. war : victory
    B. triumph : exultation
    C. tidings : jubilation
    D. emergency : desolation
    E. news : gratification

13. OINTMENT : BURN :: _____ : _____ 13._____
    A. pain : agony
    B. water : fire
    C. powder : face
    D. water : fire
    E. medicine : doctor

14. DUSK : DAWN :: _____ : _____ 14._____
    A. callow : mature
    B. light : murky
    C. diurnal : nocturnal
    D. moon : sun
    E. fall : rise

15. TABLE : LEGS :: _____ : _____ 15._____
    A. government : army
    B. men : men
    C. manuscript : thesis
    D. legislature : judiciary
    E. religion : rites

16. MANY : FEW :: _____ : _____ 16._____
    A. myriad : sparse
    B. major : minor
    C. minority : plurality
    D. plethora : innumerable
    E. predominant : sporadic

17. KING : MONARCHY :: _____ : _____ 17._____
    A. leader : executive
    B. clansman : tribe
    C. pope : papacy
    D. president : democracy
    E. queen : aristocracy

18. SQUARE : CIRCLE :: _____ : _____ 18._____
    A. acre : rod
    B. rectangle : oval
    C. sphere : cube
    D. cube : sphere
    E. hexagon : pentagon

19. DECADE : CENTURY :: _____ : _____
    A. dime : dollar
    B. time : number
    C. little : much
    D. penny : dime
    E. Decalogue : trilogy

20. ORNITHOLOGIST : BIRDS :: _____ : _____
    A. philologist : language
    B. biologist : cells
    C. pediatrician : feet
    D. botanist : animals
    E. etymologist : insects

21. DEER : VENISON :: _____ : _____
    A. lion : jackal
    B. beef : stew
    C. hog : pork
    D. mutton : sheep
    E. lamb : chops

22. INNUENDO : ASSERTION :: _____ : _____
    A. suggestion : recommendation
    B. implicit : explicit
    C. state : hint
    D. allusion : insinuation
    E. indirect : devious

23. VOLUME : BOOKLET :: _____ : _____
    A. genuine : synthetic
    B. tome : epitaph
    C. synopsis : compendium
    D. exposition : precis
    E. obese : slender

24. TOWER : DUNGEON :: _____ : _____
    A. virtue : disgrace
    B. building : foundation
    C. citadel : vault
    D. prop : cornice
    E. head : foot

25. TRANSLATE : PARAPHRASE :: _____ : _____
    A. intrinsic : extrinsic
    B. communicate : express
    C. hews : hearsay
    D. literal : free
    E. simile : metaphor

KEY (CORRECT ANSWERS)

1.	A	11.	C
2.	A	12.	B
3.	E	13.	B
4.	D	14.	E
5.	C	15.	E
6.	E	16.	A
7.	A	17.	C
8.	B	18.	B
9.	A	19.	A
10.	B	20.	A

21.	C
22.	B
23.	D
24.	C
25.	D

TEST 3

DIRECTIONS: Each question in this part consists of two capitalized words which have a certain relationship to each other, followed by five lettered pairs of words in small letters. Choose the letter of the pair of words which are related to each other in the SAME way as the words of the capitalized pair are related to each other. *PRINT THE LETTER OF THE CORRECT ANSWER IN THE SPACE AT THE RIGHT.*

1. ANCHOR : SHIP :: _____ : _____ 1._____
   A. stopper : door
   B. sound : whisper
   C. length : inch
   D. weight : paper
   E. cork : bottle

2. KING : PURPLE :: _____ : _____ 2._____
   A. sum : gold
   B. soldier : whisper
   C. soldier : khaki
   D. grass : green
   E. cork : bottle

3. HORSE : CENTAUR :: _____ : _____ 3._____
   A. fish : mermaid
   B. fish : nymph
   C. horse : man
   D. crocodile : dragon
   E. shark : whale

4. POOR : FRUGAL :: _____ : _____ 4._____
   A. rich : gorgeous
   B. wealth : prosperous
   C. well-to-do : heedless
   D. prosperous : prodigal
   E. lachrymose : indolent

5. INTEMPERATE : CRITICAL :: _____ : _____ 5._____
   A. deference : thought
   B. anger : spite
   C. emotion : reason
   D. devotion : fondness
   E. fulmination : recrimination

6. PRICES : SUBSIDY :: _____ : _____ 6._____
   A. steel : girder
   B. apex : climax
   C. tree : trunk
   D. society : law
   E. ceiling : pillar

7. GOVERNMENT : ORDER :: _____ : _____ 7._____
   A. hierarchy : peace
   B. disturbance : problem
   C. anarchy : chaos
   D. oppression : confusion
   E. dictator : democrat

8. GRUMBLE : SCOWL :: _____ : _____ 8._____
   A. laugh : smile
   B. express : restrain
   C. cry : sigh
   D. lament : condole
   E. entice : endow

9. FLEETNESS : RUNNER :: _____ : _____
   A. paint : artist
   B. imagination : artist
   C. grace : chess-player
   D. suppleness : acrobat
   E. strength : detective

10. HAND : WRIST :: _____ : _____
    A. angle : elbow
    B. compound sentence : conjunction
    C. leg : knee
    D. ribs : breastbone
    E. simile : metaphor

11. METIER : CALLING : _____ : _____
    A. heresy : hexapla
    B. purveyor : overseer
    C. minion : dominion
    D. hierarchy : organization of officials according to rank
    E. administration : oligarchy

12. SIDEREAL : STARRY :: _____ : _____
    A. bovine : piglike
    B. discrepant : discordant
    C. perspicuous : ambiguous
    D. browsing : carousing
    E. declivitous : narrow

13. DUB : DRESS :: _____ : _____
    A. acerbate : retaliate
    B. deprecate : depreciate
    C. cavil : carp
    D. cadge : lie
    E. comprise : constrain

14. EIDOLON : IMAGE :: _____ : _____
    A. tarantella : dance of the spiders
    B. covert : bevy
    C. argot : dragon
    D. nexus : link
    E. efflux : effluvium

15. DECUMAN : TENTH :: _____ : _____
    A. consummate : inchoate
    B. plethoric : insufficient
    C. callow : mature
    D. crepuscular : glimmering
    E. decumbent : lambent

16. DECOCT : PREPARE BY BOILING :: _____ : _____
    A. eviscerate : thin out
    B. skulk : hulk
    C. demean : conduct oneself
    D. concoct : evict
    E. rescind : abstain

17. HONORARIUM : FEE :: _____ : _____
    A. fatuity : crassness
    B. canard : hoax
    C. torpor : trudgen
    D. trull : trumpet
    E. truffle : trousseau

18. FRICATIVE : FORCED :: _____ : _____   18._____
    A. voracious : veracious   B. clamorous : glamorous
    C. adipose : fatty   D. vaunted : truckle
    E. bellicose : mangy

19. ASSEVERATE : AFFIRM :: _____ : _____   19._____
    A. enervate : give impetus to   B. roil : convulse
    C. impugn : call in question   D. essay : assay
    E. digest : diffuse

20. ZEITGEIST : SPIRIT OF THE TIME :: _____ : _____   20._____
    A. nimbus : atmosphere   B. lintel ; vertical support
    C. atoll : treeless plain   D. cloak : cloister

21. FUSTY : MUSTY :: _____ : _____   21._____
    A. tractable : spineless   B. maudlin : fuddled
    C. climacteric : released   D. donative : illative
    E. fictile : fictive

22. ADUMBRATE : OUTLINE :: _____ : _____   22._____
    A. derogate : detract   B. reticulate : reformulate
    C. obtrude : obtest   D. obvert : obviate
    E. abrogate : validate

23. SEQUESTER : SET APART :: _____ : _____   23._____
    A. obliquity : defamatory language
    B. junto : hunt
    C. scourge : dereliction
    D. noblesse oblige : obligation of generous behavior associated with high rank
    E. colander : calendar

24. ANOMALOUS : ABNORMAL :: _____ : _____   24._____
    A. dulcet : tame   B. cavalier : finical
    C. feigned : restricted   D. recondite : elementary
    E. esoteric : abstruse

25. ASPERSE : DISCREDIT :: _____ : _____   25._____
    A. inveigh : impound   B. inculpate : exculpate
    C. lampoon : satirize   D. accede : exceed
    E. condone : condign

KEY (CORRECT ANSWERS)

1. D
2. C
3. A
4. D
5. C

6. E
7. C
8. A
9. D
10. C

11. D
12. B
13. C
14. D
15. D

16. C
17. B
18. C
19. C
20. C

21. B
22. A
23. D
24. E
25. C

TEST 4

DIRECTIONS: Each question in this part consists of two capitalized words which have a certain relationship to each other, followed by five lettered pairs of words in small letters. Choose the letter of the pair of words which are related to each other in the SAME way as the words of the capitalized pair are related to each other. *PRINT THE LETTER OF THE CORRECT ANSWER IN THE SPACE AT THE RIGHT.*

1. INCONGRUITY : DISCREPANT :: _____ : _____ 1._____
   A. incoherent : unconsolidated
   B. unfit : absurd
   C. slacken : looseness
   D. instrument : orchestra
   E. dissonance : discordant

2. LOAF : LOITER :: _____ : _____ 2._____
   A. doze : somnolence
   B. vegetate : dormant
   C. slacken : looseness
   D. dawdler : truant
   E. eater : opium

3. HALLUCINATION : ILLUSION :: _____ : _____ 3._____
   A. phantom : apprarition
   B. phantasm : phantasmagorical
   C. fancy : visual
   D. error : deceptive
   E. ghost : appear

4. PARKING : OFFENSE :: _____ : _____ 4._____
   A. tort : wrong
   B. smuggle : contraband
   C. breach : violation
   D. void : marriage
   E. annulment : invalidation

5. SEMBLANCE : ADAPTATION :: _____ : _____ 5._____
   A. imitate : duplication
   B. mimicking : parrot
   C. satirize : parody
   D. counterfeit : forgery
   E. echo : mountain

6. OBLATION : IMMOLATION :: _____ : _____ 6._____
   A. bemusement : inaptness
   B. babbling : idiocy
   C. fatuity : inanity
   D. shallowness : asininity
   E. thralldom : freedom

7. BOWER : PERGOLA :: _____ : _____ 7._____
   A. orchard : vineyard
   B. market : agriculture
   C. greenhouse : gardening
   D. wine : apple
   E. fertilizer : vintage

8. FURROW : MOAT :: _____ : _____ 8._____
   A. carve : chisel
   B. trench : ditch
   C. engraving : offset
   D. slit : seam
   E. etch : wrinkle

9. JOINTURE : APPANAGE :: _____ : _____
   A. quarry : prey   B. sporting : blood
   C. contest : play   D. divert : entertain
   E. chase : animal

10. GHOULISH : SPIRITS :: _____ : _____
    A. devilish : ghoulish   B. demoniacal : fabulous
    C. hobgoblin : spook   D. fiendish : incubi
    E. gnome : salamander

11. LISTLESS : MOTIVATING :: _____ : _____
    A. effective : effectual   B. active : thinking
    C. enervating : stimulating D. cold : hot
    E. energizing : forcible

12. MATURATION : INCIPIENCE :: _____ : _____
    A. fertility : fruition   B. materialism : existentialism
    C. senescence : youth   D. imbecile : moron
    E. field marshal : lieutenant

13. CURSORY : CONSUMMATE :: _____ : _____
    A. pompous : pomposity   B. archaic : archeological
    C. signature : calligraphy   D. diffident : sanguine
    E. alto : contralto

14. DECEIT : FURTIVE :: _____ : _____
    A. affluence : parsimony   B. notoriety : flagrant
    C. generosity : altruism   D. perennial : decennial
    E. subterfuge : clandestine

15. WOOF : WARP :: _____ : _____
    A. windmill : water   B. smokestack : chimney
    C. forest : meadow   D. ledge : minaret
    E. supine : horizontal

16. DOCTOR : TREATMENT :: _____ : _____
    A. thief : theft   B. electors : president
    C. pirate : ship   D. nun : ministration
    E. boss : efficiency

17. DILEMMA : PUZZLE :: _____ : _____
    A. guess : choose   B. oracle : treacle
    C. maturation : condensation D. sphinx : enigma
    E. portent : foretell

18. PUNCTURE : INCISE :: _____ : _____
    A. precipice : precipitous   B. engulf : convulse
    C. holocaust : flagrant   D. burn : wound
    E. seethe : smolder

3 (#4)

19. LANGUAGE : WORDS :: _____ : _____ 19.____
    A. science : experiments   B. arithmetic : numbers
    C. center : arc   D. social science : history
    E. spelling : phonetics

20. ACQUIT : CRIME :: _____ : _____ 20.____
    A. prescription : sickness   B. repent : sin
    C. release : bail   D. presentment : jury
    E. exonerate : change

21. DECADE : CENTURY :: _____ : _____ 21.____
    A. multitude : myriads   B. second : hour
    C. youth : senescence   D. dime : dollar
    E. penny : dime

22. BROKER : INVESTOR :: _____ : _____ 22.____
    A. doctor : nurse   B. executive : subordinate
    C. student : teacher   D. merchant : marine
    E. attorney : client

23. PUNGENT : BITTER :: _____ : _____ 23.____
    A. refreshing : refreshment   B. flabby : flaccid
    C. brusque : brisk   D. acute : acerb
    E. morbid : morbidity

24. UNCTUOUS : SMOOTH :: _____ : _____ 24.____
    A. terse : succinct   B. cowardly : obsequious
    C. stalwart : pusillanimous   D. valiant : verve
    E. viscous : suave

25. NERVOUS : DEPRESSED :: _____ : _____ 25.____
    A. intensive : extensive   B. fabulous : large
    C. physical : mental   D. exultant : gratified
    E. insane : neurotic

KEY (CORRECT ANSWERS)

1.	E		11.	C
2.	C		12.	C
3.	A		13.	D
4.	A		14.	E
5.	D		15.	D
6.	A		16.	D
7.	A		17.	D
8.	B		18.	E
9.	A		19.	B
10.	D		20.	E

21.	D
22.	E
23.	D
24.	A
25.	D

TEST 5

DIRECTIONS: Each question in this part consists of two capitalized words which have a certain relationship to each other, followed by five lettered pairs of words in small letters. Choose the letter of the pair of words which are related to each other in the SAME way as the words of the capitalized pair are related to each other. *PRINT THE LETTER OF THE CORRECT ANSWER IN THE SPACE AT THE RIGHT.*

1. CHESS : PIECES :: _____ : _____ 1._____
   A. cards : bridge
   B. Mah Jongg : tiles
   C. Russian roulette : dice
   D. tennis : court
   E. letters : scrabble

2. MOOSE : NORTH AMERICA :: _____ : _____ 2._____
   A. camel : South America
   B. beaver : Egypt
   C. mosquito : malaria
   D. elk : Asia
   E. Australia : kangaroo

3. PROCESS : PARTICIPANT :: _____ : _____ 3._____
   A. vote : voter
   B. election : elector
   C. choice : chosen
   D. president : people
   E. primary : privilege

4. PUNGENT : PERCEPTIVE :: _____ : _____ 4._____
   A. poignant : sentient
   B. biting : feeling
   C. sensitive : emotional
   D. keen : piercing
   E. arouse : display

5. CARBOLIC ACID : MILK :: _____ : _____ 5._____
   A. poison : emetic
   B. catalyst : venomous
   C. infect : defect
   D. arsenic : anecdote
   E. nicotine : cigarette

6. CONIC : FUNNEL :: _____ : _____ 6._____
   A. triangular : obelisk
   B. cylindrical : column
   C. hexagonal : star
   D. cyanic : bluish
   E. rhombus : parallelogram

7. MONSOON : WIND :: _____ : _____ 7._____
   A. river : overflowing
   B. raining : excessively
   C. flood : rain
   D. cyclone : hurricane
   E. earthquake : volcano

8. ELEMENT : SUPPORT :: _____ : _____ 8._____
   A. tire : puncture
   B. gas : leak
   C. clay : mold
   D. fire : andiron
   E. paper : perforate

2 (#5)

9. IODINE : CHLORINE :: _____ : _____ 9._____
   A. calcium : enamel
   B. copper : penny
   C. carbon : diamond
   D. pure : impure
   E. cobalt : nickel

10. EXPERIMENT : CATALYST :: _____ : _____ 10._____
    A. travel : interfere
    B. business : expediter
    C. manuscript : publisher
    D. hasten : rush
    E. energy : expend

KEY (CORRECT ANSWERS)

1.	B	6.	B
2.	D	7.	C
3.	B	8.	D
4.	A	9.	E
5.	A	10.	B

VERBAL ANALOGIES – 2 BLANKS
EXAMINATION SECTION
TEST 1

DIRECTIONS: Each question in this part consists of two capitalized words which have a certain relationship to each other, followed by five lettered pairs of words in small letters. Choose the letter of the pair of words which are related to each other in the SAME way as the words of the capitalized pair are related to each other. *PRINT THE LETTER OF THE CORRECT ANSWER IN THE SPACE AT THE RIGHT.*

1. DOOR : KEY : : _____ : _____ 1._____

   A. crossword puzzle : design B. frame : window
   C. problem : solution D. suitcase : handle
   E. password : sentry

2. STORM WINDOW : COLD :: _____ : _____ 2._____

   A. Dr. Salk : polio B. roof : rain
   C. disease : vaccination D. thermos : heat
   E. vitamin D : rickets

3. ACORN : OAK : : _____ : _____ 3._____

   A. pistil : stamen B. tree : leaf
   C. bulb : tulip D. root : grass
   E. rose : thorn

4. SICKNESS : DOCTOR :: _____ : _____ 4._____

   A. dividends : stocks B. salary : laborer
   C. robbery : thief D. wind : sail
   E. leak : plumber

5. FRICTION/ : HEAT :: _____ : _____ 5._____

   A. eating : appendicitis B. grass : lawn mower
   C. typewriter : ribbon D. match : flame
   E. night : day

6. MODERATE : EXTREMIST ::_____ : _____ 6._____

   A. scribe : inscribe B. spiritual : material
   C. agnostic : prognosis D. noticeable : flagrant
   E. heathen : pagan

7. AGGRESSION : WAR :: _____ : _____ 7._____

   A. fear : dread B. neurosis : psychosis
   C. nervousness : reaction D. demise : disease
   E. illness : treatment

8. BILL : AMENDMENT : : _____ : _____ 8._____

   A. introduction : theme B. antithesis : synthesis
   C. stanza : poem D. letter : postscript
   E. summary : report

9. SPHERE : HEMISPHERE :: _____ : _____

    A. polygon : hexagon   B. circle : quadrant
    C. duality : modality   D. acute angle : obtuse angle
    E. triangle : rectangle

10. TOP : STRING :: _____ : _____

    A. hoof : horse   B. runner : sled
    C. wheel : axle   D. ramrod : rifle
    E. propeller : wing

11. AQUARIUM : FISH :: _____ : _____

    A. jungle : monkeys   B. estuary : monkeys
    C. nest : birds   D. museum : monkeys
    E. aviary : birds

12. MOTH : LARVA :: _____ : _____

    A. accomplishment : plan   B. accomplishment : community
    C. community : plan   D. populace : community
    E. train : community

13. HERESY : CHURCH :: _____ : _____

    A. treason : institution   B. institution : state
    C. orthodoxy : atheism   D. atheism : agnosticism
    E. treason : state

14. RANSOM : CAPTIVE :: _____ : _____

    A. death : suffer   B. money : prisoner
    C. war : prisoner   D. money : kidnapper
    E. blackmail : victim

15. ROCK : EROSION :: _____ : _____

    A. signature : forgery   B. landscape : flatness
    C. food : fasting   D. character : dissipation
    E. task : fatigue

16. FIBER : FABRIC :: _____ : _____

    A. appurtenance : object   B. obstinate : deadlock
    C. nucleus : cell   D. leverage : aggregate
    E. member : league

17. REST : FATIGUE :: _____ : _____

    A. relaxation : recreation   B. precipice : mountain
    C. laziness : obesity   D. diploma : graduate
    E. praise : dejection

18. RULES : BASEBALL :: _____ : _____

    A. law : jury   B. law : society
    C. jury : sentence   D. prisoner : cell
    E. prisoner : law

19. TORTOISE : HARE :: _____ : _____   19.____
    A. letter : telegram   B. truth : lie
    C. essay : thesis   D. word : number
    E. modesty : egotism

20. CANNON : CATAPULT :: _____ : _____   20.____
    A. matter : mind   B. church : temple
    C. oak : scorn   D. clock : hourglass
    E. temple : foundation

21. HOOF : HORSE :: _____ : _____   21.____
    A. wing : robin   B. egg : chicken
    C. paw : cat   D. hole : chipmunk
    E. purr : kitten

22. CLUB : SWORD :: _____ : _____   22.____
    A. pound : pierce   B. cut : parry
    C. thrust : pierce   D. cut : break
    E. break : crack

23. BIRD : EGG :: _____ : _____   23.____
    A. vegetable : earth   B. oak : acorn
    C. muscle : cell   D. flight : motion
    E. crime : implication

24. OBJECTIVE : CAMPAIGN :: _____ : _____   24.____
    A. success : talent   B. goal : motivation
    C. triumph : victory   D. consequence : misdeed
    E. destination : voyage

25. LOSE : POSSESS :: _____ : _____   25.____
    A. supply : produce   B. advance : hesitate
    C. perform : undertake   D. desist : continue
    E. recur : cease

KEY (CORRECT ANSWERS)

1.	C	11.	E
2.	B	12.	A
3.	C	13.	E
4.	E	14.	E
5.	D	15.	D
6.	D	16.	E
7.	B	17.	E
8.	D	18.	B
9.	B	19.	A
10.	C	20.	D
21.	C		
22.	A		
23.	B		
24.	E		
25.	D		

TEST 2

DIRECTIONS: Each question in this part consists of two capitalized words which have a certain relationship to each other, followed by five lettered pairs of words in small letters. Choose the letter of the pair of words which are related to each other in the SAME way as the words of the capitalized pair are related to each other.
PRINT THE LETTER OF THE CORRECT ANSWER IN THE SPACE AT THE RIGHT.

1. METAL : ALLOY :: _____ : _____　　　　　　　　　　　　　　　　　　　1._____

   A. mixture : blend　　　　　　　　B. species : hybrid
   C. plant : flower　　　　　　　　　D. rock : metal
   E. block : chip

2. INSULT : SENSITIVE :: _____ : _____　　　　　　　　　　　　　　　　2._____

   A. cheat : unassuming　　　　　　B. convince : gullible
   C. steal : starved　　　　　　　　D. suffer : fatigued
   E. fear : frightened

3. APPROBATION : APPLAUSE :: _____ : _____　　　　　　　　　　　　　3._____

   A. retaliation : injury　　　　　　B. superiority : scorn
   C. understanding : praise　　　　D. contempt : snub
   E. amusement : grimace

4. BLAME : EXCULPATE :: _____ : _____　　　　　　　　　　　　　　　　4._____

   A. honor : retract　　　　　　　　B. debt : regain
   C. duty : resent　　　　　　　　　D. position : retract
   E. obligation : absolve

5. PERJURE : RELATE :: _____ : _____　　　　　　　　　　　　　　　　　5._____

   A. examine : glance　　　　　　　B. sprawl : recline
   C. gorge : eat　　　　　　　　　　D. destroy : mar
   E. trespass : wander

6. TORPID : TEMPERATE :: _____ : _____　　　　　　　　　　　　　　　　6._____

   A. lethargic : abstemious　　　　B. pusillanimous : absent
   C. militant : irascible　　　　　　D. dogmatic : truculent
   E. latent : gregarious

7. HEADLONG : DEJECTED :: _____ : _____　　　　　　　　　　　　　　　7._____

   A. melancholy : unhappy　　　　　B. askew : explicit
   C. nebulous : credulous　　　　　D. intrinsic : fatuous
   E. precipitous : disconsolate

8. APPLAUSE : RIDICULE :: _____ : _____　　　　　　　　　　　　　　　8._____

   A. amnesia : oblivion　　　　　　　B. felon : miscreant
   C. constantly : bow　　　　　　　　D. encore : catcall
   E. generosity : lechery

65

9. PARSIMONY : MAGNANIMITY :: _____ : _____   9.___
   A. urgency : exigency   B. ribaldry : prodigality
   C. profession : avocation   D. unselfish . selfish
   E. bigotry : tolerance

10. TROPICAL. : LUXURIANT : : _____ : _____   10.___
    A. penicillin : cure   B. invigoration : exhilaration
    C. arctic : gelid   D. cold : muddy
    E. disturbed : halcyon

11. ISLAND : ARCHIPELAGO _____ : _____   11.___
    A. cerebrum : nucleus   B. strait : peninsula
    C. nucleus : cell   D. Africa : Australia
    E. individual : multitude

12. DOWNCAST : EXUBERANT : : _____ : _____   12.___
    A. melancholy : effusive   B. beaver : eager
    C. lavish : exultant   D. abundant : parsimonious
    E. dispersal : congregation

13. OBELISK : HIEROGLYPHIC :: _____ : _____   13.___
    A. statue : sphinx   B. masterpiece : signature
    C. geography : cartography   D. medicine : cardiograph
    E. blackboard : penmanship

14. CAVIAR : GOURMET :: _____ : _____   14.___
    A. art : artificer   B. edition : critic
    C. patrician : plebeian   D. seance : clairvoyant
    E. masterpiece : connoisseur

15. GRACEFUL : GAUCHE :: _____ : _____   15.___
    A. wealthy : indigent   B. poised : sad
    C. secretive : clandestine   D. melancholy : lugubrious
    E. thoughtless : inadvertent

16. DYNAMO : SWITCH :: _____ : _____   16.___
    A. ambition : aspiration   B. lamp : light
    C. spur : horse   D. man : stimulus
    E. dynamo : switch

17. RAGE : RED : : _____ : _____   17.___
    A. depressed:yellow   B. envy : green
    C. fright : chalk   D. red : henna
    E. cadaverous : ashen

18. STUDY : DIPLOMA :: _____ : _____   18.___
    A. ambition : honor   B. examination : marks
    C. diligence : bonus   D. labor : wages
    E. course : promotion

19. FEDERATION : UNION :: _____ : _____   19.____
    A. league : team   B. city : borough
    C. gender : girls   D. congregation : sect
    E. organization : club

20. BULLDOG : PUGNACITY :: _____ : _____   20.____
    A. bloodhound : odor   B. hen : cowardice
    C. truck : commodious   D. Pekingese : affectation
    E. greynound : fleetness

21. DEJECTION : FAILED :: _____ : _____   21.____
    A. disapproval : approved   B. emotion: success
    C. dejected : failed   D. angry : rejected
    E. elation : passed

22. HAZE : LABYRINTH :: _____ : _____   22.____
    A. string : labyrinth   B. matador : bull
    C. alternative : dilemma   D. riddle : enigma
    E. ancient : sphinx

23. WINE : DREGS :: _____ : _____   23.____
    A. wheat : chaff   B. dress : ore
    C. lead : gold   D. humanity : dregs
    E. wisdom : cunning

24. WARLIKE : PEACEFUL :: _____ : _____   24.____
    A. belligerent : growling   B. martial : halcyon
    C. warlike : mournful   D. Mars : sun
    E. worried : soothed

25. SAVAGE : BARBARIAN :: _____ : _____   25.____
    A. belief : peaceful   B. charm : talisman
    C. superstition : talisman D. ritual : savage
    E. experiment : antitoxin

4 (#2)

KEY (CORRECT ANSWERS)

1.	B	11.	D
2.	B	12.	A
3.	D	13.	E
4.	E	14.	E
5.	E	15.	A
6.	A	16.	E
7.	E	17.	B
8.	D	18.	D
9.	E	19.	A
10.	C	20.	E

21. E
22. D
23. A
24. B
25. C

TEST 3

DIRECTIONS: Each question in this part consists of two capitalized words which have a certain relationship to each other, followed by five lettered pairs of words in small letters. Choose the letter of the pair of words which are related to each other in the SAME way as the words of the capitalized pair are related to each other. *PRINT THE LETTER OF THE CORRECT ANSWER IN THE SPACE AT THE RIGHT.*

1. FLOOD : LEVEE :: _____ : _____   1.____
   - A. money : miser
   - B. stoic : emotion
   - C. humility : arrogant
   - D. dilemma : solution
   - E. disorder : police

2. RECONDITE : BULKY :: _____ : _____   2.____
   - A. remote : ponderous
   - B. protracted : laden
   - C. distant : momentous
   - D. hence : pensive
   - E. yonder : onerous

3. MATURITY : INFANCY :: _____ : _____   3.____
   - A. lamb : cub
   - B. pod : seed
   - C. senility : puerility
   - D. novice : fundamental
   - E. culmination : inception

4. VERSE : POET :: _____ : _____   4.____
   - A. art : sculptor
   - B. statue : sculptor
   - C. prelude : musician
   - D. house : architect
   - E. chisel : craftsman

5. FOUNDER : SHIP :: _____ : _____   5.____
   - A. fame : disgrace
   - B. illness : woman
   - C. collapse : regime
   - D. incarcerate : criminal
   - E. holocaust : earthquake

6. OBTUSE : ACUTE :: _____ : _____   6.____
   - A. knife : blade
   - B. dull : shrewd
   - C. chisel : hammer
   - D. opaque : transparent
   - E. perspicuous : perspicacious

7. CARAT : WEIGHT :: _____ : _____   7.____
   - A. fathom : depth
   - B. rod : farm
   - C. speed : knot
   - D. acre : distance
   - E. pennyweight : diamond

8. COMMUNISTS : FASCISTS :: _____ : _____   8.____
   - A. Fascists : Nazis
   - B. red : black
   - C. Liberals : Blackshirts
   - D. Whites : Brownshirts
   - E. subversive : patriotic

9. CARBINE : SOLDIER :: _____ : _____

 A. marine : sailor   B. pirate : ship
 C. book : writer   D. spear : knight
 E. test tube : chemist

10. HORSE : CARRIAGE :: _____ : _____

 A. teacher : prodigy   B. coolie : rickshaw
 C. ass : Ford   D. Shetland : pony
 E. hen : egg

11. PROBABLY : PERHAPS :: _____ : _____

 A. rarely : generally   B. necessity : invention
 C. certainly : surely   D. surely : accidentally
 E. incidentally : fortuitous

12. HARDIHOOD : HARDY :: _____ : _____

 A. egotism : selfish   B. fortitude : force
 C. solitude : indifference   D. friendship : friends
 E. great : greater

13. UNTRUTH : LIE :: _____ : _____

 A. weakness : act   B. prevaricate : deny
 C. homicide : murder   D. accident : assault
 E. hallucination : nightmare

14. MINISTER : CONGREGATION :: _____ : _____

 A. guide : tourists   B. doctor : patients
 C. scientists : knowledge   D. dean : students
 E. leader : paratroop team

15. PRAISE : DEPRESSION :: _____ : _____

 A. steam : engine   B. apathy : despair
 C. ulcer : cancer   D. bicarbonate : gastric acidity
 E. hope : despair

16. BROOK : RIVER :: _____ : _____

 A. island : peninsula   B. cove : bay
 C. lagoon : bay   D. ocean : gulf
 E. stream : outlet

17. BRASS : COPPER :: _____ : _____

 A. pewter : lead   B. tin : foil
 C. urn : copper   D. zinc : iron
 E. coin : silver

18. ENGINE : CABOOSE :: _____ : _____

 A. motor : housing   B. introduction : conclusion
 C. cabin : train   D. power : freight
 E. beginning : commencement

19. DIAMOND : CARAT :: _____ : _____   19.____
    A. bullion : silver
    B. ring : gold
    C. gold : ore
    D. potato : peck
    E. bushel : oat

20. WOODMAN : AXE :: _____ : _____   20.____
    A. mason : awl
    B. reader : novel
    C. ploughman : scythe
    D. teacher : quadrant
    E. pilot : sextant

21. ARCHEOLOGIST : ANTIQUITY :: _____ : _____   21.____
    A. philologist : stamps
    B. entomologist : words
    C. theologian : astronomy
    D. ornithologist : horticulture
    E. ichthyologist : marine life

22. SERFDOM : FEUDALISM :: _____ : _____   22.____
    A. taxation : totalitarianism
    B. independence : agriculture
    C. entrepreneur : laissez-faire
    D. nationalization : socialism
    E. reedom : dictatorship

23. RAISIN PRUNE :: _____ : _____   23.____
    A. apricot : fig
    B. grape : raisin
    C. wine : alcohol
    D. privet : barberry
    E. cherry : wine

24. PYRAMID : CUBE :: _____ : _____   24.____
    A. triangle : square
    B. square : parallelogram
    C. triangle : cone
    D. hexagon : pentagon
    E. cone : cylinder

25. COKE : COAL :: _____ : _____   25.____
    A. steel : iron
    B. oxygen : nitrogen
    C. bread : yeast
    D. charcoal : wood
    E. skeleton : body

KEY (CORRECT ANSWERS)

1. E
2. A
3. E
4. B
5. C

6. B
7. A
8. B
9. D
10. B

11. C
12. A
13. C
14. D
15. D

16. C
17. A
18. B
19. D
20. E

21. E
22. D
23. A
24. A
25. D

TEST 4

DIRECTIONS: Each question in this part consists of two capitalized words which have a certain relationship to each other, followed by five lettered pairs of words in small letters. Choose the letter of the pair of words which are related to each other in the SAME way as the words of the capitalized pair are related to each other. *PRINT THE LETTER OF THE CORRECT ANSWER IN THE SPACE AT THE RIGHT.*

1. EACH : EVERYBODY :: _____ : _____   1.____

    A. solo : ensemble   B. ocean : wave
    C. ball of wool : skein   D. spool : thread
    E. house : beams

2. NEXT : BY :: _____ : _____   2.____

    A. wit : approach   B. off : from
    C. contiguous : close   D. warmth : glow
    E. adjacent : sequence

3. TOO : VERY :: _____ : _____   3.____

    A. potion : beverage   B. of : off
    C. approach : accost   D. overdose : heaping measure
    E. copious : scanty

4. REVEREND : REVERENT :: _____ : _____   4.____

    A. intend : pretend   B. proud : haughty
    C. respected : respectful   D. kneeling : pious
    E. sycophant : king

5. HEADLONG : IMPETUOSITY :: _____ : _____   5.____

    A. dry : moderation   B. degenerate : perversity
    C. accident : recklessness D. phlegmatic : stolidity
    E. quiet : tacit

6. TRULY : FORSOOTE :: _____ : _____   6.____

    A. really : consequently   B. statement : hyperbole
    C. average : extraordinary D. in fact : indeed
    E. reality : fiction

7. ON CONDITION THAT ACCEPTANCE :: _____ : _____   7.____

    A. granted that : nevertheless   B. except : consent
    C. relying upon : enmity   D. provided that : agreement
    E. in accordance with : depending

8. NAMELY : FOR EXAMPLE :: _____ : _____   8.____

    A. like : i.e.   B. that is : such as
    C. for instance : especially D. to wit : thus
    E. viz. : ibid.

2 (#4)

9. NECESSITY : INVENTION :: _____ : _____   9.___

    A. because : out
    B. emergency : effect
    C. luxury : lethargy
    D. hardship : luck
    E. opulence : affluence

10. PARAPHRASE : VERBATIM :: _____ : _____   10.___

    A. imitate : lampoon
    B. quotation : allusion
    C. caricature : portrait
    D. similarity : likeness
    E. likeness : sketch

11. MAN : CONSCIENCE :: _____ : _____   11.___

    A. imitate : lampoon
    B. quotation : allusion
    C. caricature : portrait
    D. similarity : likeness
    E. likeness : sketch

12. PICTURE : PAINTER :: _____ : _____   12.___

    A. cement : bricklayer
    B. friendship : stranger
    C. cure : doctor
    D. magic : magician
    E. wall : mason

13. CANARY : CAGE :: _____ : _____   13.___

    A. pugilist : ring
    B. poodle : kennel
    C. tiger : zoo
    D. bird : nest
    E. fish : tackle

14. MOUNTAIN : VALLEY :: _____ : _____   14.___

    A. lake:river
    B. country:state
    C. order:cancel
    D. peak:gorge
    E. pla eap:plain

15. MACHINE : JAM :: _____ : _____   15.___

    A. stone : crack
    B. pain : throb
    C. order : cancel
    D. muscle : cramp
    E. lightning : flash

16. TOUCH : GRASP :: _____ : _____   16.___

    A. watch : search
    B. Took : see
    C. ponder : examine
    D. eye : sight
    E. glance : scrutinize

17. TAX : EXEMPTION :: _____ : _____   17.___

    A. obligation : debt
    B. custom : conformity
    C. disease : immunity
    D. change : adaptation
    E. transgression : pardon

18. IRREGULAR : SYMMETRICAL :: _____ : _____   18.___

    A. oblong : square
    B. trapezoid : parallel
    C. coastline : statue
    D. area : perimeter
    E. solid : sphere

3 (#4)

19. EVENT : PROPHECY :: _____ : _____   19.____
    A. disaster : premonition   B. fact : opinion
    C. religion : faith   D. life : dream
    E. expectation : hope

20. CURRENT : SWITCH :: _____ : _____   20.____
    A. rope : pulley   B. drawer : handle
    C. light : bulb   D. bullet : trigger
    E. gun : holster   F.

21. ALWAYS : NEVER :: _____ : _____   21.____
    A. happy : sad   B. frequently : seldom
    C. never : always   D. intermittently : occasionally
    E. constantly : ubiquitously

22. NEVADA : JAVA :: _____ : _____   22.____
    A. clever : shrewd   B. bald : stupid
    C. obtuse : acute   D. California : New York
    E. sparse : dense

23. LIBERAL : CONSERVATIVE :: _____ : _____   23.____
    A. Socialist : Monarchist   B. Whig : Tory
    C. Democrat : Republican   D. patriot : traitor
    E. Republican : Conservative

24. SPEAKER : HECKLER :: _____ : _____   24.____
    A. song : vocalist   B. cow : matador
    C. bull : picador   D. victim : executioner
    E. E. eye : mote

25. PIG : PORK :: _____ : _____   25.____
    A. youth : age   B. sheep : lamb
    C. beef : steer   D. beef : veal
    E. sheep : mutton

KEY (CORRECT ANSWERS)

1.	A	11.	D
2.	C	12.	E
3.	D	13.	B
4.	C	14.	E
5.	D	15.	D
6.	D	16.	E
7.	D	17.	C
8.	B	18.	C
9.	C	19.	A
10.	C	20.	D

21. B
22. E
23. B
24. C
25. E

———

TEST 5

DIRECTIONS: Each question in this part consists of two capitalized words which have a certain relationship to each other, followed by five lettered pairs of words in small letters. Choose the letter of the pair of words which are related to each other in the SAME way as the words of the capitalized pair are related to each other. *PRINT THE LETTER OF THE CORRECT ANSWER IN THE SPACE AT THE RIGHT.*

1. BIRDS : AVIARY :: _____ : _____   1.____

   A. apiary : bees   B. grain: barn
   C. bus : depot   D. subway : kiosk
   E. ships : drydock

2. BULLION : COIN :: _____ : _____   2.____

   A. wool : suit   B. voice : words
   C. mint : money   D. soup : dessert
   E. print : periodical

3. PROGNOSIS : DISEASE :: _____ : _____   3.____

   A. medicine : illness   B. cause : disaster
   C. hypothesis : problem   D. forecast : humidity
   E. warning : detour

4. CONDEMN : COMPLAIN :: _____ : _____   4.____

   A. laugh : titter   B. jail: sentence
   C. sigh : weep   D. laughter : anger
   E. brightness : fancy

5. WEEPING : PUNISHMENT :: _____ : _____   5.____

   A. grief : sadness   B. dying : grave
   C. peace : lose   D. evil : chastisement
   E. self-satisfaction : praise

6. FROM : TO :: _____ : _____   6.____

   A. hardship : emergency   B. apparently : really
   C. by : of   D. angrily : satirically
   E. off : down

7. RATHER : QUITE :: _____ : _____   7.____

   A. apparently : secretly   B. fault : guilt
   C. more : less   D. nearly : hardly
   E. guilt : punishment

8. IRRETRIEVABLE : MISLAID :: _____ : _____   8.____

   A. smashed : cracked   B. mend : break
   C. found : lost   D. present : gone
   E. invisible : seen

9. ARCHITECT : HOUSE :: _____ : _____
    A. general : army
    B. farm : produce
    C. priest : religion
    D. conspirators : plot
    E. government : people

10. WHEEL : CIRCLE :: _____ : _____
    A. sphere : triangle
    B. square : house
    C. orange : sphere
    D. round : sphere
    E. round : orange

KEY (CORRECT ANSWERS)

1. C
2. A
3. C
4. A
5. E
6. B
7. B
8. A
9. D
10. C

ANTONYMS/OPPOSITES
EXAMINATION SECTION
TEST 1

DIRECTIONS: Each question below consists of a word printed in capital letters, followed by five words or phrases lettered A through E. Choose the lettered word or phrase that is *most nearly* OPPOSITE in meaning to the word in capital letters. *PRINT THE LETTER OF THE CORRECT ANSWER IN THE SPACE AT THE RIGHT.*

1. ACRID   1.____
   - A. smoky
   - B. withered
   - C. sharp
   - D. mild
   - E. acerb

2. ALLERGY   2.____
   - A. extreme sensitivity
   - B. distaste
   - C. sleepiness
   - D. suppressed desire
   - E. unsusceptibility

3. AMBIGUOUS   3.____
   - A. acoustic
   - B. ambivalent
   - C. equivocal
   - D. imitating
   - E. succinct

4. AMELIORATE   4.____
   - A. bring together
   - B. settle a dispute
   - C. worsen
   - D. improve
   - E. amend

5. AUGMENT   5.____
   - A. sever
   - B. disperse
   - C. increase
   - D. diminish
   - E. argue

6. BANAL   6.____
   - A. sarcastic
   - B. trite
   - C. novel
   - D. futuristic
   - E. sagacious

7. BEATIFY   7.____
   - A. make lovely
   - B. desecrate
   - C. make happy
   - D. restore
   - E. hallow

8. BOURGEOIS   8.____
   - A. middle-class citizen
   - B. capital letters
   - C. swollen streams
   - D. nobility
   - E. peasant

9. BROMIDE   9.____
   - A. vegetable
   - B. petty bribe
   - C. pamphlet
   - D. skin abrasion
   - E. epigram

79

10. BRING

    A. fetch   B. transfer   C. relate
    D. suggest   E. dispatch

11. CAPRICIOUS

    A. fickle   B. fault-finding   C. sneering
    D. dominating   E. resolve

12. CASUAL

    A. watery   B. fated   C. fortuitous
    D. aromatic   E. moving

13. CHOLERIC

    A. dignified   B. high-tempered   C. gloomy
    D. unexcitable   E. caustic

14. CIRCULAR

    A. muscular   B. oblique   C. grouped
    D. pivotal   E. incongruous

15. CIRCUMVENT

    A. succor   B. reserve   C. fortify
    D. surround   E. delude

16. COMPASSIONATE

    A. pitiful   B. merciful   C. ruthless
    D. reluctant   E. pietistic

17. COMPLIANCE

    A. violation   B. regulation   C. attendance
    D. submission   E. conformance

18. CONDIGN

    A. punishable   B. scheming   C. undeserved
    D. merited   E. condemn

19. CONDONE

    A. demand payment   B. express sympathy   C. forget
    D. revenge   E. forgive

20. COPE

    A. fail in striving   B. contend on equal terms
    C. plug with soft material   D. crown with laurel
    E. compare with others

21. DECOROUS

    A. unseemly   B. proper   C. low cut
    D. in groups of ten   E. deteriorating

22. DESPONDENT

    A. powdery
    B. bent
    C. optional
    D. artificial
    E. elated

22.____

23. DESULTORY

    A. pompous
    B. methodical
    C. rambling
    D. oppressively hot
    E. cursory

23.____

24. DETONATE

    A. explode
    B. deafen
    C. muffle
    D. fizzle out
    E. destroy

24.____

25. DISCIPLE

    A. impostor
    B. follower
    C. antagonist
    D. paragon
    E. colleague

25.____

KEYS (CORRECT ANSWERS)

1. D
2. E
3. E
4. C
5. D

6. C
7. B
8. E
9. E
10. E

11. E
12. B
13. D
14. B
15. A

16. C
17. A
18. C
19. D
20. A

21. A
22. E
23. B
24. C
25. C

TEST 2

DIRECTIONS: Each question below consists of a word printed in capital letters, followed by five words or phrases lettered A through E. Choose the lettered word or phrase that is *most nearly* OPPOSITE in meaning to the word in capital letters. *PRINT THE LETTER OF THE CORRECT ANSWER IN THE SPACE AT THE RIGHT.*

1. DISCREET 1.___
   - A. cautious
   - B. chary
   - C. prudent
   - D. distinct
   - E. temerarious

2. DISINTER 2.___
   - A. dig up from a grave
   - B. lack interest
   - C. interrupt
   - D. inject between muscles
   - E. entomb

3. DOGGEREL 3.___
   - A. trivial verse
   - B. small canine species
   - C. stubborn behavior
   - D. sophisticated poetry
   - E. manger

4. DOLE OUT 4.___
   - A. squander
   - B. distribute piecemeal
   - C. control
   - D. deny alms
   - E. hoard

5. DOMINEERING 5.___
   - A. dictatorial
   - B. pliant
   - C. considerate
   - D. unsympathetic
   - E. recreant

6. ELEGY 6.___
   - A. inheritance
   - B. burnt offering
   - C. violin obbligato
   - D. dirge
   - E. paean

7. ELICIT 7.___
   - A. concoct with alcohol
   - B. draw out
   - C. compel approval
   - D. request sharply
   - E. ignite

8. EMOLLIENT 8.___
   - A. salve
   - B. monument
   - C. tariff charge
   - D. extra tip
   - E. abrasive

9. ENCORE 9.___
   - A. intermission
   - B. termination
   - C. heart of the matter
   - D. repetition
   - E. variation

10. ENERVATE 10.___
    - A. stumble
    - B. devitalize
    - C. stimulate
    - D. rejoice
    - E. impede

2 (#2)

11. EXPIATION 11._____
    A. reprobation B. clarification C. failure
    D. atonement E. interpretation

12. FABULOUS 12._____
    A. wealthy B. impressionistic C. realistic
    D. legendary E. fictional

13. FAIRWAY 13._____
    A. airplane landing field B. golf greensward C. captain's private quarters
    D. entrance to ferry slip E. coppice

14. FEASIBLE 14._____
    A. garish B. festive C. theoretical
    D. practicable E. pertinent

15. FIERY 15._____
    A. vehement B. irritable C. restive
    D. gay E. indifferent

16. FLORID 16._____
    A. flowing B. livid C. blotchy
    D. ruddy E. over-heated

17. FLOUT 17._____
    A. move B. mock C. obey
    D. defy E. flog

18. FOREGO 18._____
    A. prosecute B. align C. renounce
    D. look forward E. over-heated

19. FURTIVE 19._____
    A. fleeing B. hairy C. glancing
    D. stealthy E. ingenuous

20. GARBLE 20._____
    A. substantiate B. garnish C. mutilate
    D. unravel E. embroider

21. GARRULOUS 21._____
    A. talkative B. quarrelsome C. snarling
    D. laconic E. ungainly

22. GOSSAMER 22._____
    A. sleezy B. dusty C. gauzy
    D. unbreakable E. zephyr-like

83

3 (#2)

23. GOURMAND

    A. greedy eater   B. epicure   C. hungry person
    D. ascetic   E. fried pumpkin shell

23.____

24. GRIEVOUS

    A. rutty   B. gratifying   C. sorrowful
    D. vicious   E. unmentionable

24.____

25. GRIMACE

    A. happy smile   B. fruit sherbet   C. twisting of the countenance

    D. fine quality silk   E. sneer

25.____

KEYS (CORRECT ANSWERS)

1.	E	11.	A
2.	E	12.	C
3.	D	13.	E
4.	A	14.	C
5.	B	15.	E
6.	E	16.	B
7.	D	17.	C
8.	E	18.	A
9.	B	19.	E
10.	C	20.	A

21. D
22. D
23. D
24. B
25. A

TEST 3

DIRECTIONS: Each question below consists of a word printed in capital letters, followed by five words or phrases lettered A through E. Choose the lettered word or phrase that is *most nearly* OPPOSITE in meaning to the word in capital letters. *PRINT THE LETTER OF THE CORRECT ANSWER IN THE SPACE AT THE RIGHT.*

1. HEINOUS
   - A. criminal
   - B. elevated
   - C. inhuman
   - D. flagrant
   - E. moderate

   1._____

2. HUE
   - A. tint
   - B. shade
   - C. tone
   - D. tinge
   - E. etiolation

   2._____

3. IMMUNITY
   - A. protection against accident
   - B. exemption
   - C. freedom from disease
   - D. dispensation
   - E. tendency

   3._____

4. IMPLICIT
   - A. directly stated
   - B. understood though not expressed
   - C. omitted entirely by chance
   - D. stated but not for publication
   - E. inherent

   4._____

5. IMPUTE
   - A. insult
   - B. contradict
   - C. ascribe
   - D. question
   - E. refer

   5._____

6. INCIPIENT
   - A. tasteless
   - B. criminal
   - C. beginning
   - D. diseased
   - E. terminal

   6._____

7. INGENUOUS
   - A. guileful
   - B. naive
   - C. frank
   - D. uncertain
   - E. jealous

   7._____

8. INIQUITOUS
   - A. awesome
   - B. unequal
   - C. wicked
   - D. present everywhere
   - E. exemplary

   8._____

9. INTERMITTENT
   - A. continuing without break
   - B. occurring at intervals
   - C. persistently noisy
   - D. gradually subdued
   - E. intermediate

   9._____

10. INTRANSIGENT

    A. utterly fearless   B. irreconcilable   C. invalid
    D. not transferable   E. tractable

11. INTREPID

    A. fearful   B. uneasy   C. dauntless
    D. stumbling   E. insistent

12. INURE

    A. maim   B. entice   C. deplete
    D. toughen   E. endure

13. INVOKE

    A. provoke   B. denounce   C. slanderous
    D. address in prayer   E. evoke

14. NOSTALGIA

    A. homesickness   B. inertia   C. gloominess
    D. nasal catarrh   E. wanderlust

15. OCCULT

    A. abstract   B. manifest   C. secret
    D. oriental   E. acute

16. ONEROUS

    A. unwanted   B. impossible   C. delicate
    D. burdensome   E. facile

17. OPULENT

    A. expensive   B. oily   C. crafty
    D. profuse   E. jejune

18. ORDINANCE

    A. excess weight   B. anarchy   C. law
    D. military supplies   E. mound of filth

19. ORTHOGRAPHY

    A. correct accent   B. choice of words   C. misspelling
    D. derivation of words   E. clear enunciation

20. PAROCHIAL

    A. limited in range   B. sacred   C. stubborn
    D. objective   E. easily manageable

21. PEREMPTORY

    A. trifling   B. compliant   C. arbitrary
    D. binding   E. camouflaged

22. PERVADE

    A. pass along
    C. convince at length
    E. confine
    B. escape quietly
    D. to be diffused throughout

    22._____

23. PERVERSITY

    A. cruelty
    D. adherent
    B. miserliness
    E. frugality
    C. conformity

    23._____

24. PHLEGMATIC

    A. stolid
    D. sentient
    B. figurative
    E. substantial
    C. aphasic

    24._____

25. POIGNANT

    A. melancholy
    D. keen
    B. soothing
    E. reluctant
    C. doubtful

    25._____

KEYS (CORRECT ANSWERS)

1.	B	11.	A
2.	E	12.	C
3.	E	13.	B
4.	A	14.	E
5.	B	15.	B
6.	E	16.	E
7.	A	17.	E
8.	E	18.	B
9.	A	19.	C
10.	E	20.	D

21. B
22. E
23. C
24. D
25. B

TEST 4

DIRECTIONS: Each question below consists of a word printed in capital letters, followed by five words or phrases lettered A through E. Choose the lettered word or phrase that is *most nearly* OPPOSITE in meaning to the word in capital letters. *PRINT THE LETTER OF THE CORRECT ANSWER IN THE SPACE AT THE RIGHT.*

1. PRODIGIOUS   1.___
    A. extraordinary   B. commonplace   C. profound
    D. prehistoric   E. infinitesmal

2. PUERILE   2.___
    A. childish   B. mature   C. feverish
    D. immaculate   E. pusillanimous

3. PUNCTILIOUS   3.___
    A. offensively frank B. willing to admit blame C. sarcastically polite
    D. precise in conduct E. indiscriminate

4. RAZE   4.___
    A. torture   B. erect   C. salvage
    D. destroy   E. prorogue

5. RECESSIVE   5.___
    A. inclined to go back B. relating to slavery C. moving forward
    D. modest   E. allemorphic

6. RENEGADE   6.___
    A. turncoat   B. loyalist   C. habitual drunkard
    D. confirmed criminal E. one who kills a king

7. RENASCENCE   7.___
    A. unwinding   B. restoration   C. unscrewing
    D. detraining   E. perdition

8. RESPITE   8.___
    A. pardon   B. re-trial   C. stay
    D. vengeance   E. continuation

9. SALIENT   9.___
    A. hidden   B. salty   C. floating
    D. prominent   E. flagrant

10. SATELLITE   10.___
    A. falling star   B. attentive follower C. adversary
    D. flint spark   E. fellow captive

2 (#4)

11. SCRUPULOUS   11._____

    A. niggardly   B. abusive   C. conscientious
    D. unprincipled   E. guilty

12. SINEWY   12._____

    A. callused   B. enervated   C. springy
    D. slimy   E. brawny

13. SKEPTIC   13._____

    A. agnostic   B. suave   C. ingenious
    D. credulous   E. faithful

14. SPARE   14._____

    A. forbear   B. forego   C. reserve
    D. control   E. squander

15. SPORADIC   15._____

    A. isolated   B. incessant   C. dissipated
    D. involuntary   E. discrete

KEYS (CORRECT ANSWERS)

1. E   6. B
2. B   7. E
3. E   8. E
4. B   9. A
5. C   10. C

11. D
12. B
13. D
14. E
15. B

ANTONYMS/OPPOSITES
EXAMINATION SECTION

DIRECTIONS FOR THIS SECTION: Each question below consists of a word printed in capital letters, followed by five words or phrases lettered A through E. Choose the lettered word or phrase that is *most nearly* OPPOSITE in meaning to the word in capital letters. *PRINT THE LETTER OF THE CORRECT ANSWER IN THE SPACE AT THE RIGHT.*

TEST 1

1. ABEYANCE — A. revival B. following orders C. temporary inactivity D. adjournment E. concealment
2. ACADEMIC — A. unseasoned B. scholarly C. practical D. attainable E. superficial
3. AFFECTATION — A. histrionics B. conquetry C. shield D. airs E. ingeniousness
4. AFFILIATE — A. thread B. honor C. cut away D. associate oneself E. feign
5. ALLEGE — A. deny B. declare C. arouse D. arrest E. conjure
6. ALLEVIATE — A. moderate B. assign C. tax D. antagonize E. deceive
7. ANIMOSITY — A. hatred B. affection C. sprightliness D. animalism E. contempt
8. APATHY — A. hatred B. indifference C. policy D. cowardice E. fervor
9. APPAL — A. pierce B. apportion C. dismay D. attach E. gratify
10. AUTHENTIC — A. severe B. gracious C. mendacious D. reliable E. supreme
11. BRISK — A. large B. fragile C. alert D. flagging E. tolerant
12. BRUSQUE — A. keen B. smooth C. menacing D. quick E. abrupt
13. CALUMNIOUS — A. disastrous B. quartz-like C. laudatory D. slanderous E. querulous
14. CANDID — A. straightforward B. evasive C. profound D. pleasant E. contrite
15. CAROUSE — A. cajole B. revel C. decay D. induce E. abstain
16. CELIBATE — A. chaste B. spouseless C. pertaining to funerals D. relic E. conjugal
17. CLEMENCY — A. weather condition B. climbing plant C. type of cloud D. rigor E. mercy
18. COMMODIOUS — A. inutile B. spacious C. ordinary D. interchangeable E. useful
19. COMPETENT — A. equivalent B. compact C. adequate D. based on rivalry E. maladroit
20. COMPLICITY — A. deceit B. antipathy C. partnership in wrong D. collusion E. delight in society
21. CONSTERNATION — A. dissapointment B. dismay C. disapproval D. distrust E. intrepidity
22. CONTAMINATE — A. include B. expurgate C. pollute D. adjacent E. reflect upon
23. CORROBORATE — A. withdraw B. terminate C. disavow D. confirm E. correlate
24. COSMIC — A. funny B. vast C. greasy D. childish E. finite
25. CRITERION — A. standard B. anomaly C. judgment D. analysis E. probability

TEST 2

1. CRUCIAL — A. pending B. conditional C. critical D. unreasonable E. unessential   1. ...
2. CULPABILITY — A. misprint B. blame C. felony D. impeccability E. whitewash   2. ...
3. DAUB — A. alarm B. delay C. depict D. stupefy E. smear   3. ...
4. DELINEATE — A. crack B. blotch C. do twice D. make of linen E. describe   4. ...
5. DEVIATING — A. conspiring B. depressing C. indirect D. unswerving E. turning   5. ...
6. DILAPIDATED — A. lonely B. integral C. ruined D. sequestered E. old-fashioned   6. ...
7. DILATORY — A. reclining B. spiteful C. expeditious D. praiseworthy E. procrastinating   7. ...
8. DISPATCH — A. curb B. argue C. send off D. mend E. receive   8. ...
9. DOCILE — A. parasitic B. ungovernable C. mournful D. teachable E. compliant   9. ...
10. DRIFT — A. meaning B. tendency C. riot D. motion E. procession   10. ...
11. DUALITY — A. unity B. falsity C. biformity D. perversity E. intactness   11. ...
12. DUBIOUS — A. questionable B. categorical C. sufficient D. pleasant to the ear E. composed   12. ...
13. DURABLE — A. flimsy B. permanent C. ugly D. timely E. callous   13. ...
14. ECCENTRIC — A. peculiar B. convergent C. ecliptic D. eclectic E. pragmatic   14. ...
15. EMBELLISH — A. defraud B. deface C. represent symbolically D. point up E. review   15. ...
16. EMBRYONIC — A. accelerated B. many-colored C. rudimentary D. undeveloped E. perfected   16. ...
17. ENIGMATIC — A. cognitive B. fraudulent C. odious D. magical E. puzzling   17. ...
18. EPIGRAMMATIC — A. pointed B. national C. ungrammatical D. scabrous E. concise   18. ...
19. FANATICISM — A. perplexity B. indifference C. endurance D. flatulence E. excessive enthusiasm   19. ...
20. FORMIDABLE — A. menacing B. conventional C. loathsome D. apprehensive E. resolute   20. ...
21. GAWKY — A. gaudy B. clumsy C. meager D. elegant E. straightforward   21. ...
22. GENESIS — A. gender B. origin C. outcome D. inception E. exodus   22. ...
23. HILARITY — A. celerity B. mirth C. despondence D. abandon E. covetousness   23. ...
24. HOSTILE — A. singular B. convincing C. poisonous D. stimulating E. amicable   24. ...
25. HYBRID — A. mongrel B. eugenic C. exaggerated D. dwarfed E. homogenous   25. ...

TEST 3

1. IMPEDIMENT — A. accusation B. hindrance C. succor D. admission E. inhibition   1. ...
2. IMPERVIOUS — A. incomparable B. impenetrable C. inhuman D. trackless D. dissoluble   2. ...
3. INCREDIBLE — A. hard to believe B. skeptical C. bad beyond correction D. indisputable D. illogical   3. ...

4. INGENIOUS   A. frank B. deceitful C. ingenuous   4. ...
                  D. subversive E. clever
5. INTEGRITY   A. honesty B. opprobrium C. humor D. courage 5. ...
                  E. knowledge
6. INTIMIDATE   A. to defy B. to make afraid C. to come with- 6. ...
                  out invitation D. to weary E. to make less fearful
7. INTROSPECTION A. bending backwards B. insertion C. performa- 7. ...
                  tion D. self examination E. extroversion
8. JOSTLE   A. trip B. elbow C. bully D. rob E. quail   8. ...
9. LAVISH   A. niggardly B. extravagant C. prodigal   9. ...
                  D. convalescent E. plain
10. LENIENCY   A. transparent substance B. stringency   10. ...
                  C. fickleness D. forbearance E. decay
11. MERCENARY   A. egoistic B. pestilential C. altruistic   11. ...
                  D. greedy E. venal
12. MEDIOCRE   A. yellow B. boundless C. ordinary E. eminent 12. ...
                  E. tiny
13. NOVELTY   A. modernism B. pseudonym C. relic D. innova- 13. ...
                  tion E. quaintness
14. OBSOLETE   A. antiquated B. polite C. neglected   14. ...
                  D. rectangular E. vernal
15. ONSLAUGHT   A. furious attack B. murder C. repulse   15. ...
                  D. adventure E. severe punishment
16. OUST   A. evict B. banish C. injure D. admit   16. ...
                  E. cry out
17. PALATABLE   A. toothsome B. savory C. soft D. intoler-   17. ...
                  able E. vindictive
18. PALLID   A. wretched B. funereal C. ghastly D. spectral 18. ...
                  E. vivid
19. PALTRY   A. consequential B. pitiable C. grandiloquent   19. ...
                  D. prevalent E. petty
20. PARABLE   A. analogy B. pattern C. phenomenon D. fable   20. ...
                  E. allegory
21. PARAPHRASE   A. restate B. convey C. reword D. articulate   21. ...
                  E. translate
22. PARCH   A. swab B. saturate C. desiccate D. sponge   22. ...
                  E. scorch
23. PATHOLOGICAL A. morbid B. virulent C. salubrious E. diseased 23. ...
                  E. implied
24. PERMEATE   A. enfilade B. traverse C. pervade D. infil-   24. ...
                  trate E. block
25. PERPETUATE   A. obliterate B. punish C. preserve D. flourish 25. ...
                  E. enshrine

TEST 4

1. PERTINENT   A. appropriate B. awkward C. obstinate   1. ...
                 D. abusive E. irrelevant
2. PONDER   A. reflect B. hazard C. argue D. reject   2. ...
                 E. consider
3. POLLUTE   A. spread B. foul C. stain D. decontaminate   3. ...
                 E. rebut
4. POSTHUMOUS   A. hastily B. extant C. inappropriate   4. ...
                 D. happening after one's death E. unawakened

Test 4/
KEYS

5. PREDILECTION   A. maintenance B. negotiation C. investment   5. ...
                 D. inclination E. evulsion
6. PRETEXT   A. reason B. fact C. excuse D. opinion   6. ...
                 E. illusion
7. PRODIGAL   A. perturbing B. wasteful C. venal D. large   7. ...
                 E. wandering
8. REFUTE   A. disobey B. disprove C. remove D. affirm   8. ...
                 E. strike out
9. RELENTLESS   A. compassionate B. unmoved by pity C. confident 9. ...
                 D. unexciting E. graceful
10. RETICENT   A. backward B. rash C. timid D. reserved   10. ...
                 E. gushing
11. SEDENTARY   A. soothing B. calm C. migratory D. aged   11. ...
                 E. stationary
12. SKEPTICISM   A. cynicism B. simplicity C. critical state of   12. ...
                 mind D. distortion E. chariness
13. SMUG   A. uncomplaisant B. adjacent C. self-satisfied   13. ...
                 D. hazy E. cozy
14. SPASMODIC   A. continuous B. intermittent C. feverish   14. ...
                 D. gradual E. momentary
15. STILTED   A. formal B. subdued C. deprived D. archaic   15. ...
                 E. facile
16. SUCCINCT   A. superfluous B. concise C. pithy D. succu-   16. ...
                 lent E. colloquial
17. SURREPTITIOUS A. stealthy B. surprising C. authorized   17. ...
                 D. affected E. unobserved
18. SUSCEPTIBLE A. aggressive B. impotent C. cowering   18. ...
                 D. unimpressionable E. hesitant
19. TANTRUM   A. symbol B. tranquility C. commiseration   19. ...
                 D. conundrum E. display of temper
20. TATTERS   A. finery B. gossip C. sails D. riches E. rags   20. ...

KEYS (CORRECT ANSWERS)

TEST 1		TEST 2		TEST 3		TEST 4	
1. A	11. D	1. E	11. A	1. C	11. C	1. E	11. C
2. E	12. B	2. D	12. B	2. E	12. D	2. B	12. B
3. E	13. C	3. C	13. A	3. D	13. C	3. D	13. C
4. C	14. B	4. B	14. D	4. C	14. E	4. B	14. A
5. A	15. E	5. D	15. B	5. B	15. C	5. E	15. E
6. D	16. E	6. B	16. E	6. A	16. D	6. B	16. A
7. B	17. D	7. C	17. A	7. E	17. D	7. C	17. C
8. E	18. A	8. A	18. E	8. E	18. E	8. D	18. D
9. E	19. E	9. B	19. B	9. A	19. A	9. A	19. E
10. C	20. B	10. E	20. B	10. B	20. C	10. E	20. A
21. E		21. D		21. E			
22. B		22. C		22. B			
23. C		23. C		23. C			
24. E		24. E		24. E			
25. B		25. E		25. A			

ANTONYMS/OPPOSITES
EXAMINATION SECTION
TEST 1

DIRECTIONS: Each question below consists of a word printed in capital letters, followed by five words or phrases lettered A through E. Choose the lettered word or phrase that is *most nearly* OPPOSITE in meaning to the word in capital letters. *PRINT THE LETTER OF THE CORRECT ANSWER IN THE SPACE AT THE RIGHT.*

1. CELERITY 1.____
   - A. torpor
   - B. felicity
   - C. fame
   - D. acrimony
   - E. temerity

2. APATHETIC 2.____
   - A. stoical
   - B. amative
   - C. lissome
   - D. finical
   - E. redolent

3. FLACCID 3.____
   - A. cold
   - B. sterile
   - C. brave
   - D. stiff
   - E. whimsical

4. INGENUOUS 4.____
   - A. foolish
   - B. intelligent
   - C. wily
   - D. indigent
   - E. native

5. AMENABLE 5.____
   - A. prayerful
   - B. conciliatory
   - C. pliant
   - D. truculent
   - E. mendacious

6. PARSIMONIOUS 6.____
   - A. benevolent
   - B. worldly
   - C. scoffing
   - D. ungrammatical
   - E. grudging

7. INDIGENOUS 7.____
   - A. caustic
   - B. factitious
   - C. exotic
   - D. opulent
   - E. sophisticated

8. SAPIENT 8.____
   - A. distasteful
   - B. animalistic
   - C. ignorant
   - D. jejune
   - E. zestful

9. TENUOUS 9.____
   - A. substantial
   - B. decadent
   - C. salubrious
   - D. illogical
   - E. slender

10. ZENITH 10.____
    - A. acme
    - B. nadir
    - C. pentacle
    - D. azimuth
    - E. apogee

2 (#1)

11. RESTIVE
    - A. overactive
    - B. refractory
    - C. compliant
    - D. uneasy
    - E. listless

12. ADAMANT
    - A. primeval
    - B. laudatory
    - C. polite
    - D. yielding
    - E. intractable

13. DISCRETE
    - A. continuous
    - B. separate
    - C. foolish
    - D. tactful
    - E. serrated

14. SANGUINE
    - A. bloody
    - B. diffident
    - C. happy
    - D. pale
    - E. confident

15. PLACATE
    - A. retaliate
    - B. confuse
    - C. wander
    - D. nettle
    - E. condone

16. FATUOUS
    - A. inane
    - B. stout
    - C. witty
    - D. empty
    - E. vacuous

17. INNOCUOUS
    - A. toxic
    - B. guileful
    - C. gullible
    - D. criminal
    - E. culpable

18. DEARTH
    - A. demise
    - B. copiousness
    - C. nativity
    - D. distaste
    - E. lack

19. RESPITE
    - A. affirmation
    - B. intermission
    - C. continuance
    - D. colloquy
    - E. fairness

20. LACONIC
    - A. turgid
    - B. replete
    - C. tearful
    - D. negligent
    - E. draconic

21. ANIMADVERSION
    - A. censure
    - B. distaste
    - C. spirituality
    - D. bestiality
    - E. approbation

22. NOISOME
    - A. boisterous
    - B. beneficial
    - C. villous
    - D. pallid
    - E. noxious

23. EXPURGATE

    A. cleanse B. harden C. improve
    D. deflect E. smirch

24. ATAVISM

    A. progression B. favoritism C. inclination
    D. cannibalism E. reversion

25. ATTRITION

    A. appeasement B. capitulation C. wearing away
    D. calming down E. aggrandizement

KEYS (CORRECT ANSWERS)

1. A
2. B
3. D
4. C
5. D

6. A
7. C
8. C
9. A
10. B

11. C
12. D
13. A
14. B
15. D

16. C
17. A
18. B
19. C
20. A

21. E
22. B
23. E
24. A
25. E

TEST 2

DIRECTIONS: Each question below consists of a word printed in capital letters, followed by five words or phrases lettered A through E. Choose the lettered word or phrase that is *most nearly* OPPOSITE in meaning to the word in capital letters. *PRINT THE LETTER OF THE CORRECT ANSWER IN THE SPACE AT THE RIGHT*

1. FABRICATE
   - A. consume
   - B. furrow
   - C. construct
   - D. materialize
   - E. delete

2. COMMAND
   - A. mandate
   - B. consummation
   - C. correlation
   - D. commitment
   - E. supplication

3. DISSIPATE
   - A. sip
   - B. amass
   - C. disturb
   - D. outdistance
   - E. disperse

4. UNBIASED
   - A. unfair
   - B. unreasonable
   - C. uniform
   - D. equitable
   - E. disquieting

5. SATURNINE
   - A. buoyant
   - B. gloomy
   - C. aspiring
   - D. incongruous
   - E. splenetic

6. PROFITABLE
   - A. preferable
   - B. chagrined
   - C. ruinous
   - D. lucrative
   - E. profligate

7. GENERATING
   - A. generous
   - B. originating
   - C. degenerating
   - D. terminating
   - E. ingenuous

8. SANCTION
   - A. safety
   - B. performance
   - C. injunction
   - D. sanctuary
   - E. permission

9. PROBABLE
   - A. perchance
   - B. imprudent
   - C. unlikely
   - D. perilous
   - E. unsavory

10. FRUITION
    - A. exposure
    - B. harvest
    - C. frustration
    - D. neglect
    - E. attainment

2 (#2)

11. RANCOROUS 11.____
    - A. benign
    - B. confusing
    - C. satiated
    - D. complex
    - E. malicious

12. AVARICIOUS 12.____
    - A. munificent
    - B. rapacious
    - C. analogous
    - D. perverse
    - E. atonal

13. UNIQUE 13.____
    - A. uniform
    - B. single
    - C. utilitarian
    - D. senescent
    - E. unitary

14. PROCURE 14.____
    - A. decline
    - B. reap
    - C. forfeit
    - D. effect
    - E. contrive

15. RAVENOUS 15.____
    - A. birdlike
    - B. hungry
    - C. rancid
    - D. venial
    - E. sated

16. INNOCUOUS 16.____
    - A. mixed
    - B. pernicious
    - C. defiled
    - D. harmless
    - E. diffused

17. PERMEATE 17.____
    - A. smooth
    - B. pulverize
    - C. obstruct
    - D. pollute
    - E. penetrate

18. AXIOM 18.____
    - A. adage
    - B. proof
    - C. precept
    - D. dictum
    - E. hearsay

19. RELEVANT 19.____
    - A. immaterial
    - B. pertinent
    - C. relenting
    - D. capable
    - E. released

20. POTENT 20.____
    - A. secretive
    - B. powerful
    - C. restive
    - D. puissant
    - E. enervated

21. AMELIORATE 21.____
    - A. improve
    - B. embitter
    - C. alter
    - D. mellow
    - E. impair

22. IMPENDING 22.____
    - A. pendulous
    - B. impeding
    - C. fortuitous
    - D. imminent
    - E. looming

23. LATENT
    A. tricky   B. hidden   C. pompous
    D. overt   E. hateful

24. DISCERNMENT
    A. concern   B. obtuseness   C. distance
    D. sickness   E. acumen

25. SUAVE
    A. genuine   B. captive   C. gauche
    D. bland   E. captious

KEYS (CORRECT ANSWERS)

1. A   11. A
2. E   12. A
3. B   13. A
4. A   14. C
5. A   15. E

6. C   16. B
7. D   17. C
8. C   18. E
9. C   19. A
10. C   20. E

21. B
22. C
23. D
24. B
25. C

TEST 3

DIRECTIONS: Each question below consists of a word printed in capital letters, followed by five words or phrases lettered A through E. Choose the lettered word or phrase that is *most nearly* OPPOSITE in meaning to the word in capital letters. *PRINT THE LETTER OF THE CORRECT ANSWER IN THE SPACE AT THE RIGHT.*

1. WORLDLY
   - A. trifling
   - B. secular
   - C. mundane
   - D. unworthy
   - E. impractical

   1.____

2. BEG
   - A. seek
   - B. implore
   - C. convert
   - D. vaunt
   - E. donate

   2.____

3. ERUDITE
   - A. impolite
   - B. learned
   - C. correct
   - D. illiterate
   - E. contrite

   3.____

4. CURSORY
   - A. protracted
   - B. persistent
   - C. evanescent
   - D. superficial
   - E. gentle

   4.____

5. ENIGMATIC
   - A. evident
   - B. enormous
   - C. lucid
   - D. abstruse
   - E. sphinxlike

   5.____

6. PROSCRIBE
   - A. banish
   - B. condemn
   - C. diagnose poorly
   - D. transcend
   - E. prescribe

   6.____

7. TURBID
   - A. limpid
   - B. muddy
   - C. moody
   - D. settled
   - E. turgid

   7.____

8. PERSPICACITY
   - A. keenness
   - B. penetration
   - C. rudeness
   - D. discernment
   - E. insensibility

   8.____

9. CONTIGUOUS
   - A. contagious
   - B. adjoining
   - C. intolerant
   - D. unconnected
   - E. uncontaminated

   9.____

10. ASSUAGE
    - A. intensify
    - B. coagulate
    - C. alleviate
    - D. congeal
    - E. molest

    10.____

101

11. PROTAGONIST
    - A. enemy
    - B. participant
    - C. champion
    - D. protector
    - E. patron

12. VIRULENT
    - A. vehement
    - B. virtuous
    - C. deadly
    - D. reparatory
    - E. virile

13. PROLIX
    - A. tiresome
    - B. exciting
    - C. wordy
    - D. terse
    - E. pompous

14. LEVITY
    - A. lengthiness
    - B. glumness
    - C. lenience
    - D. frivolity
    - E. lewdness

15. METICULOUS
    - A. careful
    - B. approximate
    - C. untrue
    - D. metallic
    - E. indiscriminate

16. ANALOGOUS
    - A. tantamount
    - B. extracurricular
    - C. distinctive
    - D. presumptuous
    - E. cavernous

17. VICARIOUS
    - A. inconsiderate
    - B. direct
    - C. fraudulent
    - D. substitute
    - E. prestigious

18. ABROGATION
    - A. promulgation
    - B. repeal
    - C. extension
    - D. investigation
    - E. postponement

19. HOMOGENEOUS
    - A. manly
    - B. assorted
    - C. creamy
    - D. similar
    - E. parallel

20. ARRAIGN
    - A. accuse
    - B. convict
    - C. disentangle
    - D. disarrange
    - E. discharge

21. ABJURE
    - A. remove
    - B. disavow
    - C. acknowledge
    - D. imagine
    - E. entreat

22. INTESTATE
    - A. relating to inner parts
    - B. legally devised
    - C. shipped from one place to another
    - D. subject to taxation
    - E. not disposed of by will

23. ANCILLARY   23.____

    A. deterrent   B. temporary   C. auxiliary
    D. approved   E. additional

24. EXTRANEOUS   24.____

    A. foreign   B. accidental   C. mixed
    D. indigenous   E. adventitious

25. DISPARAGE   25.____

    A. divide   B. dismiss   C. depreciate
    D. discourage   E. dignify

KEYS (CORRECT ANSWERS)

1.	E	11.	A
2.	E	12.	D
3.	D	13.	D
4.	A	14.	B
5.	C	15.	E
6.	E	16.	C
7.	A	17.	B
8.	E	18.	A
9.	D	19.	B
10.	A	20.	E

21. C
22. B
23. A
24. D
25. E

TEST 4

DIRECTIONS: Each question below consists of a word printed in capital letters, followed by five words or phrases lettered A through E. Choose the lettered word or phrase that is *most nearly* OPPOSITE in meaning to the word in capital letters. PRINT THE LETTER OF THE CORRECT ANSWER IN THE SPACE AT THE RIGHT.

1. FUGACIOUS

   A. pugnacious B. tenacious C. mendacious
   D. settled   E. migratory

   1.___

2. THRASONICAL

   A. treasonable B. gingival C. vainglorious
   D. unassuming   E. lyrical

   2.___

3. PELAGIC

   A. terrestrial B. aquatic   C. noncontagious
   D. polemical   E. epigrammatic

   3.___

4. FUSCOUS

   A. importunate B. chaste   C. radiant
   D. fractious   E. amenable

   4.___

5. CREPUSCULAR

   A. glimmering B. crackling C. pussy
   D. mutable   E. distinct

   5.___

6. NOISOME

   A. attractive B. noxious   C. inoffensive
   D. winsome   E. noiseless

   6.___

7. PEJORATIVE

   A. appreciative B. acceding   C. ultimate
   D. alliterative E. conceding

   7.___

8. JEJUNE

   A. valiant B. vital   C. graceful
   D. senile   E. incipient

   8.___

9. FULGENT

   A. divergent B. lambent   C. unresplendent
   D. cogent   E. indigent

   9.___

10. LENITIVE

    A. laxative B. provocative C. menial
    D. incursive E. malevolent

   10.___

104

2 (#4)

11. IRREFRAGABLE   11.____
    A. breakable   B. desirable   C. tractable
    D. inconclusive   E. refutable

12. INCHOATE   12.____
    A. chaotic   B. disclosed   C. coherent
    D. infatuated   E. complete

13. MINATORY   13.____
    A. vanishing   B. nugatory   C. myriad
    D. malignant   E. propitious

14. AMBIENT   14.____
    A. wandering   B. pandering   C. transient
    D. remote   E. hostile

15. EUPHEMISTIC   15.____
    A. euphuistic   B. grating   C. masochistic
    D. palpable   E. insolent

16. FACTIOUS   16.____
    A. fractious   B. fictitious   C. scrupulous
    D. seemly   E. disinterested

17. FRIABLE   17.____
    A. unseasoned   B. palatable   C. renascent
    D. indestructible E. adhesive

18. HEGEMONY   18.____
    A. thraldom   B. testimony   C. followership
    D. necromancy   E. obligation

19. IMMANENT   19.____
    A. illative   B. imminent   C. emanating
    D. unessential   E. clement

20. INDEFEASIBLE   20.____
    A. defensible   B. abrogable   C. disputable
    D. deferential   E. execrable

21. EQUIVOCAL   21.____
    A. ambiguous   B. ambivalent   C. equitable
    D. esoteric   E. unquestionable

22. LIVID   22.____
    A. lurid   B. discolored   C. unrestrained
    D. rubicund   E. ghastly

105

23. MOIETY

    A. impiety
    D. harmony
    B. notoriety
    E. inconsistency
    C. unity

24. PEREMPTORY

    A. dogmatic
    D. conciliatory
    B. authoritarian
    E. whimsical
    C. indecisive

25. VENIAL

    A. mercenary
    D. aberrant
    B. venous
    E. loathsome
    C. purulent

KEYS (CORRECT ANSWERS)

1. D
2. D
3. A
4. C
5. E
6. C
7. A
8. B
9. C
10. B

11. E
12. E
13. E
14. D
15. B
16. E
17. D
18. A
19. D
20. B

21. E
22. D
23. C
24. C
25. E

ANTONYMS / OPPOSITES

EXAMINATION SECTION
TEST 1

DIRECTIONS: Each question in this test consists of a word in capital letters, followed by five words lettered A through E. Choose the letter of the word that is most nearly OPPOSITE in meaning to the word in capital letters and print the letter of the correct answer in the space at the right.

1. FLEXIBLE

    A. avoidable B. incorrigible C. rational
    D. adaptable E. negligible

    1.____

2. PERPETUATE

    A. concretize B. delay C. abrogate
    D. collate E. derive

    2.____

3. OBSTINATE

    A. resolved B. stained C. complaisant
    D. resourceful E. mindful

    3.____

4. EUPHONY

    A. melody B. harmony C. symphony
    D. rhapsody E. cacophony

    4.____

5. PROLIX

    A. plotting B. parting C. arrogant
    D. pithy E. mechanical

    5.____

6. PEACEABLE

    A. broken B. delicate C. fractious
    D. periodic E. understanding

    6.____

7. SESSILE

    A. ceasing B. mobile C. steady
    D. solvent E. searing

    7.____

8. AVERSION

    A. proclivity B. equanimity C. suitability
    D. revision E. suasion

    8.____

9. WHIMSICAL

    A. partial B. rational C. fulsome
    D. chimerical E. comical

    9.____

10. PETTY

    A. petite B. partisan C. magnanimous
    D. perilous E. long-lived

    10.____

107

11. PERMANENT
    - A. tempting
    - B. irregular
    - C. eternal
    - D. transitory
    - E. diurnal

12. EXECRABLE
    - A. incipient
    - B. executory
    - C. alienable
    - D. lamentable
    - E. exemplary

13. CONVICT
    - A. convey
    - B. conduct
    - C. exculpate
    - D. arrest
    - E. arraign

14. SALUBRIOUS
    - A. pernicious
    - B. pertinent
    - C. peripheral
    - D. intact
    - E. saline

15. FAMINE
    - A. fasting
    - B. satiety
    - C. family
    - D. hunger
    - E. canine

16. WARY
    - A. weary
    - B. worried
    - C. audacious
    - D. cautious
    - E. wearing

17. MELANCHOLY
    - A. mixed
    - B. medial
    - C. mental
    - D. debonair
    - E. ailing

18. DISAVOW
    - A. offer
    - B. display
    - C. asseverate
    - D. refute
    - E. lose

19. CONTENTIOUS
    - A. sententious
    - B. warlike
    - C. amicable
    - D. refractory
    - E. menial

20. OBJECTIVITY
    - A. purposiveness
    - B. obscurity
    - C. obversity
    - D. irrationality
    - E. entity

21. IGNOMINY
    - A. puerility
    - B. nobility
    - C. patrimony
    - D. ignorance
    - E. mentality

22. GERMANE
    - A. non-German
    - B. irrelevant
    - C. penitent
    - D. biological
    - E. gruesome

23. QUERULOUS

    A. fickle   B. bibulous   C. scrupulous
    D. nasty   E. amenable

24. EXIGUOUS

    A. copious   B. exacting   C. exigent
    D. grueling   E. brazen

25. PARSIMONIOUS

    A. frugal   B. preying   C. partial
    D. open-handed E. silly

KEY (CORRECT ANSWERS)

1. B		11. D	
2. C		12. E	
3. C		13. C	
4. E		14. A	
5. D		15. B	
6. C		16. C	
7. B		17. D	
8. A		18. C	
9. B		19. C	
10. C		20. D	

21. B
22. B
23. E
24. A
25. D

TEST 2

DIRECTIONS: Each question in this test consists of a word in capital letters, followed by five words lettered A through E. Choose the letter of the word that is most nearly OPPOSITE in meaning to the word in capital letters and print the letter of the correct answer in the space at the right.

1. ROCOCO
   - A. rocklike
   - B. brown-colored
   - C. unadorned
   - D. cagey
   - E. boxlike

   1.___

2. EQUALITY
   - A. asperity
   - B. renovation
   - C. paltry
   - D. disparity
   - E. geniality

   2.___

3. UNILATERAL
   - A. lettered
   - B. parallel
   - C. collective
   - D. partial
   - E. material

   3.___

4. HOMOGENEOUS
   - A. pertaining to man
   - B. pertaining to genius
   - C. homolosine
   - D. humid
   - E. dissimilar

   4.___

5. PSYCHOTIC
   - A. rational
   - B. neurotic
   - C. myopic
   - D. sclerotic
   - E. seasonal

   5.___

6. PRODIGAL
   - A. son
   - B. abstinent
   - C. prodigy
   - D. gallant
   - E. indicative

   6.___

7. VENIAL
   - A. prehensile
   - B. deferential
   - C. inexcusable
   - D. despondent
   - E. consistent

   7.___

8. AMBULATORY
   - A. confined
   - B. pertaining to an ambulance
   - C. laudatory
   - D. ambient
   - E. aiming

   8.___

9. GARRULOUS
   - A. gadding about
   - B. unruly
   - C. fraternal
   - D. taciturn
   - E. garnish

   9.___

10. ALLERGIC
    - A. alert
    - B. artificial
    - C. immune
    - D. elegiac
    - E. poetic

    10.___

11. AGGRAVATE

    A. growl   B. grieve   C. magnify
    D. ingrave   E. mitigate

12. PROFESSIONAL

    A. connoisseur   B. journeyman   C. dilettante
    D. processional E. public

13. HIBERNAL

    A. nameless   B. putrid   C. geometrical term
    D. vernal   E. Celtic

14. UNCHANGING

    A. unlike   B. undue   C. mutable
    D. charging   E. clanging

15. COVERT

    A. overt   B. curious   C. condign
    D. erect   E. pensive

16. DEFINITE

    A. careless   B. massive   C. dreary
    D. intangible E. concrete

17. FASTIDIOUS

    A. financial B. fiduciary C. slipshod
    D. frantic   E. final

18. RESTRAINED

    A. exulting   B. elliptical C. containing
    D. intemperate E. insidious

19. TRANSLUCENT

    A. patent   B. remarkable C. transitory
    D. apparent   E. opaque

20. DIFFIDENT

    A. different B. poised   C. distinctive
    D. loyal   E. faithless

21. PROLETARIAN

    A. fireman   B. Aryan   C. aristocratic
    D. democratic E. laborite

22. UNFEASIBLE

    A. unwary   B. terminal C. sensory
    D. viable   E. unadaptable

23. PRACTICAL
    A. puritanical   B. parietal   C. visionary
    D. complex   E. fundamental

24. DEFERENTIAL
    A. aggressive   B. submissive   C. permissive
    D. sacrosanct   E. artificial

25. SANGUINE
    A. bloody   B. sang-froid   C. squinting
    D. harsh   E. tremulous

KEY (CORRECT ANSWERS)

1. C
2. D
3. C
4. E
5. A

6. B
7. C
8. A
9. D
10. C

11. E
12. C
13. D
14. C
15. A

16. D
17. C
18. D
19. E
20. B

21. C
22. D
23. C
24. A
25. E

TEST 3

DIRECTIONS: Each question in this test consists of a word in capital letters, followed by five words lettered A through E. Choose the letter of the word that is most nearly OPPOSITE in meaning to the word in capital letters and print the letter of the correct answer in the space at the right.

1. TEMPESTUOUS
   - A. tight
   - B. unfit
   - C. chosen
   - D. serene
   - E. necessary

2. LACONIC
   - A. radial
   - B. tangible
   - C. minute
   - D. pompous
   - E. unproved

3. THRIVE
   - A. come to an end
   - B. swell
   - C. wither
   - D. enjoy
   - E. strive

4. UNDERTAKE
   - A. refrain
   - B. conceal
   - C. decide
   - D. identify
   - E. address

5. REMOVABLE
   - A. indelible
   - B. threadbare
   - C. legible
   - D. uncommon
   - E. fictitious

6. PRIOR
   - A. primary
   - B. contemporary
   - C. recent
   - D. subsequent
   - E. simultaneous

7. YIELDING
   - A. unsympathetic
   - B. moist
   - C. modern
   - D. adamant
   - E. pressing

8. CREDULOUS
   - A. buttress
   - B. hinge
   - C. skeptical
   - D. surface
   - E. oblivion

9. MOURN
   - A. lament
   - B. welcome
   - C. change
   - D. deny
   - E. exult

10. IMPROPRIETY
    - A. plaudit
    - B. indecisiveness
    - C. decorum
    - D. insight
    - E. silence

11. UNION
    - A. majority
    - B. schism
    - C. uniformity
    - D. conference
    - E. construction

113

12. BESTIAL 12.___
    A. dense   B. refractory   C. humane
    D. stable   E. concentrating

13. LEPER 13.___
    A. emetic   B. stimulant   C. paragon
    D. scapegoat   E. mendicant

14. AVERSION 14.___
    A. foible   B. flagrant   C. weakness
    D. penchant   E. mischance

15. ELATED 15.___
    A. nagging   B. exuberant   C. triumphant
    D. howling   E. plaintive

16. DISCLOSE 16.___
    A. see through B. imitate   C. express
    D. dissimulate E. invade

17. ACCLAIM 17.___
    A. aid   B. express condolence
    C. castigate   D. cover
    E. clothe

18. QUONDAM 18.___
    A. sick   B. moribund   C. extant
    D. near   E. remote

19. UNDERSTATEMENT 19.___
    A. exact statement   B. restraint   C. high spirits
    D. hyperbole   E. low spirits

20. BENEVOLENT 20.___
    A. inviolable   B. dishonorable   C. invidious
    D. public   E. commonplace

21. ORDER 21.___
    A. panic   B. rigidity   C. indolence
    D. innocence   E. discipline

22. HEALTHFUL 22.___
    A. noxious   B. balmy   C. healthy
    D. nubile   E. salubrious

23. PLENTY 23.___
    A. vastness   B. dearth   C. mass
    D. regiment   E. number

24. WAVERING

    A. pleasant   B. calm   C. peremptory
    D. inviting   E. carping

25. PLATITUDE

    A. banal   B. harsh manner   C. epigram
    D. wisdom   E. sorrow

KEY (CORRECT ANSWERS)

1.	D	11.	B
2.	D	12.	C
3.	C	13.	C
4.	A	14.	D
5.	A	15.	E
6.	D	16.	D
7.	D	17.	C
8.	C	18.	C
9.	E	19.	D
10.	C	20.	C

21. A
22. A
23. B
24. C
25. C

TEST 4

DIRECTIONS: Each question in this test consists of a word in capital letters, followed by five words lettered A through E. Choose the letter of the word that is most nearly OPPOSITE in meaning to the word in capital letters and print the letter of the correct answer in the space at the right.

1. TRUE 1.___

   A. obvious B. hidden C. equivocal
   D. frank E. wilful

2. ENRAGE 2.___

   A. support B. be angry C. yield
   D. mollify E. torment

3. MELLIFLUOUS 3.___

   A. smear B. polite C. raucous
   D. noxious E. mending

4. ABUNDANCE 4.___

   A. riches B. magnanimity C. sufficient
   D. insufficiency E. abbreviation

5. BENEFICIAL 5.___

   A. inserted B. prosperous C. benign
   D. malignant E. benighted

6. PARIAH 6.___

   A. trustful B. cynosure
   C. subject of ridicule D. evil omen
   E. iniquitous

7. INTRANSIGENT 7.___

   A. resentful B. negating C. be determined
   D. acquiescent E. unruly

8. PROFLIGATE 8.___

   A. prodigious B. costly C. luxurious
   D. prodigal E. parsimonious

9. THOUGHTFUL 9.___

   A. forget B. indifferent C. insipid
   D. proscribed E. diminished

10. PERSPICACIOUS 10.___

    A. erudite B. dull C. tactful
    D. persistent E. mandatory

116

2 (#4)

11. RECONDITE 11.____
    A. mumbling   B. poorly defined   C. concise
    D. abstract   E. verbose

12. ELEMENTARY 12.____
    A. famous   B. alimentary   C. popular
    D. recondite   E. prosaic

13. REAL 13.____
    A. normal   B. genuine   C. vicarious
    D. original   E. legendary

14. REDOLENT 14.____
    A. malodorous   B. fragrant   C. aromatic
    D. pellucid   E. redundant

15. REPELLING 15.____
    A. shy   B. diffident   C. contemptible
    D. prepossessing E. rebelling

16. DIRECT 16.____
    A. surreptitious B. naive   C. covenant
    D. guide   E. express

17. ALLURING 17.____
    A. facetious   B. dull   C. stern
    D. uninteresting E. loathsome

18. TEMERITY 18.____
    A. acerbity   B. image   C. sanity
    D. panic   E. circumspection

19. ENERGETIC 19.____
    A. prompt   B. cordial   C. apathetic
    D. effusive   E. mealy

20. LETHARGIC 20.____
    A. dormant   B. alert   C. tardy
    D. baronial   E. languid

21. DISPUTABLE 21.____
    A. untrue   B. incontrovertible C. unproven
    D. uncertain   E. recondite

22. AMICABLE 22.____
    A. reactionary   B. lonely   C. hostile
    D. alien   E. privately

23. FELICITY

   A. calm B. peace C. drought
   D. inaptness E. fortuitous

24. AVARICE

   A. munificence B. wastefulness C. kind
   D. self-seeking E. covetousness

25. PECULIAR

   A. passive B. obedient C. ubiquitous
   D. adamant E. intractable

KEY (CORRECT ANSWERS)

1. C	11. C
2. D	12. D
3. C	13. C
4. D	14. A
5. D	15. D
6. B	16. A
7. D	17. E
8. E	18. E
9. B	19. C
10. B	20. B

21. B
22. C
23. D
24. A
25. C

TEST 5

DIRECTIONS: Each question in this test consists of a word in capital letters, followed by five words lettered A through E. Choose the letter of the word that is most nearly OPPOSITE in meaning to the word in capital letters and print the letter of the correct answer in the space at the right.

1. BOMBASTIC 1.____
   - A. solicitous
   - B. rhapsodic
   - C. peaceful
   - D. unimpassioned
   - E. weightless

2. UNSALABLE 2.____
   - A. bargaining
   - B. marketable
   - C. sickly
   - D. salutary
   - E. worthless

3. HELOT 3.____
   - A. freeman
   - B. peon
   - C. universal
   - D. Roman
   - E. angel

4. SERPENTINE 4.____
   - A. circuitous
   - B. slippery
   - C. straight
   - D. alpine
   - E. cognizant

5. RITUALISTIC 5.____
   - A. irreligious
   - B. oratorical
   - C. impolite
   - D. ceremonious
   - E. informal

6. REMISS 6.____
   - A. remorseful
   - B. attentive
   - C. forgiving
   - D. negligent
   - E. permissive

7. DESOLATE 7.____
   - A. unswept
   - B. joyous
   - C. intact
   - D. decadent
   - E. miserable

8. EBB 8.____
   - A. steep
   - B. eke
   - C. abate
   - D. reactivate
   - E. flow

9. FRUGAL 9.____
   - A. humanistic
   - B. illiberal
   - C. bounteous
   - D. sparing
   - E. deductible

10. DISQUIETUDE 10.____
    - A. purity
    - B. fear
    - C. fortitude
    - D. ribaldry
    - E. field

11. HEINOUS 11.____
    - A. hindsight
    - B. unsightly
    - C. outrageous
    - D. creditable
    - E. venal

119

12. HERCULEAN 12.___
    - A. ponderous
    - B. deistic
    - C. elephantine
    - D. puny
    - E. indecent

13. DAWDLE 13.___
    - A. hasten
    - B. sketch
    - C. parade
    - D. avoid
    - E. loiter

14. THRALLDOM 14.___
    - A. plebeian
    - B. independence
    - C. prescience
    - D. allegiance
    - E. holding

15. INTEGRAL 15.___
    - A. realistic
    - B. profane
    - C. fragmentary
    - D. spiritual
    - E. wordy

16. MARTIAL 16.___
    - A. bachelor
    - B. unmarriageable
    - C. peaceful
    - D. solar
    - E. bellicose

17. LURE 17.___
    - A. refuse
    - B. repel
    - C. curb
    - D. decoy
    - E. misconstrue

18. MUNIFICENT 18.___
    - A. maleficent
    - B. cringing
    - C. unworldly
    - D. magnanimous
    - E. stingy

19. PROFFER 19.___
    - A. misappropriate
    - B. tender
    - C. renege
    - D. spurn
    - E. cajole

20. ENTICE 20.___
    - A. frighten
    - B. disperse
    - C. exit
    - D. expunge
    - E. disarrange

21. PACIFIC 21.___
    - A. argument
    - B. quiet
    - C. Atlantic
    - D. conciliatory
    - E. belligerent

22. PERPLEXITY 22.___
    - A. deadly
    - B. pomposity
    - C. perspicacity
    - D. acuity
    - E. certitude

23. DESICCATE 23.___
    - A. upgrade
    - B. collate
    - C. saturate
    - D. obfuscate
    - E. resuscitate

24. FELICITOUS

 A. effeminate   B. inexact   C. sensuous
 D. notorious   E. inappropriate

24.____

25. INVALUABLE

 A. worthless   B. ponderable   C. valuable
 D. cowardly   E. verifiable

25.____

KEY (CORRECT ANSWERS)

1.	D	11.	D
2.	B	12.	D
3.	A	13.	A
4.	C	14.	B
5.	E	15.	C
6.	B	16.	C
7.	B	17.	B
8.	E	18.	E
9.	C	19.	C
10.	C	20.	A

21. E
22. E
23. C
24. E
25. A

TESTS IN SENTENCE COMPLETION / 1 BLANK
EXAMINATION SECTION
TEST 1

DIRECTIONS: Each question in this section consists of a sentence in which one word is missing; a blank line indicates where the word has been removed from the sentence. Beneath each sentence are five words, *one* of which is the missing word. You are to select the letter of the missing word by deciding which one of the five words BEST fits in with the meaning of the sentence. *PRINT THE LETTER OF THE CORRECT ANSWER IN THE SPACE AT THE RIGHT.*

1. A man who cannot win honor in his own _____ will have a very small chance of winning it from posterity.

   A. right   B. field   C. country   D. way   E. age

2. The latent period for the contractile response to direct stimulation of the muscle has quite another and shorte value, encompassing only a utilization period. Hence it is that the term *latent period* must be _____ carefully each time that it is used.

   A. checked   B. timed   C. introduced
   D. defined   E. selected

3. Many television watchers enjoy stories which contain violence. Consequently those television producers who are dominated by rating systems aim to _____ the popular taste.

   A. raise   B. control   C. gratify   D. ignore   E. lower

4. No other man loses so much, so _____, so absolutely, as the beaten candidate for high public office.

   A. bewilderingly   B. predictably   C. disgracefully
   D. publicly   E. cheerfully

5. Mathematics is the product of thought operating by means of _____ for the purpose of expressing general laws.

   A. reasoning   B. symbols   C. words
   D. examples   E. science

6. Deductive reasoning is that form of reasoning in which the conclusion must necessarily follow if we accept the premise as true. In deduction, it is _____ the premise to be true and the conclusion false.

   A. impossible   B. inevitable   C. reasonable
   D. surprising   E. unlikely

7. Because in the administration it hath respect not to the group but to the _____, our form of government is called a democracy.

   A. courts   B. people   C. majority
   D. individual   E. law

8. Before criticizing the work of an artist one needs to _____ the artist's purpose.

    A. understand   B. reveal   C. defend
    D. correct   E. change

9. Their work was commemorative in character and consisted largely of _____ erected upon the occasion of victories.

    A. towers   B. tombs   C. monuments
    D. castles   E. fortresses

10. Every good story is carefully contrived: the elements of the story are _____ to fit with one another in order to
    make an effect on the reader.

    A. read   B. learned   C. emphasized
    D. reduced   E. planned

KEY (CORRECT ANSWERS)

1. E   6. A
2. D   7. D
3. C   8. A
4. D   9. C
5. B   10. E

TEST 2

DIRECTIONS: Each question in this section consists of a sentence in which one word is missing; a blank line indicates where the word has been removed from the sentence. Beneath each sentence are five words, *one* of which is the missing word. You are to select the letter of the missing word by deciding which one of the five words BEST fits in with the meaning of the sentence. *PRINT THE LETTER OF THE CORRECT ANSWER IN THE SPACE AT THE RIGHT.*

1. One of the most prevalent erroneous contentions is that Argentina is a country of _____ agricultural resources and needs only the arrival of ambitious settlers.   1._____

   A. modernized   B. flourishing   C. undeveloped
   D. waning   E. limited

2. The last official statistics for the town indicated the presence of 24,212 Italians, 6,450 Magyars, and 2,315 Germans, which ensures to the _____ a numerical preponderance.   2._____

   A. Germans   B. figures   C. town   D. Magyars   E. Italians

3. Precision of wording is necessary in good writing; by choosing words that exactly convey the desired meaning, one can avoid _____.   3._____

   A. duplicity   B. incongruity   C. complexity
   D. ambiguity   E. implications

4. Various civilians of the liberal school in the British Parliament remonstrated that there were no grounds for _____ of French aggression, since the Emperor showed less disposition to augment the navy than had Louis Philippe.   4._____

   A. suppression   B. retaliation   C. apprehension
   D. concealment   E. commencement

5. _____ is as clear and definite as any of our urges; we wonder what is in a sealed letter or what is being said in a telephone booth.   5._____

   A. Envy   B. Curiosity   C. Knowledge
   D. Communication   E. Ambition

6. It is a rarely philosophic soul who can make a _____ the other alternative forever into the limbo of forgotten things.   6._____

   A. mistake   B. wish   C. change   D. choice   E. plan

7. A creditor is worse than a master. A master owns only your person, but a creditor owns your _____ as well.   7._____

   A. aspirations   B. potentialities   C. ideas
   D. dignity   E. wealth

8. People _____ small faults, in order to insinuate that they have no great ones.   8._____

   A. create   B. display   C. confess   D. seek   E. reject

9. Andrew Jackson believed that wars were inevitable, and to him the length and irregularity of our coast presented a _____ that called for a more than merely passive navy.

    A. defense   B. barrier   C. provocation
    D. vulnerability   E. dispute

10. The progressive yearly _____ of the land, caused by the depositing of mud from the river, makes it possible to estimate the age of excavated remains by noting the depth at which they are found below the present level of the valley.

    A. erosion   B. elevation   C. improvement
    D. irrigation   E. displacement

KEY (CORRECT ANSWERS)

1.	C	6.	D
2.	E	7.	D
3.	D	8.	C
4.	C	9.	D
5.	B	10.	B

TEST 3

DIRECTIONS: Each question in this section consists of a sentence in which one word is missing; a blank line indicates where the word has been removed from the sentence. Beneath each sentence are five words, *one* of which is the missing word. You are to select the letter of the missing word by deciding which one of the five words BEST fits in with the meaning of the sentence. *PRINT THE LETTER OF THE CORRECT ANSWER IN THE SPACE AT THE RIGHT.*

1. The judge exercised commendable _____ dismissing the charge against the prisoner. In spite of the clamor that surrounded the trial, and the heinousness of the offense, the judge could not be swayed to overlook the lack of facts in the case. 1.____

    A. avidity
    B. meticulousness
    C. clemency
    D. balance
    E. querulousness

2. The pianist played the concerto _____, displaying such facility and skill as has rarely been matched in this old auditorium. 2.____

    A. strenuous
    B. spiritedly
    C. passionately
    D. casually
    E. deftly

3. The Tanglewood Symphony Orchestra holds its outdoor concerts far from city turmoil in a _____, bucolic setting. 3.____

    A. spectacular
    B. atavistic
    C. serene
    D. chaotic
    E. catholic

4. Honest satire gives true joy to the thinking man. Thus, the satirist is most _____ when he points out the hypocrisy in human actions. 4.____

    A. elated
    B. humiliated
    C. ungainly
    D. repressed
    E. disdainful

5. She was a(n) _____ preferred the company of her books to the pleasures of cafe society. 5.____

    A. philanthropist
    B. stoic
    C. exhibitionist
    D. extrovert
    E. introvert

6. So many people are so convinced that people are driven by _____ motives that they cannot believe that anybody is unselfish! 6.____

    A. interior
    B. ulterior
    C. unworth
    D. selfish
    E. destructive

7. These _____ results were brought about by a chain of fortuitous events. 7.____

    A. unfortunate
    B. odd
    C. harmful
    D. haphazard
    E. propitious

8. The bank teller's _____ of the funds was discovered the following month when the auditors examined the books. 8.____

    A. embezzlement
    B. burglary
    C. borrowing
    D. assignment
    E. theft

127

9. The monks gathered in the _____ for their evening meal.

    A. lounge   B. auditorium   C. refectory
    D. rectory   E. solarium

10. Local officials usually have the responsibility in each area of determining when the need is sufficiently great to _____ withdrawals from the community water supply.

    A. encourage   B. justify   C. discontinue
    D. advocate   E. forbid

KEY (CORRECT ANSWERS)

1. D   6. B
2. E   7. D
3. C   8. A
4. A   9. C
5. E   10. B

TEST 4

DIRECTIONS: Each question in this section consists of a sentence in which one word is missing; a blank line indicates where the word has been removed from the sentence. Beneath each sentence are five words, *one* of which is the missing word. You are to select the letter of the missing word by deciding which one of the five words BEST fits in with the meaning of the sentence. *PRINT THE LETTER OF THE CORRECT ANSWER IN THE SPACE AT THE RIGHT*

1. The life of the mining camps as portrayed by Bret Harte–boisterous, material, brawling—was in direct _____ to the contemporary Eastern world of conventional morals and staid deportment depicted by other men of letters.

   A. model B. parallel C. antithesis D. relationship E. response

2. The agreements were to remain in force for three years and were subject to automatic _____ unless terminated by the parties concerned on one month's notice.

   A. renewal B. abrogation C. amendment D. confiscation E. option

3. In a democracy, people are recognized for what they do rather than for their _____.

   A. alacrity B. ability C. reputation D. skill E. pedigree

4. Although he had often loudly proclaimed his _____ concerning world affairs, he actually read widely and was usually the best informed person in his circle.

   A. weariness B. complacency C. condolence D. indifference E. worry

5. This student holds the _____ record of being the sole failure in his class.

   A. flagrant B. unhappy C. egregious D. dubious E. unusual

6. She became enamored _____ acrobat when she witnessed his act.

   A. of B. with C. for D. by E. about

7. This will _____ all previous wills.

   A. abrogates B. denies C. supersedes D. prevents E. continues

8. In the recent terrible Chicago _____, over ninety children were found dead as a result of the fire.

   A. hurricane B. destruction C. panic D. holocaust E. accident

9. I can ascribe no better reason why he shunned society than that he was a _____.

   A. mentor B. Centaur C. aristocrat D. misanthrope E. failure

10. One who attempts to learn all the known facts before he comes to a conclusion may most aptly be described as a _____.

    A. realist   B. philosopher   C. cynic
    D. pessimist   E. skeptic

KEY (CORRECT ANSWERS)

1.	C	6.	A
2.	A	7.	C
3.	E	8.	D
4.	D	9.	D
5.	D	10.	E

TEST 5

DIRECTIONS: Each question in this section consists of a sentence in which one word is missing; a blank line indicates where the word has been removed from the sentence. Beneath each sentence are five words, *one* of which is the missing word. You are to select the letter of the missing word by deciding which one of the five words BEST fits in with the meaning of the sentence. *PRINT THE LETTER OF THE CORRECT ANSWER IN THE SPACE AT THE RIGHT.*

1. The prime minister, fleeing from the rebels who had seized the government, sought _____ in the church.

    A. revenge B. mercy C. relief
    D. salvation E. sanctuary

2. It does not take us long to conclude that it is foolish to fight the _____, and that it is far wiser to accept it.

    A. inevitable B. inconsequential C. impossible
    D. choice E. invasion

3. _____ is usually defined as an excessively high rate of interest.

    A. Injustice B. Perjury C. Exorbitant
    D. Embezzlement E. Usury

4. "I ask you, gentlemen of the jury, to find this man guilty since I have _____ the charges brought about him."

    A. documented B. questioned C. revised
    D. selected E. confused

5. Although the critic was a close friend of the producer, he told him that he could not _____ his play.

    A. condemn B. prefer C. congratulate
    D. endorse E. revile

6. Knowledge of human nature and motivation is an important _____ in all areas of endeavor.

    A. object B. incentive C. opportunity
    D. asset E. goal

7. Numbered among the audience were kings, princes, dukes, and even a maharajah, all attempting to _____ another in the glitter of their habiliments and the number of their escorts.

    A. supersede B. outdo C. guide
    D. vanquish E. equal

8. There seems to be a widespread feeling that peoples who are located below us in respect to latitude are _____ also in respect to intellect and ability.

    A. superior B. melodramatic C. inferior
    D. ulterior E. contemptible

9. This should be considered a(n) _____ rather than the usual occurrence.

    A. coincidence   B. specialty   C. development
    D. outgrowth   E. mirage

10. Those who were considered states' rights adherents in the early part of our history, espoused the diminution of the powers of the national government because they had always been _____ of these powers.

    A. solicitous   B. advocates   C. apprehensive
    D. mindful   E. respectful

KEY (CORRECT ANSWERS)

1. E   6. D
2. A   7. B
3. E   8. C
4. A   9. A
5. D   10. C

TEST 6

DIRECTIONS: Each question in this section consists of a sentence in which one word is missing; a blank line indicates where the word has been removed from the sentence. Beneath each sentence are five words, *one* of which is the missing word. You are to select the letter of the missing word by deciding which one of the five words BEST fits in with the meaning of the sentence. *PRINT THE LETTER OF THE CORRECT ANSWER IN THE SPACE AT THE RIGHT.*

1. We can see in retrospect that the high hopes for lasting peace conceived at Versailles in 1919 were _____.

   A. ingenuous
   B. transient
   C. nostalgic
   D. ingenious
   E. specious

   1._____

2. One of the constructive effects of Nazism was the passage by the U.N. of a resolution to combat _____.

   A. armaments
   B. nationalism
   C. colonialism
   D. genocide
   E. geriatrics

   2._____

3. In our prisons, the role of _____ often gains for certain inmates a powerful position among their fellow prisoners.

   A. informer   B. clerk   C. warden   D. trusty   E. turnkey

   3._____

4. It is the _____ liar, experienced in the ways of the world, who finally trips upon some incongruous detail.

   A. consummate
   B. incorrigible
   C. congenital
   D. lagrant
   E. contemptible

   4._____

5. Anyone who is called a misogynist can hardly be expected to look upon women with _____ contemptuous eyes.

   A. more than
   B. nothing less than
   C. decidedly
   D. other than
   E. always

   5._____

6. Demagogues such as Hitler and Mussolini aroused the masses by appealing to their _____ rather than to their intellect.

   A. emotions
   B. reason
   C. nationalism
   D. conquests
   E. duty

   6._____

7. He was in great demand as an entertainer for his _____ abilities: he could sing, dance, tell a joke, or relate a story with equally great skill and facility.

   A. versatile
   B. logical
   C. culinary
   D. histrionic
   E. creative

   7._____

8. The wise politician is aware that, next to knowing when to seize an opportunity, it is also important to know when to _____ an advantage.

   A. develop
   B. seek
   C. revise
   D. proclaim
   E. forego

   8._____

133

9. Books on psychology inform us that the best way to break a bad habit is to _____ a new habit in its place.

   A. expel
   B. substitute
   C. conceal
   D. curtail
   E. supplant

10. The author who uses one word where another uses a whole paragraph, should be considered a _____ writer.

    A. successful
    B. grandiloquent
    C. experienced
    D. prolix
    E. succinct

KEY (CORRECT ANSWERS)

1. A
2. D
3. A
4. A
5. D
6. A
7. A
8. E
9. B
10. E

READING COMPREHENSION
UNDERSTANDING AND INTERPRETING WRITTEN MATERIAL
EXAMINATION SECTION
TEST 1

DIRECTIONS: Each question or incomplete statement is followed by several suggested answers or completions. Select the one that BEST answers the question or completes the statement. PRINT THE LETTER OF THE CORRECT ANSWER IN THE SPACE AT THE RIGHT.

PASSAGE

It is a common belief that a thing is desirable because it is scarce and thereby has ostentation value. The notion that such a standard of value is an inescapable condition of settled social existence rests on one of two implicit assumptions. The first is that the attempt to educate the human race so that the desire to display one's possessions is not a significant feature of man's social behavior, is an infringement against personal freedom. The greatest obstacle to lucid discourse in these matters is the psychological anti-vaccinationist who uses the word freedom to signify the natural right of men and women to be unhappy and unhealthy through scientific ignorance instead of being healthy and happy through the knowledge which science confers. Haunted by a perpetual fear of the dark, the last lesson which man learns in the difficult process of growing up is "ye shall know the truth, and the truth shall make you free." The professional economist who is too sophisticated to retreat Into the obscurities of this curious conception of liberty may prefer to adopt the second assumption, that the truth does not and cannot make us free because the need for ostentation is a universal species characteristic, and all attempts to eradicate the unconscionable nuisance and discord which arise from overdeveloped craving for personal distinction artificially fostered by advertisement propaganda and so-called good breeding are therefore destined to failure. It may be earnestly, hoped that those who entertain this view have divine guidance. No rational basis for it will be found in textbooks of economics. Whatever can be said with any plausibility in the existing state of knowledge rests on the laboratory materials supplied by anthropology and social history.

1. According to the writer, the second assumption

    A. Is fostered by propaganda and so-called good breeding
    B. is basically opposite to the view of the psychological anti-vaccinationist
    C. is not so curious a conception of liberty as Is the first assumption
    D. is unsubstantiated
    E. is a religious explanation of an economic phenomenon

1.____

2. The author's purpose in writing this paragraph is MOST probably to

    A. denounce the psychological anti-vaccinationists
    B. demonstrate that the question under discussion is an economic rather than a psychological problem
    C. prove the maxim "ye shall know the truth, and the truth shall make you free"
    D. prove that ostentation is not an inescapable pheonomenon of settled social existence
    E. prove the inability of economics to account for ostentation

2.____

3. The writer implies that

   A. neither the psychological anti-vaccinationist nor the professional economist recognizes the undesirability of ostentation
   B. our cultural standards are at fault in enhancing ostentation value
   C. scarcity as a criterion of value Is an inexplicable concept
   D. his main objection Is to the inescapable standard of values
   E. the results of studies of ostentation in anthropology and social history are Irrational

4. The writer believes that both assumptions

   A. are invalid because they ignore the lesson "ye shall know the truth, and the truth shall make you free"
   B. are fallacious because they agree that a thing is desirable because it is scarce
   C. arise from overdeveloped craving for personal distinction
   D. are implicit in the conception of ostentation value
   E. dispute the efficacy of education in eliminating ostentation

5. In his reference to divine guidance, the writer is

   A. being ironic
   B. implying that only divine guidance can solve the problem
   C. showing how the professional economist is opposing divine laws
   D. referring to opposition which exists between religion and science
   E. indicating that the problem is not a matter for divine guidance

6. The writer believes that personal freedom is

   A. less important than is scientific knowledge
   B. a requisite for the attainment of truth
   C. attained by eradicating false beliefs
   D. no concern of the professional economist
   E. an unsophisticated concept

7. We may infer that this writer does NOT believe that

   A. education can solve the problem
   B. people have any "natural rights"
   C. science can solve the problem
   D. the psychological anti-vaccinationist is more than a lipservant of the cause of freedom
   E. people can be happy under the present value system

8. The writer would consider as MOST comparable to the effect of a vaccination on the body, the effect of

   A. fear upon personality
   B. science upon the supposed need for ostentation
   C. truth upon the mind
   D. knowledge upon ignorance
   E. knowledge upon happiness

KEY (CORRECT ANSWERS)

1. D
2. D
3. B
4. D
5. A
6. C
7. E
8. C

TEST 2

DIRECTIONS: Each question or incomplete statement is followed by several suggested answers or completions. Select the one that *BEST* answers the question or completes the statement. *PRINT THE LETTER OF THE CORRECT ANSWER IN THE SPACE AT THE RIGHT.*

PASSAGE

In any country the wages commanded by laborers who have comparable skills but who work in various industries are determined by the productivity of the least productive unit of labor, i.e., that unit of labor which works in the industry which has the greatest economic disadvantage. We will represent the various opportunities of employment in a country like the United States by symbols: A, standing for a group of industries in which we have exceptional economic advantages over foreign countries; B, for a group in which our advantages are less; C, one in which they are still less; D, the group of industries in which they are least of all.

When our population is so small that all our labor can be engaged in the group represented by A, productivity of labor (and therefore wages) will be at their maximum. When our population increases so that some of the labor will have to be set to work in group B, the wages of all labor must decline to the level of the productivity in that group. But no employer, without government aid, will yet be able to afford to hire labor to exploit the opportunities represented by C and D, unless there is a further increase in population.

But suppose that the political party in power holds the belief that we should produce everything that we consume, that the opportunities represented by C and D should be exploited. The commodities that the industries composing C and D will produce have been hitherto obtained from abroad in exchange for commodities produced by A and B. The government now renders this difficult by placing high duties upon the former class of commodities. This means that workers in A and B must pay higher prices for what they buy, but do not receive higher prices for what they sell.

After the duty has gone into effect and the prices of commodities that can be produced by C and D have risen sufficiently, enterprisers will be able to hire labor at the wages prevailing in A and B, and establish industries in C and D. So far as the remaining laborers in A and B buy the products of C and D, the difference between the price which they pay for those products and the price that they would pay if they were permitted to import those products duty-free is a tax paid not to the government, but to the producers in C and D, to enable the latter to remain in business. It is an uncompensated deduction from the natural earnings of the laborers in A and B. Nor are the workers in C and D paid as much, estimated in purchasing power, as they would have received if they had been allowed to remain in A and B under the earlier conditions.

1. When C and D are established, workers in these industries

    A. receive higher wages than do the workers in A and B
    B. receive lower wages than do the workers in A and B
    C. must be paid by government funds collected from the duties on imports
    D. are not affected so adversely by the levying of duties as are workers in A and B
    E. receive wages equal to those workers in A and B

2. We cannot exploit C and D unless

   A. the productivity of labor in all industries is increased
   B. the prices of commodities produced by A and B are raised
   C. we export large quantities of commodities produced by A and B
   D. the producers in C and D are compensated for the disadvantages under which they operate
   E. we allow duties to be paid to the producers in C and D rather than to the government

3. "No employer; without government aid, will yet be able to afford to hire labor to exploit the opportunities represented by C and D" because

   A. productivity of labor is not at the maximum
   B. we cannot produce everything we consume
   C. the population has increased
   D. enterprisers would have to pay wages equivalent to those obtained by workers in A and B, while producing under greater economic disadvantages
   E. productivity would drop correspondingly with the wages of labor

4. The government, when it places high duties on imported commodities of classes C and D,

   A. raises the price of commodities produced by A and B
   B. is, in effect, taxing the workers in A and B
   C. raises the wages of workers in C and D at the expense of the workers in A and B
   D. does not affect the productivity of the workers in A and B, although the wages of these workers are reduced
   E. is adopting a policy made necessary by the stability of the population

5. The author's MAIN point is that

   A. it is impossible to attain national self-sufficiency
   B. the varying productivity of the various industries leads to the inequalities in wages of workers in these industries
   C. a policy that draws labor from the fields of greater natural productiveness to fields of lower natural productiveness tends to reduce purchasing power
   D. wages ought to be independent of international trade
   E. the government ought to subsidize C and D.

6. The author's arguments in this passage could BEST be used to

   A. refute the belief that it is theoretically possible for us to produce everything that we consume
   B. disprove the theory that national self-sufficiency can be obtained by means of protective tariffs
   C. advocate the levying of duties on imported goods
   D. advocate equal wages for workers who have comparable skills but who work in various industries
   E. advocate free trade

3 (#2)

7. When could C and D, as here defined, be exploited without the assistance of an artificially boosted price and without resultant lowering of wage levels?   7.___

   A. When a duty is placed on competing products from other countries
   B. When the products of C and D are exchanged in trade for other commodities
   C. When the country becomes economically self-sufficient
   D. When there is a favorable balance of trade
   E. At no time

8. In the last sentence in the selection, the statement is made: "Nor are the workers in C and D paid as much, estimated in purchasing power, as they would have received if they had been allowed to remain in A and B under the earlier conditions." This is because   8.___

   A. they must pay higher prices for commodities produced by C and D
   B. C and D cannot pay so high wages as can A and B
   C. products of C and D do not command sufficiently high prices
   D. there has not been an increase in population
   E. wages in all groups have declined

KEY (CORRECT ANSWERS)

1. E	5. C
2. D	6. E
3. D	7. B
4. B	8. E

TEST 3

DIRECTIONS: Each question or incomplete statement is followed by several suggested answers or completions. Select the one that BEST answers the question or completes the statement. PRINT THE LETTER OF THE CORRECT ANSWER IN THE SPACE AT THE RIGHT.

PASSAGE

In the Federal Convention of 1787, the members were fairly well agreed as to the desirability of some check on state laws; but there was sharp difference of opinion whether this check should be political in character as in the form of a congressional veto, or whether the principle of judicial review should be adopted.

Madison was one of the most persistent advocates of the congressional veto and in his discussion of the subject he referred several times to the former imperial prerogative of disallowing provincial statutes. In March, 1787, he wrote to Jefferson, urging the necessity of a federal negative upon state laws. He referred to previous colonial experience in the suggestion that there should be "some emanation" of the federal prerogative "within the several states, so far as to enable them to give a temporary sanction to laws of immediate necessity." This had been provided for in the imperial system through the action of the royal governor in giving immediate effect to statutes, which nevertheless remained subject to royal disallowance. In a letter to Randolph a few weeks later, Madison referred more explicitly to the British practice, urging that the national government be given "a negative, in all cases whatsoever, on the Legislative acts of the States, as the King of Great Britain heretofore had." Jefferson did not agree with Madison; on practical grounds rather than as a matter of principle, he expressed his preference for some form of judicial control.

On July 17, Madison came forward with a speech in support of the congressional veto, again supporting his contention by reference to the royal disallowance of colonial laws: "Its utility is sufficiently displayed in the British System. Nothing could maintain the harmony and subordination of the various parts of the empire, but the prerogative by which the Crown stifles in the birth every Act of every part tending to discord or encroachment. It is true the prerogative is sometimes misapplied thro' ignorance or a partiality to one particular part of the empire: but we have not the same reason to fear such misapplications in our System." This is almost precisely Jefferson's theory of the legitimate function of an imperial veto.

This whole issue shows that the leaders who wrestled with confederation problems during and after the war understood, in some measure at least, the attitude of British administrators when confronted with the stubborn localism of a provincial assembly.

1. Madison was advocating

   A. royal disallowance of state legislation
   B. a political check on state laws
   C. the supremacy of the states over the federal government
   D. the maintenance of a royal governor to give immediate effect to statutes
   E. discord and encroachment among the states

1.____

2. From this passage there is no indication

   A. of what the British System entailed
   B. of Jefferson's stand on the question of a check on state laws
   C. that the royal negative had been misapplied in the past
   D. that Jefferson understood the attitude of British administrators
   E. of what judicial review would entail

3. According to this passage, Madison believed that the federal government

   A. ought to legislate for the states
   B. should recognize the sovereignty of the several states
   C. ought to exercise judicial control over state legislation
   D. should assume the king's veto power
   E. was equivalent to a provincial assembly

4. Madison's conception of a congressional veto

   A. was opposed to Jefferson's conception of a congressional veto
   B. developed from fear that the imperial negative might be misused
   C. was that the federal prerogative should be exercised in disallowing state laws
   D. was that its primary function was to give temporary sanction to laws of immediate necessity
   E. was that its primary function was to prevent such injustices as "taxation without representation"

5. Madison believed that

   A. the congressional veto would not be abused
   B. the royal prerogative ought to have some form of check to correct misapplications
   C. the review of state legislation by the federal government ought to remain subject to a higher veto
   D. the imperial veto had not been misused
   E. utility rather than freedom is the criterion for governmental institutions

6. Jefferson believed that

   A. the congressional veto would interfere with states' rights
   B. Madison's proposal smacked of imperialism
   C. the veto of state legislation was outside the limits of the federal prerogative
   D. the British System would be harmful if applied in the United States
   E. an imperial veto should include the disallowance of all legislation leading to discord

7. Madison's MAIN principle was that

   A. the national interest is more important than the interests of any one state
   B. the national government should have compulsive power over the states
   C. the king can do no wrong
   D. the United States should follow the English pattern of government
   E. the veto power of the royal governor should be included in the federal prerogative

8. Madison thought of the states as 8._____

   A. emanations of the federal government
   B. comparable to provinces of a colonial empire
   C. incapable of creating sound legislation
   D. having no rights specifically delegated to them
   E. incapable of applying judicial review of their legislation

9. Which of the following is the BEST argument which could be made against Madison's proposition? 9._____

   A. The United States has no king.
   B. The federal government is an entity outside the jurisdiction of the states.
   C. Each state has local problems concerning which representatives from other states are not equipped to pass judgment.
   D. The federal prerogative had been misused in the past.
   E. It provides no means of dealing with stubborn localism.

KEY (CORRECT ANSWERS)

1.	B	5.	A
2.	E	6.	D
3.	D	7.	B
4.	C	8.	B
		9.	C

TEST 4

DIRECTIONS: Each question or incomplete statement is followed by several suggested answers or completions. Select the one that BEST answers the question or completes the statement. PRINT THE LETTER OF THE CORRECT ANSWER IN THE SPACE AT THE RIGHT.

PASSAGE

The nucleus of its population is the local businessmen, whose interests constitute the municipal policy and control its municipal administration. These local businessmen are such as the local bankers, merchants of many kinds and degrees, real estate promoters, local lawyers, local clergymen...The businessmen, who take up the local traffic in merchandising, litigation, church enterprise and the like, commonly begin with some share in the real estate speculation. This affords a common bond and a common ground of pecuniary interest, which commonly masquerades under the name of local patriotism, public spirit, civic pride, and the like. This pretense of public spirit is so consistently maintained that most of these men come presently to believe in their own professions on that head. Pecuniary interest in local land values involves an interest in the continued growth of the town. Hence any creditable misrepresentation of the town's volume of business traffic, population, tributary farming community, or natural resources, is rated as serviceable to the common good. And any member of this business-like community will be rated as a meritorious citizen in proportion as he is serviceable to this joint pecuniary interest of these "influential citizens."

1. The tone of the paragraph is

   A. bitter
   B. didactic
   C. complaining
   D. satirical
   E. informative

2. The foundation for the "influential citizens" interest in their community is

   A. their control of the municipal administration
   B. their interests in trade and merchandising
   C. their natural feeling of civic pride
   D. a pretense of public spirit
   E. ownership of land for speculation

3. The "influential citizens" type of civic pride may be compared with the patriotism of believers in

   A. a balance of power in international diplomacy
   B. racial superiority
   C. laissez faire
   D. a high tariff
   E. dollar diplomacy

4. The IMPORTANT men in the town

   A. are consciously insincere in their local patriotism
   B. are drawn together for political reasons
   C. do not scruple to give their community a false boost
   D. regard strict economy as a necessary virtue
   E. are extremely jealous of their prestige

5. The writer considers that the influential men of the town

   A. are entirely hypocritical in their conception of their motives
   B. are blinded to facts by their patriotic spirit
   C. have deceived themselves into thinking they are altruistic
   D. look upon the welfare of their community as of paramount importance
   E. form a closed corporation devoted to the interests of the town

6. PROBABLY the author's own view of patriotism is that it

   A. should be a disinterested passion untinged by commercial motives
   B. is found only among the poorer classes
   C. is usually found in urban society
   D. grows out of a combination of the motives of selfinterest and altruism
   E. consists in the main of a feeling of local pride

KEY (CORRECT ANSWERS)

1. B   4. C
2. E   5. C
3. E   6. A

TEST 5

DIRECTIONS: Each question or incomplete statement is followed by several suggested answers or completions. Select the one that *BEST* answers the question or completes the statement. *PRINT THE LETTER OF THE CORRECT ANSWER IN THE SPACE AT THE RIGHT.*

PASSAGE

Negative thinking and lack of confidence in oneself or in the pupils are probably the greatest hindrances to inspirational teaching. Confronted with a new idea, one teacher will exclaim: "Oh, my children couldn't do that! They're too young." Another will mutter, "If I tried that stunt, the whole class would be in an uproar." Such are the self-justifications for mediocrity.

Here and there it is good to see a teacher take a bold step away from the humdrum approach. For example, Natalie Robinson Cole was given a class of fourth-year pupils who could hardly speak English. Yet in her book, THE ARTS IN THE CLASSROOM, she describes how she tried clay work, creative writing, interpretive dancing and many other exciting activities with them. Did her control of the class suffer? Were the results poor? Was morale adversely affected? The answer is *NO* on all three counts.

But someone may point out that what Mrs. Cole could do on the fourth-grade could not be done in the primary grades. Wrong again! The young child is more malleable than his older brother. Furthermore, his radiant heritage of originality has not been enveloped in clouds of self-consciousness. Given the proper encouragement, he will paint an interesting design on the easel, contribute a sparkling expression to the "class poem" as it takes shape on the blackboard, make a puppet speak his innermost thoughts, and react with sensitivity in scores of other ways.

All teachers on all grade levels need to think positively and act confidently. Of course, any departure from the commonplace must be buttressed by careful preparation, firm handling of the situation, and consistent attention to routines. Since these assets are within the reach of all teachers there should be no excuse for not putting some imagination into their work.

1. The central idea of the above passage is BEST conveyed by the

    A. first sentence in the first paragraph
    B. last sentence in the first paragraph
    C. first sentence in the second paragraph
    D. last sentence in the passage
    E. third sentence in the third paragraph

2. If the concepts of this passage were to be expanded into a book, the one of the following titles which would be MOST suitable is

    A. THE ARTS IN THE CLASSROOM
    B. THE POWER OF POSITIVE THINKING
    C. THE HIDDEN PERSUADERS
    D. KIDS SAY THE DARNDEST THINGS
    E. ARMS AND THE MAN

146

3. Of the following reasons for uninspired teaching, the one which is NOT given explicitly in the passage is   3.____

   A. negative thinking
   B. teachers' underestimation of pupils' ability or stability
   C. teachers' failure to broaden themselves culturally
   D. teachers' lack of self-assurance
   E. teachers' rationalizations

4. From reading the passage one can gather that Natalie R. Cole   4.____

   A. teaches in New York City
   B. has been married
   C. is an expert in art
   D. teaches in the primary grades
   E. is a specialist in child psychology

5. An activity for children in the primary grades which is NOT mentioned in the passage is   5.____

   A. creative expression
   B. art work
   C. puppetry
   D. constructing with blocks
   E. work on the blackboard

6. A basic asset of the inspirational teacher NOT mentioned in the passage is   6.____

   A. a pleasant, outgoing personality
   B. a firm hand
   C. a thorough, careful plan
   D. consistent attention to routines
   E. acting confidently

KEY (CORRECT ANSWERS)

1. A   4. B
2. B   5. D
3. C   6. A

TEST 6

DIRECTIONS: Each question or incomplete statement is followed by several suggested answers or completions. Select the one that BEST answers the question or completes the statement. PRINT THE LETTER OF THE CORRECT ANSWER IN THE SPACE AT THE RIGHT.

PASSAGE

Of all the areas of learning the most important is the development of attitudes. Emotional reactions as well as logical thought processes affect the behavior of most people. "The burnt child fears the fire" is one instance; another is the rise of despots like Hitler. Both these examples also point up the fact that attitudes stem from experience. In the one case the experience was direct and impressive; in the other it was indirect and cumulative. The Nazis were indoctrinated largely by the speeches they heard and the books they read.

The classroom teacher in the elementary school is in a strategic position to influence attitudes. This is true partly because children acquire attitudes from these adults whose word they respect. Another reason it is true is that pupils often delve somewhat deeply into a subject in school that has only been touched upon at home or has possibly never occurred to them before. To a child who had previously acquired little knowledge of Mexico, his teacher's method of handling such a unit would greatly affect his attitude toward Mexicans.

The media through which the teacher can develop wholesome attitudes are innumerable. Social studies (with special reference to races, creeds and nationalities), science, matters of health and safety, the very atmosphere of the classroom... these are a few of the fertile fields for the inculcation of proper emotional reactions.

However, when children come to school with undesirable attitudes, it is unwise for the teacher to attempt to change their feelings by cajoling or scolding them. She can achieve the proper effect by helping them obtain constructive experiences. To illustrate, firstgrade pupils afraid of policemen will probably alter their attitudes after a classroom chat with the neighborhood officer in which he explains how he protects them. In the same way, a class of older children can develop attitudes through discussion, research, outside reading and all-day trips.

Finally, a teacher must constantly evaluate her own attitude because her influence can be deleterious if she has personal prejudices. This is especially true in respect to controversial issues and questions on which children should be encouraged to reach their own decisions as a result of objective analysis of all the facts.

1. The central idea conveyed in the above passage is that 1.__

   A. attitudes affect our actions
   B. teachers play a significant role in developing or changing pupils' attitudes
   C. by their attitudes, teachers inadvertently affect pupils' attitudes
   D. attitudes can be changed by some classroom experiences
   E. attitudes are affected by experience

2. The author implies that

   A. children's attitudes often come from those of other children
   B. in some aspects of social studies a greater variety of methods can be used in the upper grades than in the lower grades
   C. the teacher should guide all discussions by revealing her own attitude
   D. people usually act on the basis of reasoning rather than on emotion
   E. parents' and teachers' attitudes are more often in harmony than in conflict

3. A statement NOT made or implied in the passage is that

   A. attitudes cannot easily be changed by rewards and lectures
   B. a child can develop in the classroom an attitude about the importance of brushing his teeth
   C. attitudes can be based on the learning of falsehoods
   D. the attitudes of children are influenced by all the adults in their environment
   E. the children should accept the teacher's judgment in controversial matters

4. The passage SPECIFICALLY states that

   A. teachers should always conceal their own attitudes
   B. whatever attitudes a child learns in school have already been introduced at home
   C. direct experiences are more valuable than indirect ones
   D. teachers can sometimes have an unwholesome influence on children
   E. it is unwise for the teacher to attempt to change children's attitudes

5. The first and fourth paragraphs have all the following points in common EXCEPT

   A. how reading affects attitudes
   B. the importance of experience in building attitudes
   C. how attitudes can be changed in the classroom
   D. how fear sometimes governs attitudes
   E. how differences in approach change attitudes

KEY (CORRECT ANSWERS)

1. B
2. B
3. D
4. D
5. C

TEST 7

DIRECTIONS: Each question or incomplete statement is followed by several suggested answers or completions. Select the one that *BEST* answers the question or completes the statement. *PRINT THE LETTER OF THE CORRECT ANSWER IN THE SPACE AT THE RIGHT.*

PASSAGE

The word <u>geology</u> refers to the study of the composition, structure, and history of the earth. The term is derived from the Latin, <u>geologia</u>. coined by Bishop Richard de Bury in 1473 to distinguish lawyers who study "earthy things" from theologians. It was first consistently used in its present sense in the latter part of the 17th century. The great mass of detail that constitutes geology is classified under a number of subdivisions which, in turn, depend upon the fundamental sciences, physics, chemistry and biology.

The principal subdivisions of geology are: mineralogy, petrology, structural geology, physiography (geomorphology), usually grouped under <u>physical or dynamical geology</u>; and paleontology, stratigraphy and paleogeography, grouped under <u>historical geology</u>. The term <u>economic geology</u> usually refers to the study of valuable mineral "ore" deposits, including coal and oil. The economic aspects of geology are, however, much more embracive, including many subjects associated with civil engineering, economic geography, and conservation. Some of the more important of these subjects are: meteorology, hydrology, agriculture, and seismology. Subjects which are also distinctly allied to geology are geophysics, geochemistry, and cosmogony.

1. The statement that geology treats of the history of the earth and its life, especially as recorded in the rocks, is

    A. contrary to the paragraph
    B. made in the paragraph
    C. neither made nor implied in the paragraph
    D. not made, but implied in the paragraph
    E. unclear from the passage

2. The statement that the principal branches or phases of geology are dynamical geology and historical geology are

    A. contrary to the paragraph
    B. made in the paragraph
    C. neither made nor implied in the paragraph
    D. not made, but implied in the paragraph
    E. unclear from the passage

3. The statement that mining geology is a subdivision of geophysics is

    A. contrary to the paragraph
    B. made in the paragraph
    C. neither made nor implied in the paragraph
    D. not made, but implied in the paragraph
    E. unclear from the passage

2 (#7)

4. The statement that the study of both the exterior of the earth and its inner constitution constitutes the fundamental subject matter of geology is   4.____

   A. contrary to the paragraph
   B. made in the paragraph
   C. neither made nor implied in the paragraph
   D. not made, but implied in the paragraph
   E. unclear from the passage

5. The statement that geology utilizes the principles of astronomy, zoology, and botany is   5.____

   A. contrary to the paragraph
   B. made in the paragraph
   C. neither made nor implied in the paragraph
   D. not made, but implied in the paragraph
   E. unclear from the passage

6. The statement that geology is synonymous with the study of the attributes of rocks, rock formation, or rock attributes is   6.____

   A. contrary to the paragraph
   B. made in the paragraph
   C. neither made nor implied in the paragraph
   D. not made, but implied in the paragraph
   E. unclear from the passage

KEY (CORRECT ANSWERS)

1. D   4. D
2. B   5. D
3. C   6. A

TEST 8

DIRECTIONS: Each question or incomplete statement is followed by several suggested answers or completions. Select the one that *BEST* answers the question or completes the statement. *PRINT THE LETTER OF THE CORRECT ANSWER IN THE SPACE AT THE RIGHT.*

PASSAGE

1 Schiller was the first to ring a change on this state of things
2 by addressing himself courageously to the entire population of his
3 country in all its social strata at one time. He was the great popularizer of our
4 theatre, and remained for almost a century the guiding
5 spirit of the German drama of which Schiller's matchless tragedies
6 are still by many people regarded as the surpassing manifestoes.
7 Schiller's position, while it demonstrates a whole people's gratitude
8 to those who respond to its desires, does not however furnish a
9 weapon of self-defense to the "popularizers" of drama, or rather its
10 diluters. Schiller's case rather proves that the power of popular
11 influence wrought upon a poet may be vastly inferior to the strength
12 that radiates from his own personality. Indeed, whereas the secret
13 of ephemeral power is only too often found in paltriness or mediocrity,
14 an influence of enduring force such as Schiller exerts on the Germans
15 can only emanate from a strong and self-assertive character. No poet
16 lives beyond his day who does not exceed the average in mental stature
17 or who, through a selfish sense of fear of the general, allows
18 himself to be ground down to the conventional size and shape.
19 Schiller, no less than Ibsen, forced his moral demands tyrannically
20 upon his contemporaries. And in the long run your moral despot, pro-
21 vided he be high-minded, vigorous, and able, has a better chance of
22 fame than the pliant time-server. However, there is a great difference
23 between the two cases. For quite apart from the striking dissimilarities
24 between the poets themselves, the public, through the
25 gradual growth of social organization, has become greatly altered.

1. Schiller's lasting popularity may be attributed to 1.___

    A. his meeting the desires of a whole people, not just a segment of the people
    B. his abiding by his inmost convictions
    C. his mediocrity and paltriness
    D. his courageous facing up to the problems of his day
    E. his ability to popularize the unknown

2. In the first line, "on this state of things" refers to 2.___

    A. romantic drama
    B. the French play of contrived construction
    C. drama directed to the rich and well-born
    D. the popularizers of the theatre of today
    E. the ruling class

3. In the second sentence from the last, "the two cases" refer to

    A. pliant time-server and moral despot
    B. the one who exceeds the average In mental stature and the one who allows himself to be ground down to conventional size
    C. the popularizer and the poet of enduring fame
    D. Ibsen and Schiller
    E. the man of character and the man of wealth

4. We may assume that the author

    A. is no believer in the democratic processes
    B. has no high opinions of the "compact majority"
    C. regards popularity with the people as a measure of enduring success
    D. is opposed to the aristocracy
    E. has no fixed opinions

5. A word used in an ambiguous sense (having two or more possible meanings) in this passage is

    A. "poet" (lines 11, 15, 24)
    B. "power" (lines 10, 13)
    C. "people" (lines 6, 7)
    D. "popularizer" (lines 3, 9)
    E. "moral" (lines 19, 20)

KEY (CORRECT ANSWERS)

1. B
2. C
3. D
4. B
5. D

TEST 9

DIRECTIONS: Each question or incomplete statement is followed by several suggested answers or completions. Select the one that *BEST* answers the question or completes the statement. *PRINT THE LETTER OF THE CORRECT ANSWER IN THE SPACE AT THE RIGHT.*

PASSAGE

In one sense, of course, this is not a new insight: all our great social and philosophical thinkers have been keenly aware of the fact of individual differences. It has remained, however, for psychologists to give the insight scientific precision.

What all this adds up to is more than just a working body of information about this and that skill. It adds up to a basic recognition of one important factor in the maturing of the individual. If each individual has a certain uniqueness of power, his maturing will best be accomplished along the line of that power. To try to develop him along lines that go in directions contrary to that of his major strength is to condition him to defeat. Thus, the non-mechanical person who is arbitrarily thrust into a mechanical occupation cannot help but do his work poorly and reluctantly, with some deep part of himself in conscious or unconscious rebellion.

He may blame himself for the low level of his accomplishment or for his persistent discontent; but not all his self-berating, nor even all his efforts to become more competent by further training, can make up for the original aptitude-lack. Unless he discovers his aptitude-lack, he may be doomed to a lifetime of self-blame, with a consequent loss of self-confidence and a halting of his psychological growth.

Or he may take refuge in self-pity – finding reason to believe that his failure is due to one or another bad break, to the jealousy of a superior, to lack of sympathy and help at home, to an initial bad start, to a lack of appreciation of what he does. If he thus goes the way of self-pity, he is doomed to a lifetime of self-commiseration that makes sound growth impossible.

The characteristic of the mature person is that he affirms life. To affirm life he must be involved, heart and soul, in the process of living. Neither the person who feels himself a failure nor the person who consciously or unconsciously resents what life has done to him can feel his heart and soul engaged in the process of living. That experience is reserved for the person whose full powers are enlisted. This, then, is what this fourth insight signifies: to mature, the individual must know what his powers are and must make them competent for life.

1. It is the author's view that   1.__

   A. "all men are created equal"
   B. "each man in his life plays many parts"
   C. "all comes to him who waits"
   D. "no kernel of nourishing corn can come to one but through his toil bestowed on that plot of ground given to him to till...."
   E. "that is what it is not to be alive. To move about in a cloud of ignorance... to live with envy... in quiet despair... to feel oneself sunk into a common grey mass..."

2. Ignorance of this fourth insight

   A. may very likely cause one to take refuge in self pity or conscious or unconscious rebellion
   B. constitutes a failure to understand that each individual is different and must cultivate his special powers in socially rewarding ways
   C. is a major deterrent to a growth to maturity
   D. means unawareness of the fact that each must use all his energy and powers to the best of his ability to make him competent for life
   E. may becloud the use of scientific precision

   2._____

3. Two possible maladjustments of a man thrust into a position he is unfitted for may be summed up in the phrase,

   A. conscious and unconscious rebellion
   B. guilt-feelings and scapegoating
   C. halting of psychological growth and blaming the "breaks"
   D. "Peccavi—I have sinned" and "all the world is made except thee and me and I am not so sure of thee"
   E. light and darkness

   3._____

4. We will expect a person placed in a job he is unequal to, to

   A. strike out for himself as an entrepreneur
   B. display quick angers and fixed prejudices
   C. show a great love of life outside of his work
   D. engage in labor union activities
   E. join political and social movements

   4._____

KEY (CORRECT ANSWERS)

1. D   3. B
2. B   4. B

TEST 10

DIRECTIONS: Each question or incomplete statement is followed by several suggested answers or completions. Select the one that *BEST* answers the question or completes the statement. *PRINT THE LETTER OF THE CORRECT ANSWER IN THE SPACE AT THE RIGHT.*

PASSAGE

1 "For the ease and pleasure of treading the old road, accepting
2 the fashions, the education, the religion of society, he takes the
3 cross of making his own, and, of course, the self-accusation, the
4 faint heart, the frequent uncertainty and loss of time, which are the
5 nettles and tangling vines in the way of the self-relying and self-
6 directed; and the state of virtual hositility in which he seems to
7 stand to society, and especially to educated society. For all this
8 loss and scorn, what offset? He is to find consolation in exercising
9 the highest functions of human nature. He is one who raises himself
10 from private consideration and breathes and lives on public and
11 illustrious thoughts. He is the world's eye. He is the world's
12 heart. He is to resist the vulgar prosperity that retrogrades ever
13 to barbarism, by preserving and communicating heroic sentiments,
14 noble biographies, melodious verse, and the conclusions of history.
15 Whatsoever oracles the human heart, in all emergencies, in all solemn
16 hours, has uttered as its commentary on the world of actions – these
17 he shall receive and impart. And whatsoever new verdict Reason from
18 her inviolable seat pronounces on the passing men and events of
19 today – this he shall hear and promulgate.
20   "These being his functions, it becomes him to feel all confidence
21 in himself, and to defer never to the popular cry. He and he only
22 knows the world. The world of any moment is the merest appearance.
23 Some great decorum, some fetish of a government, some ephemeral
24 trade, or war, or man, is cried up by half mankind and cried down by
25 the other half, as if all depended on this particular up or down.
26 The odds are that the whole question is not worth the poorest thought
27 which the scholar has lost in listening to the controversy. Let him
28 not quit his belief that a popgun is a popgun, though the ancient and
29 honorable of the earth affirm it to be the crack of doom. In silence,
30 in steadiness, in severe abstraction, let him hold by himself; add
31 observation to observation, patient of neglect, patient of reproach,
32 and bide his own time – happy enough if he can satisfy himself alone
33 that this day he has seen something truly. Success treads on every
34 right step. For the instinct is sure, that prompts him to tell his
35 brother what he thinks. He then learns that in going down into the
36 secrets of his own mind he has descended into the secrets of all
37 minds. He learns that he who has mastered any law in his private
38 thoughts, is master to the extent of all translated. The poet, in
39 utter solitude remembering his spontaneous thoughts and recording
40 them, is found to have recorded that which men in crowded cities
41 find true for them also. The orator distrusts at first the fitness

```
42   of his frank confessions, his want of knowledge of the persons he
43   addresses, until he finds that he is the complement of his hearers–
44   that they drink his words because he fulfills for them their own
45   nature; the deeper he delves into his privatest, secretest presentiment,
46   to his wonder he finds this is the most acceptable, most public, and
47   universally true. The people delight in it; the better part of every
48   man feels. This is my music; this is myself."
```

1. It is a frequent criticism of the scholar that he lives by himself, in an "ivory tower," remote from the problems and business of the world. Which of these below constitutes the *BEST* refutation by the writer of the passage to the criticism here noted?

    A. The world's concern being ephemeral, the scholar does well to renounce them and the world.
    B. The scholar lives in the past to interpret the present.
    C. The scholar at his truest is the spokesman of the people.
    D. The scholar is not concerned with the world's doing because he is not selfish and therefore not engrossed in matters of importance to himself and neighbors.
    E. The scholar's academic researches of today are the businessman's practical products of tomorrow.

2. The scholar's road is rough, according to the passage. Which of these is his GREATEST difficulty?

    A. He must renounce religion.
    B. He must pioneer new approaches.
    C. He must express scorn for, and hostility to, society.
    D. He is uncertain of his course.
    E. There is a pleasure in the main-traveled roads in education, religion, and all social fashions.

3. When the writer speaks of the "world's eye" and the "world's heart" he means

    A. the same thing
    B. culture and conscience
    C. culture and wisdom
    D. a scanning of all the world's geography and a deep sympathy for every living thing
    E. mind and love

4. By the phrase, "nettles and tangling vines," the author PROBABLY refers to

    A. "self-accusation" and "loss of time"
    B. "faint heart" and "self accusation"
    C. "the slings and arrows of outrageous fortune"
    D. a general term for the difficulties of a scholar's life
    E. "self-accusation" and "uncertainty"

5. The various ideas in the passage are BEST summarized in which of these groups?
   1. (a) truth versus society
      (b) the scholar and books
      (c) the world and the scholar
   2. (a) the ease of living traditionally
      (b) the glory of a scholar's life
      (c) true knowledge versus trivia
   3. (a) the hardships of the scholar
      (b) the scholar's function
      (c) the scholar's justifications for disregarding the world's business

   A. 1 and 3 together
   B. 3 only
   C. 1 and 2 together
   D. 1 only
   E. 1, 2, and 3 together

6. "seems to stand" (lines 6 and 7) means

   A. is
   B. gives the false impression of being
   C. ends probably in becoming
   D. is seen to be
   E. the quicksands of time

7. "public and illustrious thoughts" (lines 10 and 11) means

   A. what the people think
   B. thoughts for the good of mankind
   C. thoughts in the open
   D. thoughts transmitted by the people
   E. the conclusions of history

KEY (CORRECT ANSWERS)

1. C   5. B
2. B   6. B
3. C   7. B
4. E

READING COMPREHENSION
UNDERSTANDING AND INTERPRETING
WRITTEN MATERIAL

EXAMINATION SECTION

TEST 1

DIRECTIONS: Each question or incomplete statement is followed by several suggested answers or completions. Select the one that BEST answers the question or completes the statement. *PRINT THE LETTER OF THE CORRECT ANSWER IN THE SPACE AT THE RIGHT.*

In its current application to art, the term *"primitive"* is as vague and unspecific as the term "heathen" is in its application to religion. A heathen sect is simply one which is not affiliated with one or another of three or four organized systems of theology. Similarly, a primitive art is one which flourishes outside the small number of cultures which we have chosen to designate as civilizations. Such arts differ vastly and it is correspondingly difficult to generalize about them. Any statements which will hold true for such diverse aesthetic experiences as the pictographs of the Australians, the woven designs of the Peruvians, and the abstract sculptures of the African tribes must be of the broadest and simplest sort. Moreover, the problem is complicated by the meaning attached to the term "primitive" in its other uses. It stands for something simple, undeveloped, and, by implication, ancestral to more evolved forms. Its application to arts and cultures other than our own is an unfortunate heritage from the nineteenth-century scientists who laid the foundations of anthropology. Elated by the newly enunciated doctrines of evolution, these students saw all cultures as stages in a single line of development and assigned them to places in this series on the simple basis of the degree to which they differed from European culture, which was blandly assumed to be the final and perfect flower of the evolutionary process. This idea has long since been abandoned by anthropologists, but before its demise it diffused to other social sciences and became a part of the general body of popular misinformation. It still tinges a great deal of the thought and writing about the arts of non-European peoples and has been responsible for many misunderstandings.

1. The MAIN purpose of the passage is to
   A. explain the various definitions of the term "primitive"
   B. show that the term "primitive" can be applied validly to art
   C. compare the use of the term "primitive" to the use of the term "heathen"
   D. deprecate the use of the term "primitive" as applied to art
   E. show that "primitive" arts vary greatly among themselves

1._____

2. The nineteenth-century scientists believed that the theory of evolution
   A. could be applied to the development of culture
   B. was demonstrated in all social sciences
   C. was substantiated by the diversity of "primitive" art
   D. could be applied only to European culture
   E. disproved the idea that some arts are more "primitive" than others

2._____

3. With which of the following would the author agree?
   A. The term "primitive" is used only by the misinformed.
   B. "Primitive" arts may be as highly developed as "civilized" arts.
   C. The arts of a culture often indicated how advanced that culture was.
   D. Australian, Peruvian, and African tribal arts are much like the ancestral forms from which European art evolved.
   E. A simple culture is likely to have a simple art.

4. According to the author, many misunderstandings have been caused by the belief that
   A. most cultures are fundamentally different
   B. inferior works of art in any culture are "primitive" art
   C. "primitive" arts are diverse
   D. non-European arts are diverse
   E. European civilization is the final product of the evolutionary process

KEY (CORRECT ANSWERS)

1. D
2. A
3. B
4. E

TEST 2

DIRECTIONS: Each question or incomplete statement is followed by several suggested answers or completions. Select the one that BEST answers the question or completes the statement. *PRINT THE LETTER OF THE CORRECT ANSWER IN THE SPACE AT THE RIGHT.*

    One of the ways the intellectual *avant-garde* affects the technical intelligentsia is through the medium of art, and art is, if only implicitly, a critique of experience. The turning upon itself of modern culture in the forms of the new visual art, the utilization of the detritus of daily experience to mock that experience, constitutes a mode of social criticism. Pop art, it is true, does not go beyond the surface of the visual and tactile experience of an industrial (and a commercialized) culture. Dwelling on the surface, it allows its consumers to mock the elements of their daily life, without abandoning it. Indeed, the consumption of art in the organized market for leisure serves at times to encapsulate the social criticism of the *avant-garde*. However, the recent engagement of writers, artists, and theater people in contemporary issues suggests that this sort of containment may have begun to reach its limits.
    In an atmosphere in which the intellectually dominant group insists on the contradictions inherent in daily experience, the technical intelligentsia will find it difficult to remain unconscious of those contradictions. The technical intelligentsia have until now avoided contradictions by accepting large rewards for their expertise. As expertise becomes increasingly difficult to distinguish from ordinary service on the one hand, and merges on the other with the change of the social environment, the technical intelligentsia's psychic security may be jeopardized. Rendering of labor services casts it back into spiritual proletarianization; a challenge to the social control exercised by elites, who use the technical intelligentsia's labor power, pushes it forward to social criticism and revolutionary politics. That these are matters, for the moment, of primarily spiritual import does not diminish their ultimate political significance. A psychological precondition for radical action is usually far more important than an "objectively" revolutionary situation—whatever that may be.
    The chances for a radicalization of the technical intelligentsia, thus extending the student revolt cannot be even approximated. I believe I have shown there is a chance.

1. It may be *inferred* that the technical intelligentsia are
   I. The executives and employers in society
   II. Critics of *avant-garde* art
   III. Highly skilled technical workers
   The CORRECT answer is:
   A. I only   B. I and III   C. I, II, and III
   D. III only   E. I and II

2. The engagement of the intellectual *avant-garde* in contemporary issues
   A. indicates that people tire of questioning the contradictions inherent in day-to-day living
   B. indicates that the technical intelligentsia are close to the point where they will rebel against the *avant-garde*
   C. could cause a challenge to the social control of the elites
   D. could cause the public to become more leisure-oriented
   E. could cause an increase in the consumption of art in the organized market for leisure services

3. The *possible* effect of the intellectual *avant-garde* on the technical intelligentsia is   3.____
   that
   A. the intellectual *avant-garde* makes the technical intelligentsia conscious of society's contradictions
   B. rapid curtailment of large rewards for expertise will result
   C. it may cause a strong likelihood of a radicalization of the technical intelligentsia
   D. the *avant-garde* will replace the employment of the technical intelligentsia in contemporary issues
   E. the rendering of labor services will be eliminated

4. If it is assumed that the technical intelligentsia becomes fully aware of the   4.____
   contradictions of modern life, it is the author's position that
   A. revolution will result
   B. the technical intelligentsia may refuse to perform manual labor
   C. the technical intelligentsia will be pushed forward to social criticism and revolutionary politics
   D. the technical intelligentsia will experience some psychic dislocation
   E. ordinary service will replace technical expertise

5. According to the author,   5.____
   A. the state of mind of a particular group may have more influence on its action than the effect of environmental factors
   B. the influence of art will often cause social upheaval
   C. matters of primarily spiritual import necessarily lack political significance
   D. the detritus of day-to-day living should be mocked by the intellectual *avant-garde*
   E. the technical intelligentsia can only protect their psychic security by self-expression through art

6. With which of the following would the author agree?   6.____
   I. As contradictions are less contained, the psychic security of all members of the working class would be jeopardized.
   II. The expertise of the technical intelligentsia evolved from the ownership and management of property.
   III. The technical intelligentsia is not accustomed to rendering labor services.
   The CORRECT answer is:
   A. I only   B. III only   C. I and III
   D. II only   E. None of the above

7. The MAIN purpose of the passage is to   7.____
   A. discuss the influence of the *avant-garde* art form on the expertise of the technical intelligentsia
   B. discuss the effect of the intellectual *avant-garde* on the working classes
   C. discuss the social significance of the technical intelligentsia
   D. discuss the possible effects of the de-encapsulation of *avant-garde* social criticism
   E. point out that before a change psychological preconditions are first established

KEY (CORRECT ANSWERS)

1. D   5. A
2. C   6. B
3. A   7. D
4. D

TEST 3

DIRECTIONS: Each question or incomplete statement is followed by several suggested answers or completions. Select the one that BEST answers the question or completes the statement. *PRINT THE LETTER OF THE CORRECT ANSWER IN THE SPACE AT THE RIGHT.*

Turbulent flow over a boundary is a complex phenomenon for which there is no really complete theory even in simple laboratory cases. Nevertheless, a great deal of experimental data has been collected on flows over solid surfaces, both in the laboratory and in nature, so that, from an engineering point of view at least, the situation is fairly well understood. The force exerted on a surface varies with the roughness of that surface and approximately with the square of the wind speed at some fixed height above it. A wind of 10 meters per second (about 20 knots, or 22 miles per hour) measured at a height of 10 meters will produce a force of some 30 tons per square kilometer on a field of mown grass or of about 70 tons per square kilometer on a ripe wheat field. On a really smooth surface, such as glass, the force is only about 10 tons per square kilometer.

When the wind blows over water, the whole thing is much more complicated. The roughness of the water is not a given characteristic of the surface but depends on the wind itself. Not only that, the elements that constitute the roughness—the waves—themselves move more or less in the direction of the wind. Recent evidence indicates that a large portion of the momentum transferred from the air into the water goes into waves rather than directly into making currents in the water; only as the waves break, or otherwise lose energy, does their momentum become available to generate currents, or produce Ekman layers. Waves carry a substantial amount of both energy and momentum (typically about as much as is carried by the wind in a layer about one wavelength thick), and so the wave-generation process is far from negligible. A violently wavy surface belies its appearance by acting, as far as the wind is concerned, as though it were very smooth. At 10 meters per second, recent measurements seem to agree, the force on the surface is quite a lot less than the force over mown grass and scarcely more than it is over glass; some observations in light winds of two or three meters per second indicate that the force on the wavy surface is less than it is on a surface as smooth as glass. In some way the motion of the waves seems to modify the airflow so that air slips over the surface even more freely than it would without the waves. This seems not to be the case at higher wind speeds, above about five meters per second, but the force remains strikingly low compared with that over other natural surfaces.

One serious deficiency is the fact that there are no direct observations at all in those important cases in which the wind speed is greater than about 12 meters per second and has had time and fetch (the distance over water) enough to raise substantial waves. The few indirect studies indicate that the apparent roughness of the surface increases somewhat under high-wind conditions, so that the force on the surface increases rather more rapidly than as the square of the wind speed.

Assuming that the force increases at least as the square of the wind speed, it is evident that high-wind conditions produce effects far more important than their frequency of occurrence would suggest. Five hours of 60-knot storm winds will put more momentum into the water than a week of 10-knot breezes. If it should be shown that, for high winds, the force on the surface increases appreciably more rapidly than as the square of the wind speed, then the transfer of momentum to the ocean will turn out to be dominated by what happens during the occasional storm rather than by the long-term average winds.

1. According to the passage, several hours of storm winds (60 miles per hour) over the ocean would
    A. be similar to the force exerted by light winds for several hours over glass
    B. create an ocean roughness which reduces the force exerted by the high winds
    C. have proved to be more significant in creating ocean momentum than light winds
    D. create a force not greater than 6 times the force of a 10-mile-per-hour wind
    E. eventually affect ocean current

2. According to the passage, a rough-like ocean surface
    A. is independent of the force of the wind
    B. has the same force exerted against it by high and light winds
    C. is more likely to have been caused by a storm than by continuous light winds
    D. nearly always allows airflow to be modified so as to cause the force of the wind to be less than on glass
    E. is a condition under which the approximate square of wind speed can never be an accurate figure in measuring the wind force

3. The author indicates that, where a hurricane is followed by light winds of 10 meters per second or less,
    I. ocean current will be unaffected by the light winds
    II. ocean current will be more affected by the hurricane winds than the following light winds
    III. the force of the light winds on the ocean would be less than that exerted on a wheat field.
    The CORRECT combination is:
    A. I only   B. III only   C. II and III   D. I and III   E. II only

4. The MAIN purpose of the passage is to discuss
    A. oceanic momentum and current
    B. turbulent flow of wind over water
    C. wind blowing over water as related to causing tidal flow
    D. the significance of high wind conditions on ocean momentum
    E. experiments in wind force

5. The author would be incorrect in concluding that the transfer of momentum to the ocean is dominated by the occasional storm if
    A. air momentum went directly into making ocean current
    B. high speed winds slipped over waves as easily as low speed winds
    C. waves did not move in the direction of wind
    D. the force exerted on a wheat field was the same as on mown grass
    E. the force of wind under normal conditions increased as the square of wind speed

6. A wind of 10 meters per second measured at a height of 10 meters will produce   6._____
   a force close to 30 tons per square mile on which of the following?
   A. Unmown grass B. Mown grass C. Glass
   D. Water E. A football field

KEY (CORRECT ANSWERS)

1. E
2. C
3. C
4. B
5. B
6. A

TEST 4

DIRECTIONS: Each question or incomplete statement is followed by several suggested answers or completions. Select the one that BEST answers the question or completes the statement. *PRINT THE LETTER OF THE CORRECT ANSWER IN THE SPACE AT THE RIGHT.*

Political scientists, as practitioners of a negligibly formalized discipline, tend to be accommodating to formulations and suggested techniques developed in related behavioral sciences. They even tend, on occasion, to speak of psychology, sociology, and anthropology as "hard core sciences." Such a characterization seems hardly justified. The disposition to uncritically adopt into political science non-indigenous sociological and general systems concepts tends, at times, to involve little more than the adoption of a specific, and sometimes barbarous, academic vocabulary which is used to redescribe reasonably well-confirmed or intuitively-grasped low-order empirical generalizations.

At its worst, what results in such instances is a runic explanation, a redescription in a singular language style, i.e., no explanation at all. At their best, functional accounts as they are found in the contemporary literature provide explanation sketches, the type of elliptical explanation characteristic of historical and psychoanalytic accounts. For each such account there is an indeterminate number of equally plausible ones, the consequence of either the complexity of the subject matter, differing perspectives, conceptual vagueness, the variety of sometimes mutually exclusive empirical or quasi-empirical generalizations employed, or syntactical obscurity, or all of them together.

Functional explanations have been most reliable in biology and physiology (where they originated) and in the analysis of servo mechanical and cybernetic systems (to which they have been effectively extended). In these areas we possess a well-standardized body of lawlike generalizations. Neither sociology nor political science has as yet the same resource of well-confirmed lawlike statements. Certainly sociology has few more than political science. What passes for functional explanation in sociology is all too frequently parasitic upon suggestive analogy and metaphor, trafficking on our familiarity with goal-directed systems.

What is advanced as "theory" in sociology is frequently a non-theoretic effort at classification or "codification," the search for an analytic conceptual schema which provides a typology or a classificatory system serviceable for convenient storage and ready retrieval of independently established empirical regularities. That such a schema takes on a hierarchic and deductive character, imparting to the collection of propositions a *prima facie* theoretical appearance, may mean no more than that the terms employed in the high-order propositions are so vague that they can accommodate almost any inference and consequently can be made to any conceivable state of affairs.

1. The author *implies* that, when the political scientist is at his best, his explanations   1.____
   A. are essentially a retelling of events
   B. only then form the basis of an organized discipline
   C. plausibly account for past occurrences
   D. are prophetic of future events
   E. are confirmed principles forming part of the political scientist's theory

2. With which of the following would the author probably agree?
   I. Because of an abundance of reasonable explanations for past conduct, there is the possibility of contending schools within the field of political science developing.
   II. Political science is largely devoid of predictive power.
   III. Political science has very few verified axioms.
   The CORRECT answer is:
   A. III only   B. I and III   C. I and II   D. I, II, III   E. I only

3. The passage *implies* that many sociological theories
   A. are capable of being widely applied to various situations
   B. do not even appear to be superficially theoretical in appearance
   C. contrast with those of political science in that there are many more confirmed lawlike statements
   D. are derived from deep analysis and exhaustive research
   E. appear theoretical but are really very well proved

4. The author's thesis would be UNSUPPORTABLE if
   A. the theories of the political scientist possessed predictive power
   B. political science did not consist of redescription
   C. political scientists were not restricted to "hard core sciences"
   D. political science consisted of a body of theories capable of application to any situation
   E. none of the above

5. The author believe that sociology as a "hard core science," contains reliable and functional explanations
   A. is never more than a compilation of conceptual schema
   B. is in nearly every respect unlike political science
   C. is a discipline which allows for varied inferences to be drawn from its general propositions
   D. is a science indigenous *prima facie* theoretical appearance containing very little codification posing as theory

KEY (CORRECT ANSWERS)

1. C
2. D
3. A
4. A
5. D

TEST 5

DIRECTIONS: Each question or incomplete statement is followed by several suggested answers or completions. Select the one that BEST answers the question or completes the statement. *PRINT THE LETTER OF THE CORRECT ANSWER IN THE SPACE AT THE RIGHT.*

James' own prefaces to his works were devoted to structural composition and analytics and his approach in those prefaces has only recently begun to be understood. One of his contemporary critics, with the purest intention to blame, wrote what might be recognized today as sophisticated praise when he spoke of the later James as "an impassioned geometer" and remarked that "what interested him was not the figures but their relations, the relations which alone make pawns significant." James's explanations of his works often are so bereft of interpretation as to make some of our own austere defenses against interpretation seem almost embarrassingly rich with psychological meanings. They offer, with a kind of brazen unselfconsciousness, an astonishingly artificial, even mechanical view of novelistic invention. It's not merely that James asserts the importance of technique; more radically, he tends to discuss character and situation almost entirely as functions of technical ingenuities. The very elements in a Jamesian story which may strike us as requiring the most explanation are presented by James either as a *solution* to a problem of compositional harmony or else as the *donnee* about which it would be irrelevant to ask any questions at all.

James should constantly be referred to as a model of structuralist criticism. He consistently redirects our attention from the referential aspect of a work of art (its extensions into "reality") to its own structural coherence as the principal source of inspiration.

What is most interesting about James's structurally functional view of character is that a certain devaluation of what we ordinarily think of as psychological interest is perfectly consistent with an attempt to portray reality. It's as if he came to feel that a kind of autonomous geometric pattern, in which the parts appeal for their value to nothing but their contributive place in the essentially abstract pattern, is the artist's most successful representation of life. Thus, he could perhaps even think that verisimilitude—a word he liked—has less to do with the probability of the events the novelist describes than with those processes, deeply characteristic of life, by which he creates sense and coherence from any event. The only faithful picture of life in art is not in the choice of a significant subject (James always argues against the pseudo realistic prejudice), but rather in the illustration of sense- or design-making processes. James proves the novel's connection with life by deprecating its derivation from life; and it's when he is most abstractly articulating the growth of a structure that James is almost most successfully defending the mimetic function of art (and of criticism). His deceptively banal position that only execution matters means most profoundly that verisimilitude, properly considered, is the grace and the truth of a formal unity.

1. The author suggests that James, in explanations of his own art,   1.____
    A. was not bound by formalistic strictures but concentrated on verisimilitude
    B. was deeply psychological and concentrated on personal insight
    C. felt that his art had a one-to-one connection with reality
    D. was basically mechanical and concentrated on geometrical form
    E. was event-and-character-oriented rather than technique-oriented

2. The passage indicates that James's method of approaching reality was
   A. that objective reality did not exist and was patterned only by the mind
   B. that formalism and pattern were excellent means of approaching reality
   C. not to concentrate on specific events but rather on character development
   D. that the only objective reality is the psychological processes of the mind
   E. that in reality events occur which are not structured but rather as random occurrences

3. The MAIN purpose of the paragraph is to
   A. indicate that James's own approach to his work is only now beginning to be understood
   B. deprecate the geometrical approach towards the novel
   C. question whether James's novels were related to reality
   D. indicate that James felt that society itself could be seen as a geometric structure
   E. discuss James's explanation of his works

4. In discussing his own works, James
   I. talks of people and events as a function of technique to the exclusion of all else
   II. is quick to emphasize the referential aspect of the work
   III. felt that verisimilitude could be derived not from character but rather from the ordering of event
   The CORRECT answer is:
   A. I only   B. II only   C. III only   D. I and III   E. I and II

5. The author
   A. *approves* of James's explanations of his work but *disapproves* his lack of discussion into the psychological makings of his characters
   B. *disapproves* of James's explanation of his own work and his lack of discussion into the psychological makings of his characters
   C. *approves* of James's explanations of his works in terms of structure as being well-rated to life
   D. *disapproves* of James's explanation of his works in terms of structure as lacking verisimilitude
   E. *approves* of James's explanation of his works because of the significance of the subjects chosen

6. The following is NOT true of James's explanation of his own works: He
   A. did not explain intriguing elements of a story except as part of a geometric whole
   B. felt the artist could represent life by its patterns rather than its events
   C. defended the imitative function of art by detailing the growth of a structure
   D. attempted to give the reader insight into the psychology of his characters by insuring that his explanation followed a strict geometrical pattern
   E. was able to devalue psychological interest and yet be consistent with an attempt to truly represent life

7. James believed it to be *essential* to
   A. carefully choose a subject which would lend itself to processes by which sense and cohesion is achieved
   B. defend the mimetic function of art by emphasizing verisimilitude
   C. emphasize the manner in which different facets of a story could fit together
   D. explain character in order to achieve literary harmony
   E. be artificial and unconcerned with representing life

KEY (CORRECT ANSWERS)

1. D
2. B
3. E
4. C
5. C
6. D
7. C

TEST 6

DIRECTIONS: Each question or incomplete statement is followed by several suggested answers or completions. Select the one that BEST answers the question or completes the statement. *PRINT THE LETTER OF THE CORRECT ANSWER IN THE SPACE AT THE RIGHT.*

    The popular image of the city as it is now is a place of decay, crime, of fouled streets, and of people who are poor or foreign or odd. But what is the image of the city of the future? In the plans for the huge redevelopment projects to come, we are being shown a new image of the city. Gone are the dirt and the noise—and the variety and the excitement and the spirit. That it is an ideal makes it all the worse; these bleak new utopias are not bleak because they have to be; they are the concrete manifestation—and how literally—of a deep, and at times arrogant, misunderstanding of the function of the city.

    Being made up of human beings, the city is, of course, a wonderfully resilient institution. Already it has reasserted itself as an industrial and business center. Not so many years ago, there was much talk of decentralizing to campus-like offices, and a wholesale exodus of business to the countryside seemed imminent. But a business pastoral is something of a contradiction in terms, and for the simple reason that the city is the center of things because it is a center, the suburban heresy never came off. Many industrial campuses have been built, but the overwhelming proportion of new office building has been taking place in the big cities. But the rebuilding of downtown is not enough; a city deserted at night by its leading citizens is only half a city. If it is to continue as the dominant cultural force in American life, the city must have a core of people to support its theatres and museums, its shops and its restaurants—even a Bohemia of sorts can be of help. For it is the people who like living in the city who make it an attraction to the visitors who don't. It is the city dwellers who support its style; without them there is nothing to come downtown to.

    The cities have a magnificent opportunity. There are definite signs of a small but significant move back from suburbia. There is also evidence that many people who will be moving to suburbia would prefer to stay in the city—and it would not take too much more in amenities to make them stay. But the cities seem on the verge of muffing their opportunity and muffing it for generations to come. In a striking failure to apply marketing principles and an even more striking failure of aesthetics, the cities are freezing on a design for living ideally calculated to keep everybody in suburbia. These vast, barracks-like superblocks are not designed for people who like cities, but for people who have no other choice. A few imaginative architects and planners have shown that redeveloped blocks don't have to be repellent to make money, but so far their ideas have had little effect. The institutional approach is dominant, and, unless the assumptions embalmed in it are re-examined, the city is going to be turned into a gigantic bore.

1. The author would NOT be pleased with
   A. a crowded, varied, stimulating city
   B. the dedication of new funds to the reconstruction of the cities
   C. a more detailed understanding of the poor
   D. the elimination of assumptions which do not reflect the function of the city
   E. the adoption of a laissez-faire attitude by those in charge of redevelopment

2. "The rebuilding of downtown" (1st sentence, 3rd paragraph) refers to
   A. huge redevelopment projects to come
   B. the application of marketing and aesthetic principles to rejuvenating the city
   C. keeping the city as the center of business
   D. attracting a core of people to support the city's functions
   E. the doing away with barracks-like structures

3. According to the author the city, in order to better itself, *must*
   A. increase its downtown population
   B. attract an interested core of people to support its cultural institutions
   C. adhere to an institutional approach rather than be satisfied with the status quo
   D. erect campus-like business complexes
   E. establish an ideal for orderly future growth

4. The MAIN purpose of the passage is to
   A. show that the present people inhabiting the city do not make the city viable
   B. discuss the types of construction which should and should not take place in the city's future
   C. indicate that imaginative architects and planners have shown that redeveloped areas don't have to be ugly to make money
   D. discuss the human element in the city
   E. point out the lack of understanding by many city planners of the city's functions

5. The author's thesis would be LESS supportable if
   I. city planners presently understood that stereotyped reconstruction is doomed to ultimate failure
   II. the institutional approach referred to in the passage was based upon assumptions which took into account the function of the city
   III. there were signs that a shift back to the city from suburbia were occurring
   The CORRECT answer is:
   A. II only   B. II and III   C. I and II   D. I only   E. III only

KEY (CORRECT ANSWERS)

1. D
2. C
3. B
4. E
5. C

TEST 7

DIRECTIONS: Each question or incomplete statement is followed by several suggested answers or completions. Select the one that BEST answers the question or completes the statement. *PRINT THE LETTER OF THE CORRECT ANSWER IN THE SPACE AT THE RIGHT.*

In estimating the child's conceptions of the world, the first question is to decide whether external reality is as external and objective for the child as it is for adults. In other words, can the child distinguish the self from the external world? So long as the child supposes that everyone necessarily thinks like himself, he will not spontaneously seek to convince others, nor to accept common truths, nor, above all, to prove or test his opinions. If his logic lacks exactitude and objectivity, it is because the social impulses of mature years are counteracted by an innate egocentricity. In studying the child's thought, not in this case in relation to others but to things, one is faced at the outset with the analogous problem of the child's capacity to dissociate thought from self in order to form an objective conception of reality.

The child, like the uncultured adult, appears exclusively concerned with things. He is indifferent to the life of thought and the originality of individual points of view escape him. His earliest interests, his first games, his drawings are all concerned solely with the imitation of what is. In short, the child's thought has every appearance of being exclusively realistic.

But realism is of two types, or, rather, objectivity must be distinguished from realism. Objectivity consists in so fully realizing the countless intrusions of the self in everyday thought and the countless illusions which result—illusions of sense, language, point of view, value, etc.—that the preliminary step to every judgment is the effort to exclude the intrusive self. Realism, on the contrary, consists in ignoring the existence of self and thence regarding one's own perspective as immediately objective and absolute. Realism is thus anthropocentric illusion, finality—in short, all those illusions which teem in the history of science. So long as thought has not become conscious of self, it is a prey to perpetual confusions between objective and subjective, between the real and the ostensible; it values the entire content of consciousness on a single lane in which ostensible realities and the unconscious interventions of the self are inextricably mixed. It is thus not futile, but, on the contrary, indispensable to establish clearly and before all else the boundary the child draws between the self and the external world.

1. The result of a child's not learning that others think differently than he does is that 1.____
   A. the child will not be able to function as an adult
   B. when the child has matured, he will be innately egocentric
   C. when the child has matured, his reasoning will be poor
   D. upon maturity, the child will not be able to distinguish thought from objects
   E. upon maturity, the child will not be able to make non-ego-influenced value

2. Objectivity is the ability to 2.____
   A. distinguish ego from the external world
   B. dissociate oneself from others
   C. realize that others have a different point of view
   D. dissociate ego from thought

3. When thought is not conscious of self,
   A. one is able to draw the correct conclusions from his perceptions
   B. the apparent may not be distinguishable from the actual
   C. conscious thought may not be distinguishable from the unconscious
   D. the ego may influence the actual
   E. ontogeny recapitulates phylogony

4. The MAIN purpose of the passage is to
   A. argue that the child should be made to realize that others may not think like he does
   B. estimate the child's conception of the world
   C. explain the importance of distinguishing the mind from external objects
   D. emphasize the importance of non-ego-influenced perspective
   E. show how the child establishes the boundary between himself and the external world

5. The author *implies* that, if an adult is to think logically,
   A. his reasoning, as he matures, must be tempered by other viewpoints
   B. he must be able to distinguish one physical object from another
   C. he must be exclusively concerned with thought instead of things
   D. he must be able to perceive reality without the intrusions of the self
   E. he must not value the content of consciousness on a single plain

6. Realism, according to the passage, is
   A. the realization of the countless intrusions of the self
   B. final and complete objectivity
   C. a desire to be truly objective and absolute
   D. the ability to be perceptive and discerning
   E. none of the above

7. The child who is exclusively concerned with things
   A. thinks only objectivity
   B. is concerned with imitating the things he sees
   C. must learn to distinguish between realism and anthropomorphism
   D. has no innate ability
   E. will, through interaction with others, often prove his opinions

KEY (CORRECT ANSWERS)

1. C   5. A
2. E   6. E
3. B   7. B
4. D

TEST 8

DIRECTIONS: Each question or incomplete statement is followed by several suggested answers or completions. Select the one that BEST answers the question or completes the statement. *PRINT THE LETTER OF THE CORRECT ANSWER IN THE SPACE AT THE RIGHT.*

    Democracy is not logically antipathetic to most doctrines of natural rights, fundamental or higher law, individual rights, or any similar ideals—but merely asks citizens to take note of the fact that the preservation of these rights rests with the majority, in political processes, and does not depend upon a legal or constitutional Maginot line. Democracy may, then, be supported by believers in individual rights providing they believe that rights—or any transcendental ends—are likely to be better safeguarded under such a system. Support for democracy on such instrumental ground may, of course, lead to the dilemma of loyalty to the system vs. loyalty to a natural right—but the same kind of dilemma may arise for anyone, over any prized value, and in any political system, and is insoluble in advance.
    There is unanimous agreement that—as a matter of fact and law, not of conjecture—no single right can be realized, except at the expense of other rights and claims. For that reason their absolute status, in some philosophic sense, is of little political relevance. Political policies involve much more than very generable principles or rights. The main error of the older natural rights school was not that it had an absolute right, but that it had too many absolute rights. There must be compromise, and, as any compromise destroys the claim to absoluteness, the natural outcome of experience was the repudiation of all of them. And now the name of "natural right" can only creep into sight with the reassuring placard, "changing content guaranteed." Nor is it at all easy to see how many doctrine of inalienable, natural, individual rights can be reconciled with a political doctrine of common consent—except in an anarchist society, or one of saints. Every natural right ever put forward, and the lists are elusive and capricious, is every day invaded by governments, in the public interest and with widespread public approval.
    To talk of relatively attainable justice or rights in politics is not to plump for a moral relativism—in the sense that all values are equally good. But while values may be objective, the specific value judgments and policies are inevitably relative to a context, and is only when a judgment divorces context from general principle that it looks like moral relativism. Neither, of course, does the fact of moral diversity invalidate all moral rules.
    Any political system, then, deals only with relatively attainable rights, as with relative justice and freedoms. Hence, we may differ in given instances on specific policies, despite agreement on broad basic principles such as a right or a moral "ought"; and, per contra, we may agree on specific policies while differing on fundamental principles or long-range objectives or natural rights. Politics and through politics, law and policies, give these rights—and moral principles—their substance and limits. There is no getting away from the political nature of this or any other prescriptive ideal in a free society.

1. With which of the following would the author *agree*? 1._____
    A. Natural and individual rights can exist at all only under a democracy.
    B. While natural rights may exist, they are only relatively attainable.
    C. Civil disobedience has no place in a democracy where natural rights have no philosophic relevance.
    D. Utilitarianism, which draws its criteria from the happiness and welfare of individuals, cannot logically be a goal of a democratic state.
    E. Some natural rights should never be compromised for the sake of political policy.

2. It can be *inferred* that a democratic form of government
   A. can be supported by natural rightists as the best pragmatic method of achieving their aims
   B. is a form of government wherein fundamental or higher law is irrelevant
   C. will inn time repudiate all inalienable rights
   D. forces a rejection of moral absolutism
   E. will soon exist in undeveloped areas of the world

3. The MAIN purpose of the passage is to
   A. discuss natural rights doctrine
   B. compare and contrast democracy to individual rights
   C. discuss the reconciliation of a doctrine of inalienable natural rights with a political system
   D. discuss the safeguarding of natural rights in a democratic society
   E. indicate that moral relativism is antipathetic to democracy

4. The author indicates that natural rights
   I. are sometimes difficult to define
   II. are easily definable but at times unreconcilable with a system of government predicated upon majority rule
   III. form a basis for moral relativism
   The CORRECT answer is:
   A. I only   B. II only   C. I and II   D. III only   E. II and III

5. The fact that any political system deals with relatively attainable rights
   A. shows that all values are equally good or bad
   B. is cause for divorcing political reality from moral rules
   C. shows that the list of natural rights is elusive and capricious
   D. is inconsistent with the author's thesis
   E. does not necessarily mean that natural rights do not exist

6. The passage indicates that an important conflict which can exist in a democracy is the rights of competing groups, i.e., labor versus management
   A. adherence to the democratic process versus non-democratic actions by government
   B. difficulty in choosing between two effective compromises
   C. adherence to the democratic process versus the desire to support a specific right
   D. difficulty in reconciling conflict by natural rights

KEY (CORRECT ANSWERS)

1. B   4. A
2. A   5. E
3. C   6. D

READING COMPREHENSION
UNDERSTANDING AND INTERPRETING WRITTEN MATERIAL
EXAMINATION SECTION
TEST 1

DIRECTIONS: Each question or incomplete statement is followed by several suggested answers or completions. Select the one that BEST answers the question or completes the statement. *PRINT THE LETTER OF THE CORRECT ANSWER IN THE SPACE AT THE RIGHT.*

1. Most managers make the mistake of using absolutes as signals of trouble or its absence. A quality problem emerges—that means trouble; a test is passed—we have no problems. Outside of routine organizations, there are always going to be such signals of trouble or success, but they are not very meaningful. Many times everything looks good, but the roof is about to cave in because something no one thought about and for which there is no rule, procedure, or test has been neglected. The specifics of such problems cannot be predicted, but they are often signaled in advance by changes in the organizational system: Managers spend less time on the project; minor problems proliferate; friction in the relationships between adjacent work groups or departments increases; verbal progress reports become overly glib, or overly reticent; change occur in the rate at which certain events happen, not in whether or not they happen. And they are monitored by random probes into the organization—seeing how things are going.
According to the above paragraph,
   A. managers do not spend enough time managing
   B. managers have a tendency to become overly glib when writing reports
   C. managers should be aware that problems that exist in the organization may not exhibit predictable signals of trouble
   D. managers should attempt to alleviate friction in the relationship between adjacent work groups by monitoring random probes into the organization's problems

1.____

2. *Lack of challenge* and *excessive zeal* are opposite villains. You cannot do your best on a problem unless you are motivated. Professional problem solvers learn to be motivated somewhat by money and future work that may come their way if they succeed. However, challenge must be present for at least some of the time, or the process ceases to be rewarding. On the other hand, an excessive motivation to succeed, especially to succeed quickly, can inhibit the creative process. The tortoise-and-the-hare phenomenon is often apparent in problem solving. The person who thinks up the simple elegant solution, although he or she may take longer in doing so, often wins. As in the race, the tortoise depends upon an inconsistent performance from the rabbit. And if the rabbit spends so little time on conceptualization that the rabbit merely chooses the first answers that occur, such inconsistency is almost guaranteed.

2.____

According to the above paragraph,
- A. excessive motivation to succeed can be harmful in problem solving
- B. it is best to spend a long time on solving problems
- C. motivation is the most important component in problem solving
- D. choosing the first solution that occurs is a valid method of problem solving

3. Virginia Woolf's approach to the question of women and fiction, about which she wrote extensively, polemically, and in a profoundly feminist way, was grounded in a general theory of literature. She argued that the writer was the product of her or his historical circumstances and that material conditions were of crucial importance. Secondly, she claimed that these material circumstances had a profound effect on the psychological aspects of writing, and that they could be seen to influence the nature of the creative work itself. According to this paragraph,
    - A. the material conditions and historical circumstances in which male and female writers find themselves greatly influence their work
    - B. a woman must have an independent income to succeed as a writer
    - C. Virginia Woolf preferred the writings of female authors, as their experiences more clearly reflected hers
    - D. male writers are less likely than women writers to be influenced by material circumstances

3.____

4. A young person's first manager is likely to be the most influential person in his or her career. If this manager is unable or unwilling to develop the skills the young employee needs to perform effectively, the latter will set lower personal standards than he or she is capable of achieving, that person's self-image will be impaired, and he or she will develop negative attitudes toward the job, the employer—in all probability—his or her career. Since the chances of building a successful career with the employer will decline rapidly, he or she will leave, if that person has high aspirations, in hope of finding a better opportunity. If, on the other hand, the manager helps the employee to achieve maximum potential, he or she will build a foundation for a successful career.
According to the above paragraph,
    - A. If an employee has negative attitudes towards his or her job, the manager is to blame
    - B. managers of young people often have a great influence upon their careers
    - C. good employees will leave a job they like if they are not given a chance to develop their skills
    - D. managers should develop the full potential of their young employees

4.____

5. The reason for these difference is not that the Greeks had a superior sense of form or an inferior imagination or joy in life, but that they thought differently. Perhaps an illustration will make this clear. With the historical plays of Shakespeare in mind, let the reader contemplate the only extant Greek play on a historical subject, the Persians of Aeschylus, a play written less than ten years after the event which it deals with, and performed before the Athenian people who had played so notable a part in the struggle—incidentally,

5.____

immediately below the Acropolis which the Persians had sacked and defiled. Any Elizabethan dramatist would have given us a panorama of the whole war, its moments of despair, hope, and triumph; we should see on the stage the leaders who planned and some of the soldiers who won the victory. In the Persians we see nothing of the sort. The scene is laid in the Persian capital, one action is seen only through Persian eyes, the course of the war is simplified so much that the naval battle of Artemisium is not mentioned, nor even the heroic defense of Thermopylae, and not a single Greek is mentioned by name. The contrast could hardly be more complete.
Which sentence is BEST supported by the above paragraph?
- A. Greek plays are more interesting than Elizabethan plays.
- B. Elizabethan dramatists were more talented than Greek dramatists.
- C. If early Greek dramatists had the same historical material as Shakespeare had, the final form the Greek work would take would be very different from the Elizabethan work.
- D. Greeks were historically more inaccurate than Elizabethans.

6. The problem with present planning systems, public or private, is that accountability is weak. Private planning systems in the global corporations operate on a set of narrow incentives that frustrate sensible public policies such as full employment, environmental protection, and price stability. Public planning is Olympian and confused because there is neither a clear consensus on social values nor political priorities. To accomplish anything, explicit choices must be made, but these choices can be made effectively only with the active participation of the people most directly involved. This, not nostalgia for small-town times gone forever, is the reason that devolution of political power to local communities is a political necessity. The power to plan locally is a precondition for sensible integration of cities, regions, and countries into the world economy.
According to the author,
- A. people most directly affected by issues should participate in deciding those issues
- B. private planning systems are preferable to public planning systems
- C. there is no good system of government
- D. county governments are more effective than state governments

6._____

Questions 7-11.

DIRECTIONS: Questions 7 through 11 are to be answered SOLELY on the basis of the following passage.

The ideal relationship for the interview is one of mutual confidence. To try to pretend, to put on a front of cordiality and friendship is extremely unwise for the interviewer because he will certainly convey, by subtle means, his real feelings. It is the interviewer's responsibility to take the lead in establishing a relationship of mutual confidence.

As the interviewer, you should help the interviewee to feel at ease and ready to talk. One of the best ways to do this is to be at ease yourself. If you are, it will probably be evident; if you are not, it will almost certainly be apparent to the interviewee. Begin the interview with topics for discussion which are easy to talk about and non-menacing. This interchange can be like the conversation of people when they are waiting for a bus, at the ballgame, or discussing the weather. However, do not prolong this warm-up too long since the interviewee knows as well as you do that these are not the things he came to discuss. Delaying too long in betting down too business may suggest to him that you are reluctant to deal with the topic.

Once you get onto the main topics, do all that you can to get the interviewee to talk freely with a little prodding from you as possible. This will probably require that you give him some idea of the area and of ways of looking at it. Avoid, however, prejudicing or coloring his remarks by what you say; especially, do not in any way indicate that there are certain things you want to hear, others which you do not want to hear. It is essential that he feel free to express his own ideas unhampered by your ideas, your values and preconceptions.

Do not appear to dominate the interview, nor have even the suggestion of a patronizing attitude. Ask some questions which will enable the interviewee to take pride in his knowledge. Take the attitude that the interviewee sincerely wants the interview to achieve its purpose. This creates a warm, permissive atmosphere that is most important in all interviews.

7. Of the following, the BEST title for the above passage is 7.____
   A. PERMISSIVENESS IN INTERVIEWING
   B. INTERVIEW TECHNIQUES
   C. THE FACTOR OF PRETENSE IN THE INTERVIEW
   D. THE CORDIAL INTERVIEW

8. Which of the following recommendations on the conduct of an interview is made by the above passage? 8.____
   A. Conduct the interview as if it were an interchange between people discussing the weather.
   B. The interview should be conducted in a highly impersonal manner.
   C. Allow enough time for the interview so that the interviewee does not feel rushed.
   D. Start the interview with topics which are not threatening to the interviewee.

9. The above passage indicates that the interviewer should 9.____
   A. feel free to express his opinions
   B. patronize the interviewee and display a permissive attitude
   C. permit the interviewee to give the needed information in his own fashion
   D. provide for privacy when conducting the interview

10. The meaning of the word *unhampered*, as it is used in the last sentence of the fourth paragraph of the above passage, is MOST NEARLY 10.____
    A. unheeded   B. unobstructed   C. hindered   D. aided

11. It can be INFERRED from the above passage that 11.____
    A. interviewers, while generally mature, lack confidence
    B. certain methods in interviewing are more successful than others in obtaining information
    C. there is usually a reluctance on the part of interviewers to deal with unpleasant topics
    D. it is best for the interviewer not to waiver from the use of hard and fast rules when dealing with clients

Questions 12-19.

DIRECTIONS: Questions 12 through 19 are to be answered SOLELY on the basis of the following passage.

Disabled cars pose a great danger to bridge traffic at any time, but during rush hours it is especially important that such vehicles be promptly detected and removed. The term *disable car* is an all-inclusive label referring to cars stalled due to a flat tire, mechanical failure, an accident, or locked bumpers. Flat tires are the most common reason why cars become disabled. The presence of disabled vehicles caused 68% of all traffic accidents last year. Of these, 75% were serious enough to require hospitalization of at least one of the vehicle's occupants.

The basic problem in the removal of disabled vehicles is detection of the car. Several methods have been proposed to aid detection. At a 1980 meeting of traffic experts and engineers, the idea of sinking electronic eyes into roadways was first suggested. Such *eyes* let officers know when traffic falls below normal speed and becomes congested. The basic argument against this approach is the high cost of installation of these eyes. One Midwestern state has, since 1978, employed closed circuit television to detect the existence and locations of stalled vehicles. When stalled vehicles are seen on the closed circuit television screen, the information is immediately communicated by radio to units stationed along the roadway, thus enabling the prompt removal of these obstructions to traffic. However, many cities lack the necessary manpower and equipment to use this approach. For the past five years, several east-coast cities have used the method known as *safety chains*, consisting of mobile units which represent the links at the *safety chain*. These mobile units are stationed as posts one or two miles apart along roadways to detect disabled cars. Standard procedure is for the units in the *safety chain* to have roof blinker lights turned on to full rotation. The officer, upon spotting a disabled car, at once assumes a post that gives him the most control in directing traffic around the obstruction. Only after gaining such control does he investigate and decide what action should be taken.

12. From the above passage, The PERCENTAGE of accidents caused by disabled cars in which hospitalization was required by at least one of the occupants of a vehicle last year was
    A. 17%   B. 51%   C. 68%   D. 75%

13. According to the above passage, vehicles are MOST frequently disabled because of
    A. flat tires
    B. locked bumpers
    C. brake failure
    D. overheated motors

14. According to the above passage, in the electronic eye method of detection, the *eyes* are placed
    A. on lights along the roadway
    B. on patrol cars stationed along the roadway
    C. in booths spaced two miles apart
    D. into the roadway

6 (#1)

15. According to the above passage, the factor COMMON to both the *safety chain* method and the *closed circuit television* method of detecting disabled vehicles is that both
    A. require the use of *electronic eyes*
    B. may be used where there is a shortage of officers
    C. employ units that are stationed along the highway
    D. require the use of trucks to move the heavy equipment used

15.____

16. The one of the following which is NOT discussed in the above passage as a method that may be used to detect disabled vehicles is
    A. closed circuit television   B. radar
    C. electronic eyes   D. safety chains

16.____

17. One DRAWBACK mentioned by the above passage to the use of the closed circuit television method for detection of disabled cars is that this technique
    A. cannot be used during bad weather
    B. does not provide for actual removal of the cars
    C. must be operated by a highly skilled staff of traffic engineers
    D. requires a large amount of manpower and equipment

17.____

18. The NEWEST of the methods discussed in the above passage for detection of disabled vehicles is
    A. electronic eyes   B. the mobile unit
    C. the safety chain   D. closed circuit television

18.____

19. When the *safety chain* method is being used, an officer who spots a disabled vehicle should FIRST
    A. turn off his roof blinker lights
    B. direct traffic around the disabled vehicle
    C. send a ratio message to the nearest mobile unit
    D. conduct an investigation

19.____

20. The universe is 15 billion years old, and the geological underpinnings of the earth were formed long before the first sea creature slithered out of the slime. But it is only in the last 6,000 years or so that men have descended into mines to chop and scratch at the earth's crust. Human history is, as Carl Sagan has put it, the equivalent of a few seconds in the 15 billion year life of the earth. What alarms those who keep track of the earth's crust is that since 1950 human beings have managed to consume more minerals than were mined in all previous history, a splurge of a millisecond in geologic time that cannot be long repeated without using up the finite riches of the earth.
    Of the following, the MAIN idea of this paragraph is:
    A. There is true cause for concern at the escalating consumption of the earth's minerals in recent years.
    B. Human history is the equivalent of a few seconds in the 15 billion year life of the earth
    C. The earth will soon run out of vital mineral resources

20.____

21. The authors of the Economic Report of the President are collectively aware, despite their vision of the asset-rich household, of the real economy in which millions of Americans live. There are glimpses, throughout the Report, of the underworld in which about 23 million people do not have public or private health insurance; in which the number of people receiving unemployment compensation was 41 percent of the total unemployed, in which the average dole for the compensated unemployed is about one-half of take-home pay. The authors understand, for example, that a worker may become physically disabled and that individuals generally do not like the risk of losing their ability to earn income. But such realities justify no more than the most limited interference in the (imperfect) market for disability insurance. There is only, as far as I can tell, one moment of genuine emotion in the entire Report when the authors' passions are stirred beyond market principles. They are discussing the leasing provisions of the 1981 Tax Act (conditions which so reduce tax revenues that they are apparently opposed in their present form by the Business Roundtable, the American Business Conference, and the National Association of Manufacturers).

    In the dark days before the 1981 ACT, according to the Report, (*firms with temporary tax losses* (a condition especially characteristic of new enterprises) were often unable to take advantage of investment tax incentives. The reason was that temporarily unprofitable companies had no taxable income against which to apply the investment tax deduction. It was a piteous contingency for the truly needy entrepreneur. But all was made right with the Tax Act. Social Security for the disabled incompetent corporation: the compassionate soul of Reagan's new economy.

    According to the above passage,
    A. the National Association of Manufacturers and those companies that are temporarily unprofitable oppose the leasing provisions of the 1981 Tax Act
    B. the authors of the Report are willing to ignore market principles in order to assist corporations unable to take advantage of tax incentives
    C. the authors of the Report feel the National Association of Manufacturers and the Business Roundtable are wrong in opposing the leasing provisions of the 1981 Tax Act
    D. the authors of the Report have more compassion for incompetent corporations than for disabled workers

21.____

22. Much of the lore of management in the West regards ambiguity as a symptom of a variety of organizational ills whose cure is larger doses of rationality, specificity, and decisiveness. But is ambiguity sometimes desirable? Ambiguity may be thought of as a shroud of the unknown surrounding certain events. The Japanese have a word for it, *ma*, for which there is no English translation. The word is valuable because it gives an explicit place to the unknowable aspect of things. In English, we may refer to an empty space between the chair and the table; the Japanese don't say the space is empty but *full of nothing*. However amusing the illustration, it goes to the core of the issue. Westerners speak of what is unknown primarily in reference to what is known (like the space between the chair and the table, while most eastern languages give honor to the unknown in its own right.

22.____

Of course, there are many situations that a manager finds himself in where being explicit and decisive is not only helpful but necessary. There is considerable advantage, however, in having a dual frame of reference—recognizing the value of both the clear and the ambiguous. The point to bear in mind is that in certain situations, ambiguity may serve better than absolute clarity.

Which sentence is BEST supported by the above passage?
- A. We should cultivate the art of being ambiguous.
- B. Ambiguity may sometimes be an effective managerial tool,
- C. Westerners do not have a dual frame of reference.
- D. It is important to recognize the ambiguous aspects of all situations.

23. Everyone ought to accustom himself to grasp in his thought at the same time facts that are at once so few and so simple, that he shall never believe that he has knowledge of anything which he does not mentally behold with a distinctiveness equal to that of the objects which he knows most distinctly of all. It is true that some people are born with a much greater aptitude for such discernment than others, but the mind can be made much more expert at such work by art and exercise. But there is one fact which I should here emphasize above all others; and that is everyone should firmly persuade himself that none of the sciences, however abstruse, is to be deduced from lofty and obscure matters, but that they all proceed only from what is easy and more readily understood.

   According to the author,
   - A. people should concentrate primarily on simple facts
   - B. intellectually gifted people have a great advantage over others
   - C. even difficult material and theories proceed from what is readily understood
   - D. if a scientist cannot grasp a simple theory, he or she is destined to fail

24. Goethe's casual observations about language contain a profound truth. Every word in every language is a part of a system of thinking unlike any other. Speakers of different languages live in different worlds; or rather, they live in the same world but can't help looking at it in different ways. Words stand for patterns of experience. As one generation hand its language down to the next, it also hands down a fixed pattern of thinking, seeing, and feeling. When we go from one language to another, nothing stays put; different peoples carry different nerve patterns in their brains, and there's no point where they fully match.

   According to the above passage,
   - A. language differences and their ramifications are a major cause of tensions between nations
   - B. it is not a good use of one's time to read novels that have been translated from another language because of the tremendous differences in interpretation
   - C. differences in languages reflect the different experiences of people the world over
   - D. language students should be especially careful to retain awareness of the subtleties of their native language

Questions 25-27.

DIRECTIONS: Questions 25 through 27 are to be answered SOLELY on the basis of the following passage.

The context of all education is twofold—individual and social. Its business is to make us more and more ourselves, too cultivate in each of us our own distinctive genius, however modest it may be, while showing us how this genius may be reconciled with the needs and claims of the society of which we are a part. Thought it is not education's aim to cultivate eccentrics, that society is richest, most flexible, and most humane that best uses and most tolerates eccentricity. Conformity beyond a point breeds sterile minds and, therefore, a sterile society.
The function of secondary—and still more of higher education is to affect the environment. Teachers are not, and should not be, social reformers. But they should be the catalytic agents by means of which young minds are influenced to desire and execute reform. To aspire to better things is a logical and desirable part of mental and spiritual growth.

25. Of the following, the MOST suitable title for the above passage is　　　　25._____
   A. EDUCATION'S FUNCTION IN CREATING INDIVIDUAL DIFFERENCES
   B. THE NEED FOR EDUCATION TO ACQUAINT US WITH OUR SOCIAL ENVIRONMENT
   C. THE RESPONSIBILITY OF EDUCATION TOWARD THE INDIVIDUAL AND SOCIETY
   D. THE ROLE OF EDUCATION IN EXPLAINIING THE NEEDS OF SOCIETY

26. On the basis of the above passage, it may be inferred that　　　　26._____
   A. conformity is one of the forerunners of totalitarianism
   B. education should be designed to create at least a modest amount of genius in everyone
   C. tolerance of individual differences tends to give society opportunities for improvement
   D. reforms are usually initiated by people who are somewhat eccentric

27. On the basis of the above passage, it may be inferred that　　　　27._____
   A. genius is likely to be accompanied by a desire for social reform
   B. nonconformity is an indication of the inquiring mind
   C. people who are not high school or college graduates are not able to affect the environment
   D. teachers may or may not be social reformers

Questions 28-30.

DIRECTIONS: Questions 28 through 30 are to be answered SOLELY on the basis of the following passage.

Disregard for odds and complete confidence in one's self have produced many of our great successes. But every young man who wants to go into business for himself should appraise himself as a candidate for the one percent to survive. What has he to offer that is new or better? Has he special talents, special know-how, a new invention or service, or more capital than the average competitor? Has he the most important qualification of all, a willingness to work harder than anyone else? A man who is working for himself without limitation of hours or personal sacrifice can run circles around any operation that relies on paid help. But he must forget the eight-hour day, the forty-hour week, and the annual vacation. When he stops work, his income stops unless he hires a substitute. Most small operations have their busiest day on Saturday, and the owner uses Sunday to catch up on his correspondence, bookkeeping, inventorying, and maintenance chores. The successful self-employed man invariably works harder and worries more than the man on a salary. His wife and children make corresponding sacrifices of family unity and continuity; they never know whether their man will be home or in a mood to enjoy family activities.

28. The title that BEST expresses the ideas of the above passage is   28._____
    A. OVERCOMING OBSTACLES
    B. RUNNING ONE'S OWN BUSINESS
    C. HOW TO BECOME A SUCCESS
    D. WHY SMALL BUSINESSES FAIL

29. The above passage suggests that   29._____
    A. small businesses are the ones that last
    B. salaried workers are untrustworthy
    C. a willingness to work will overcome loss of income
    D. working for one's self may lead to success

30. The author of the above passage would MOST likely believe in   30._____
    A. individual initiative   B. socialism
    C. corporations   D. government aid to small business

KEY (CORRECT ANSWERS)

1. C	11. B	21. D
2. A	12. B	22. B
3. A	13. A	23. C
4. B	14. D	24. C
5. C	15. C	25. C
6. A	16. B	26. D
7. B	17. D	27. D
8. D	18. A	28. B
9. C	19. B	29. D
10. B	20. A	30. A

READING COMPREHENSION
UNDERSTANDING AND INTERPRETING WRITTEN MATERIAL
EXAMINATION SECTION
TEST 1

DIRECTIONS: Each question or incomplete statement is followed by several suggested answers or completions. Select the one that BEST answers the question or completes the statement. *PRINT THE LETTER OF THE CORRECT ANSWER IN THE SPACE AT THE RIGHT.*

1. The National Assessment of Educational Progress recently released the results of the first statistically valid national sampling of young adult reading skills in the United States. According to the survey, ninety-five percent of United States young adults (aged 21-25) can read at a fourth-grade level or better. This means they can read well enough to apply for a job, understand a movie guide or join the Army. This is a higher literacy rate than the eighty to eighty-five percent usually estimated for all adults. The study also found that ninety-nine percent can write their names, eighty percent can read a map or write a check for a bill, seventy percent can understand an appliance warranty or write a letter about a billing error, twenty-five percent can calculate the amount of a tip correctly, and fewer than ten percent can correctly figure the cost of a catalog or understand a complex bus schedule.
   Which statement about the study is BEST supported by the above passage?
   A. United States literacy rates among young adults are at an all-time high.
   B. Forty percent of young people in the United States cannot write a letter about a billing error.
   C. Twenty percent of United States teenagers cannot read a map,
   D. More than ninety percent of United States young adults cannot correctly calculate the cost of a catalog order.

   1.____

2. It is now widely recognized that salaries, benefits, and working conditions have more of an impact on job satisfaction than on motivation. If they aren't satisfactory, work performance and morale will suffer. But even when they are high, employees will not necessarily be motivated to work well. For example, THE WALL STREET JOURNAL recently reported that as many as forty or fifty percent of newly hired Wall Street lawyers (whose salaries start at upwards of $50,000) quit within the first three years, citing long hours, pressures, and monotony as the prime offenders. It seems there's just not enough of an intellectual challenge in their jobs. An up and coming money-market executive concluded: *Whether it was $1 million or $100 million, the procedure was the same. Except for the tension, a baboon could do my job.* When money and benefits are adequate, the most important additional determinants of job satisfaction are: more responsibility, a sense of achievement, recognition, and a chance to advance. All of these factors have a more significant influence on employee motivation and performance. As a footnote, several studies have found that the absence of these non-monetary factors can lead to serious stress-related illnesses.

   2.____

Which statement is BEST supported by the above passage?
- A. A worker's motivation to perform well is most affected by salaries, benefits, and working conditions.
- B. Low pay can lead to high levels of job stress.
- C. Work performance will suffer if workers feel they are not paid well.
- D. After satisfaction with pay and benefits, the next most important factor is more responsibility.

3. The establishment of joint labor-management production committees occurred in the United States during World War I and again during World War II. Their use was greatly encouraged by the National War Labor Board in World War I and the War Production Board in 1942. Because of the war, labor-management cooperation was especially desired to produce enough goods for the war effort, to reduce conflict, and to control inflation. The committees focused on how to achieve greater efficiency, and consulted on health and safety, training, absenteeism, and people issues in general. During the second world war, there were approximately five thousand labor-management committees in factories, affecting over six million workers. While research has found that only a few hundred committees made significant contributions to productivity, there were additional benefits in many cases. It became obvious to many that workers had ideas to contribute to the running of the organization, and that efficient enterprises could become even more so. Labor-management cooperation was also extended to industries that had never experienced it before. Directly after each war, however, few United States labor-management committees were in operation.
Which statement is BEST supported by the above passage?
- A. The majority of United States labor-management committees during the second world war accomplished little.
- B. A major goal of United States labor-management committees during the first and second world wars was to increase productivity.
- C. There were more United States labor-management committees during the second world war than during the first world war.
- D. There are few United States labor-management committees in operation today.

4. Studies have found that stress levels among employees who have a great deal of customer contact or a great deal of contact with the public can be very high. There are many reasons for this. Sometimes stress results when the employee is caught in the middle—an organization wants things done one way, but the customer wants them done another way. The situation becomes even worse for the employee's stress levels when he or she knows was to more effectively provide the service, but isn't allowed to, by the organization. An example is the bank teller who is required to ask a customer for two forms of identification before he or she can cash a check, even though the teller knows the customer well. If organizational mishaps occur or if there are problems with job design, the employee may be powerless to satisfy the customer, and also powerless to protect himself or herself from the customer's wrath. An example of this is the waitress who is forced to serve poorly prepared food. Studies have also found,

however, that if the organization and the employee design the positions and the service encounter well, and encourage the use of effective stress management techniques, stress can be reduced to levels that are well below average.
Which statement is BEST supported by the above passage?
- A. It is likely that knowledgeable employees will experience greater levels of job-related stress.
- B. The highest levels of occupational stress are found among those employees who have a great deal of customer contact.
- C. Organizations can contribute to the stress levels of their employees by poorly designing customer contact situations.
- D. Stress levels are generally higher in banks and restaurants.

5. It is estimated that approximately half of the United States population suffers from varying degrees of adrenal malfunction. When under stress for long periods of time, the adrenals produce extra cortisol and norepinephrine. By producing more hormones than they were designed to comfortably manufacture and secrete, the adrenals can *burn out* over time and then decrease their secretion. When this happens, the body loses its capacity to cope with stress, and the individual becomes sicker more easily and for longer periods of time. A result of adrenal malfunction may be a diminished output of cortisol. Symptoms of diminished cortisol output include any of the following: craving substances that will temporarily raise serum glucose levels such as caffeine, sweets, soda, juice, or tobacco; becoming dizzy when standing up too quickly; irritability; headaches; and erratic energy levels. Since cortisol is an anti-inflammatory hormone, a decreased output over extended periods of time can make one prone to inflammatory disease such ass arthritis, bursitis, colitis, and allergies. (Many food and pollen allergies disappear when adrenal function is restored to normal.) The patient will have no reserve energy, and infections can spread quickly. Excessive cortisol production, on the other hand, can decrease immunity, leading to frequent and prolonged illnesses.
Which statement is BEST supported by the above passage?
- A. Those who suffer from adrenal malfunction are most likely to be prone to inflammatory diseases such as arthritis and allergies.
- B. The majority of Americans suffer from varying degrees of adrenal malfunction.
- C. It is better for the health of the adrenals to drink juice instead of soda.
- D. Too much cortisol can inhibit the body's ability to resist disease.

5.____

6. Psychologist B.F. Skinner pointed out long ago that gambling is reinforced either by design or accidentally, by what he called a variable ratio schedule. A slot machine, for example, is cleverly designed to provide a payoff after it has been played a variable number of times. Although the person who plays it and wins while playing receives a great deal of monetary reinforcement, over the long run the machine will take in much more money than it pays out. Research on both animals and humans has consistently found that such variable reward schedules maintain a very high rate of repeat behavior, and that this behavior is particularly resistant to extinction.

6.____

Which statement is BEST supported by the above passage?
- A. Gambling, because it is reinforced by the variable ratio schedule, is more difficult to eliminate than most addictions.
- B. If someone is rewarded or wins consistently, even if it is not that often, he or she is likely to continue that behavior.
- C. Playing slot machines is the safest form of gambling because they are designed so that eventually the player will indeed win.
- D. A cat is likely to come when called if its owner has trained it correctly.

7. Paper entrepreneurialism is an offshoot of scientific management that has become so extreme that it has lost all connection to the actual workplace. It generates profits by cleverly manipulating rules and numbers that only in theory represent real products and real assets. At its worst, paper entrepreneurialism involves very little more than imposing losses on others for the sake of short-term profits. The others may be taxpayers, shareholders who end up indirectly subsidizing other shar holders, consumers, or investors. Paper entrepreneurialism has replaced product entrepreneurialism, is seriously threatening the United States economy, and is hurting our necessary attempts to transform the nation's industrial and productive economic base. An example is the United States company that complained loudly in 1979 that it did not have the $200 million needed to develop a video-cassette recorder, though demand for them had been very high. The company, however, did not hesitate to spend $1.2 billion that same year to buy a mediocre finance company. The video recorder market was handed over to other countries, who did not hesitate to manufacture them.

    Which statement is BEST supported by the above passage?
    - A. Paper entrepreneurialism involves very little more than imposing losses on others for the sake of short-term profits.
    - B. Shareholders are likely to benefit most from paper entrepreneurialism.
    - C. Paper entrepreneurialism is hurting the United States economy.
    - D. The United States could have made better video-cassette recorders than the Japanese but we ceded the market to them in 1979.

8. The *prisoner's dilemma* is an almost 40-year-old game-theory model psychologists, biologists, economists, and political scientists use to try to understand the dynamics of competition and cooperation. Participants in the basic version of the experiment are told that they and their *accomplice* have been caught red-handed. Together, their best strategy is to cooperate by remaining silent. If they do this, each will get off with a 30-day sentence. But either person can do better for himself or herself. If you double-cross your partner, you will go scot free while he or she serves ten years. The problem is, if you each betray the other, you will both go to prison for eight years, not thirty days. No matter what your partner chooses, you are logically better off choosing betrayal. Unfortunately, your partner realizes this too, and so the odds are good that you will both get eight years. That's the dilemma. (The length of the prison sentences is always the same for each variation.) Participants at a recent symposium on behavioral economics at Harvard University discussed the many variations on the game that have been used

over the years. In one standard version, subjects are paired with a supervisor who pays them a dollar for each point they score. Over the long run, both subjects will do best if they cooperate every time. Yet in each round, there is a great temptation to betray the other because no one knows what the other will do. The best overall strategy for this variation was found to be *tit for tat*, doing unto your opponent as he or she has just done unto you. It is a simple strategy, but very effective. The partner can easily recognize it and respond. It is retaliatory enough not to be easily exploited, but forgiving enough to allow a pattern of mutual cooperation to develop.
Which statement is BEST supported by the above passage?
   A. The best strategy for playing *prisoner's dilemma* is to cooperate and remain silent.
   B. If you double-cross your partner, and he or she does not double-cross you, your partner will receive a sentence of eight years.
   C. When playing *prisoner's dilemma*, it is best to double-cross your partner.
   D. If you double-cross your partner, and he or she double-crosses you, you will receive an eight-year sentence.

9. After many years of experience as the vice president and general manager of a large company, I feel that I know what I'm looking for in a good manager. First, the manager has to be comfortable with himself or herself, and not be arrogant or defensive. Secondly, he or she has to have a genuine interest in people. There are some managers who love ideas—and that's fine—but to be a manager, you must love people, and you must make a hobby of understanding them, believing in them and trusting them. Third, I look for a willingness and a facility to manage conflict. Gandhi defined conflict as a way of getting at the truth. Each person brings his or her own grain of truth and the conflict washes away the illusion and fantasy. Finally, a manager has to have a vision, and the ability and charisma to articulate it. A manager should be seen as a little bit crazy. Some eccentricity is an asset. People don't want to follow vanilla leaders. They want to follow chocolate-fudge-ripple leaders.
Which statement is BEST supported by the above passage?
   A. It is very important that a good manager spend time studying people.
   B. It is critical for good managers to love ideas.
   C. Managers should try to minimize or avoid conflict.
   D. Managers should be familiar with people's reactions to different flavors of ice cream.

9._____

10. Most societies maintain a certain set of values and assumptions that make their members feel either good or bad about themselves, and either better or worse than other people. In most developed countries, these values are based on the assumption that we are all free to be what we want to be, and that differences in income, work, and education are a result of our own efforts. This may make us believe that people with more income work that is more skilled, more education, and more power are somehow *better* people. We may view their achievements as proof that they have more intelligence, more motivation, and more initiative than those with lower status. The myth tells us that power, income, and education are freely and equally available to all, and that our

10._____

failure to achieve them is due to our own personal inadequacy. This simply is not the case.

The possessions we own may also seem to point to our real worth as individuals. The more we own, the more worthy of respect we may feel we are. Or, the acquisition of possessions may be a way of trying to fulfill ourselves, to make up for the loss of community and/or purpose. It is a futile pursuit because lost community and purpose can never be compensated for by better cars or fancier houses. And too often, when these things fail to satisfy, we believe it is only because we don't have enough money to buy better quality items, or more items. We feel bad that we haven't been successful enough to get all that we think we need. No matter how much we do have, goods never really satisfy for long. There is always something else to acquire, and true satisfaction eludes many, many of us.
Which statement is BEST supported by the above passage?
   A. The author would agree with the theory of *survival of the fittest*.
   B. The possessions an individual owns are not a proper measure of his or her real worth.
   C. Many countries make a sincere attempt to ensure equal access to quality education for their citizens.
   D. The effect a society's value system has on the lives of its members is greatly exaggerated.

11. *De nihilo nihil* is Latin for *nothing comes from nothing*. In the first century, the Roman poet Persius advised that if anything is to be produced of value, effort must be expended. He also said, *In nihilum nil posse revorti*—anything once produced cannot become nothing again. It is thought that Persius was parodying Lucretius, who expounded the 500-year-old physical theories of Epicurus. *De nihilo nihil* can also be used as a cynical comment, to negatively comment on something that is of poor quality produced by a person of little talent. The implication here is: *What can you expect from such a source?*
Which statement is BEST supported by the above passage?
   A. *In nihilum nil posse revorti* can be interpreted as meaning, *If anything is to be produced of value, then effort must be expended.*
   B. *De nihilo nihil* can be understood in two different ways,
   C. Lucretius was a great physicist.
   D. Persius felt that Epicurus put in little effort while developing his theories.

12. A Cornell University study has found that less than one percent of the billion pounds of pesticides used in this country annually strike their intended targets. The study found that the pesticides, which are somewhat haphazardly applied to 370 million acres, or about sixteen percent of the nation's total land area, end up polluting the environment and contaminating almost all 200,000 species of plants and animals, including humans. While the effect of indirect contamination on human cancer rates was not estimated, the study found that approximately 45,000 human pesticide poisonings occur annually, including about 3,000 cases admitted to hospitals and approximately 200 fatalities.

Which statement is BEST supported by the above passage?
  A. It is likely that indirect pesticide contamination affects human health.
  B. Pesticides are applied to over one-quarter of the total United States land area.
  C. If pesticides were applied more carefully, fewer pesticide-resistant strains of pests would develop.
  D. Human cancer rates in this country would drop considerably if pesticide use was cut in half.

13. The new conservative philosophy presents a unified, coherent approach to the world. It offers to explain much of our experience since the turbulent 1960s, and it shows what we've learned since about the dangers of indulgence and permissiveness. But it also warns that the world has become more ruthless, and that as individuals and as a nation, we must struggle for survival. It is necessary to impose responsibility and discipline in order to defeat those forces that threaten us. This lesson is dramatically clear, and can be applied to a wide range of issues.
    Which statement is BEST supported by the above passage?
      A. The 1970s were a time of permissiveness and indulgence.
      B. The new conservative philosophy may help in imposing discipline and a sense of responsibility in order to meet the difficult challenges facing this country.
      C. The world faced greater challenges during the second world war than it faces at the present time.
      D. More people identify themselves today as conservative in their political philosophy.

13.____

14. One of the most puzzling questions in management in recent years has been how usually honest, compassionate, intelligent managers can sometimes act in ways that are dishonest, uncaring, and unethical. How could top-level managers at the Manville Corporation, for example, suppress evidence for decades that proved beyond all doubt that asbestos inhalation was killing their own employees? What drove the managers of a Midwest bank to continue to act in a way that threatened to bankrupt the institution, ruin its reputation, and cost thousands of employees and investors their jobs and their savings? It's been estimated that about two out of three of America's five hundred largest corporations have been involved in some form of illegal behavior. There are, of course, some common rationalizations used to justify unethical conduct: believing that the activity is in the organization's or the individual's best interest, believing that the activity is not *really* immoral or illegal, believing that no one will ever know, or believing that the organization will sanction the behavior because it helps the organization. Ambition can distort one's sense of *duty*.
    Which statement is BEST supported by the above passage?
      A. Top-level managers of corporations are currently involved in a plan to increase ethical behavior among their employees.
      B. There are many good reasons why a manager may act unethically.
      C. Some managers allow their ambitions to override their sense of ethics,
      D. In order to successfully compete, some organizations may have to indulge in unethical or illegal behavior from time to time.

14.____

15. Some managers and supervisors believe that they are leaders because they occupy positions of responsibility and authority. But leadership is more than holding a position. It is often defined in management literature as *the ability to influence the opinions, attitudes and behaviors of others.* Obviously, there are some managers that would not qualify as leaders, and some leaders that are not *technically* managers. Research has found that many people overrate their own leadership abilities. In one recent study, seventy percent of those surveyed rated themselves in the top quartile in leadership abilities, and only two percent felt they were below average as leaders.
Which statement is BEST supported by the above passage?
    A. In a recent study, the majority of people surveyed rated themselves in the top twenty-five percent in leadership abilities.
    B. Ninety-eight percent of the people surveyed in a recent study had average or above-average leadership skills.
    C. In order to be a leader, one should hold a management position.
    D. Leadership is best defined as the ability to be liked by those one must lead.

15.____

KEY (CORRECT ANSWERS)

1.	D	6.	B	11.	B
2.	C	7.	C	12.	A
3.	B	8.	D	13.	B
4.	C	9.	A	14.	C
5.	D	10.	B	15.	A

INTERPRETING STATISTICAL DATA
GRAPHS, CHARTS AND TABLES
EXAMINATION SECTION
TEST 1

DIRECTIONS: Each question or incomplete statement is followed by several suggested answers or completions. Select the one that BEST answers the question or completes the statement. *PRINT THE LETTER OF THE CORRECT ANSWER IN THE SPACE AT THE RIGHT.*

1. The following chart shows the number of persons employed in a certain industry for each year from 2016 through 2021.

	Thousands of Employees
2016	5.7
2017	6.8
2018	7.0
2019	7.1
2020	7.4
2021	6.4

   In making a forecast of future trends, the one of the following steps which should be taken FIRST is to
   A. take the six-year average
   B. fit a curvilinear trend to the data
   C. fit a straight line, omitting 2021 as an *outlier*, i.e., as an unusually low reading
   D. check on what happened to the industry in 2021

   1._____

2. Of the following concepts, the one which CANNOT be represented suitably by a pie chart is
   A. percent shares
   B. shares in absolute units
   C. time trends
   D. successive totals over time, with their shares

   2._____

3. A pictogram is ESSENTIALLY another version of a(n) _____ chart.
   A. plain bar   B. component bar
   C. pie   D. area

   3._____

4. A time series for a certain cost is presented in a graph. It is drawn so that the vertical (cost) axis starts at a point well above zero.
   This is a legitimate method of presentation for some purpose, but it may have the effect of

   4._____

A. hiding fixed components of the cost
B. exaggerating changes which, in actual amounts, may be insignificant
C. magnifying fixed components of the cost
D. impairing correlation analysis

5. Certain budgetary data may be represented by bar, area, or volume charts. Which one of the following BEST expresses the most appropriate order of usefulness?
   A. Descends from bar to volume and area charts, the last being about the same
   B. Descends from volume to area to bar charts
   C. Depends on the nature of the data presented
   D. Descends from bar to area to volume charts

Questions 6-7.

DIRECTIONS: Questions 6 and 7 are to be answered on the basis of the layout below.

LAYOUT OF CONFERENCE ROOM
BUREAU OF RODENT CONTROL

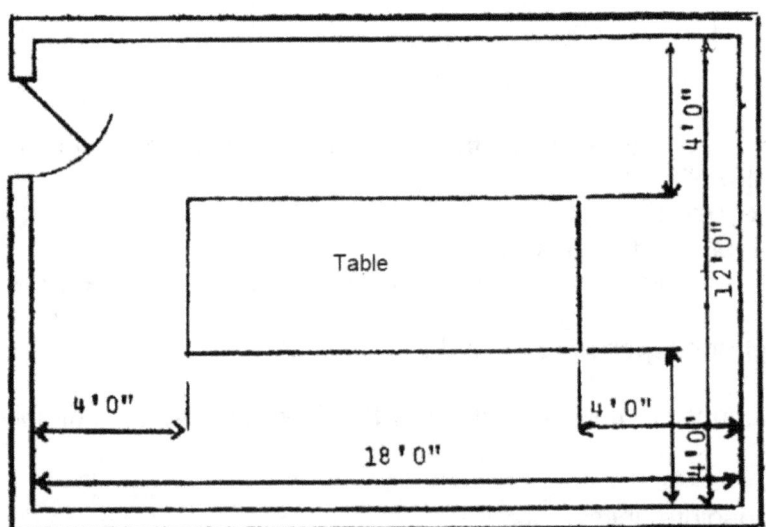

6. The LARGEST number of persons that can be accommodated in the area shown in the layout is
   A. 16   B. 10   C. 8   D. 6

7. Assume that the Bureau's programs undergo expansion and the Director indicates that the feasibility of increasing the size of the conference room should be explored.
   For every two additional persons that are to be accommodated, the analyst should recommend that _____ be added to table length and _____ be added to room length.
   A. 2'-6"; 2'-6"   B. 5'-0"; 5'-0"   C. 2'-6"; 5'-0"   D. 5'-0"; 2'-6"

Questions 8-9.

DIRECTIONS: Questions 8 and 9 are to be answered on the basis of the following groups, both of which depict the same information in different ways. The x and y axes in graphs A and B are not necessarily drawn in the same scale. The points along the curves on both graphs represent corresponding points and are the upper limits of class intervals.

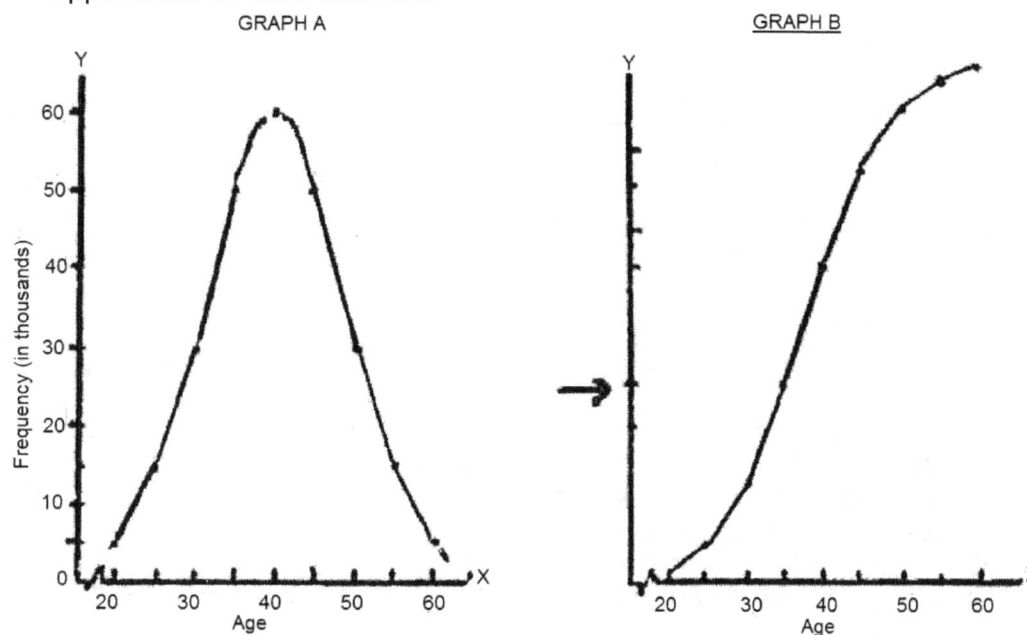

8. The ordinate (y-axis) in graph B is
    A. frequency
    B. cumulative frequency
    C. average frequency
    D. log frequency

8.____

9. The arrow on the y-axis in graph B indicates a particular number. That number is MOST NEARLY
    A. 100 B. 50,000 C. 100,000 D. 150,000

9.____

Questions 10-11.

DIRECTIONS: Questions 10 and 11 are to be answered on the basis of the graphs shown on the following page.

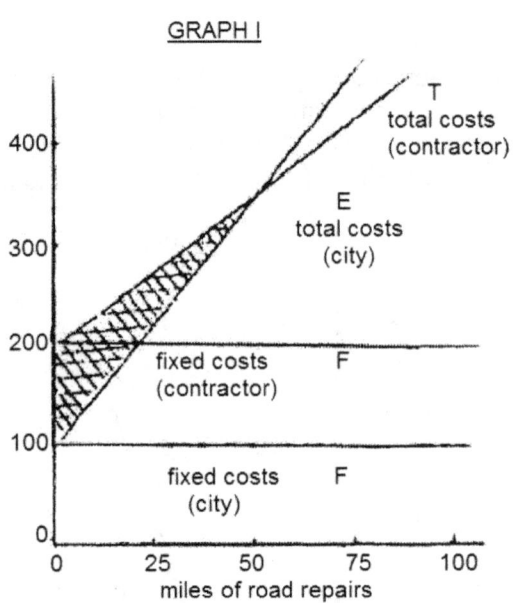
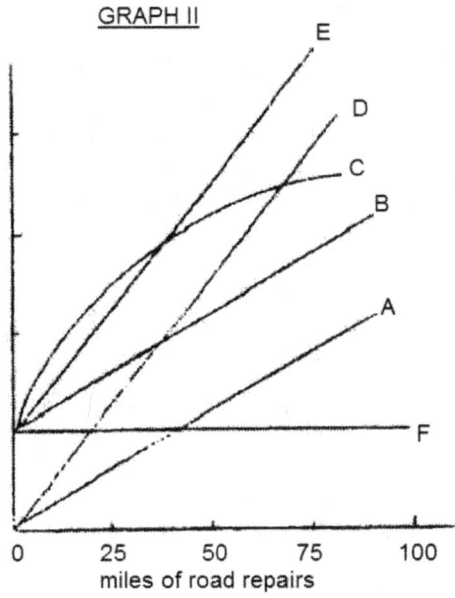

10. In Graph I, the vertical distance between lines E and T within the crosshatched area represents the _____ than 50 miles is performing by the city.
    A. savings to the city if work of less
    B. loss to the city if work of less
    C. savings to the city if work of more
    D. loss to the city if work of more

10.____

11. Graph II is identical to Graph I except that contractor costs have been eliminated. Total costs (line E) are the sum of fixed costs (line F) and variable costs.
    Variable costs are represented by line
    A. A   B. B   C. C   D. D

11.____

Questions 12-13.

DIRECTIONS: Questions 12 and 13 are to be answered on the basis of the following chart. In a hypothetical problems involving four criteria and four alternatives, the following data have been assembled.

Cost Criterion	Effectiveness Criterion	Timing Criterion	Feasibility Criterion
Alternative A $500,000	50 units	3 months	probably feasible
Alternative B $300,000	1 100 units	6 months	probably feasible
Alternative C $400,000	50 units	12 months	probably feasible
Alternative D $ 200,000	75 units	3 months	probably infeasible

12. On the basis of the above data, it appears that the one alternative which is dominated by another alternative is Alternative 12.____
    A. A B. B C. C D. D

13. If the feasibility constraint is absolute and fixed, then the critical trade-off is between lower cost _____ on the other. 13.____
    A. on the one hand and faster timing and higher effectiveness
    B. and higher effectiveness on one hand and faster timing
    C. and faster timing on the one hand and higher effectiveness
    D. on the one hand and higher effectiveness

14. The following illustration depicts the structure of a municipal agency. 14.____

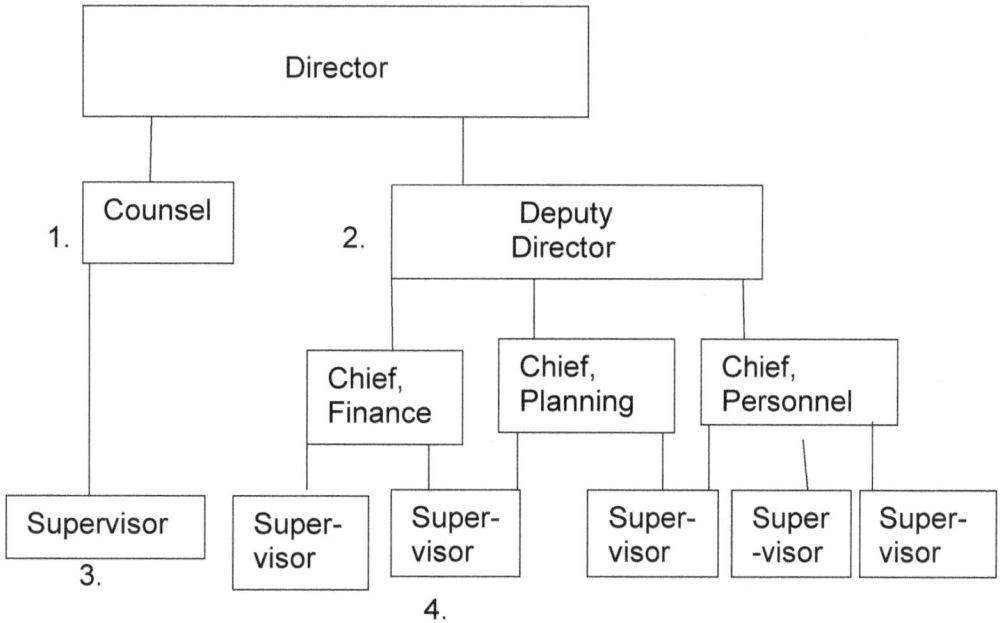

In the above illustration, which individual would generally be expected to encounter the MOST difficulty in carrying out his organizational functions?
    A. 1 B. 2 C. 3 D. 4

Questions 15-16.

DIRECTIONS: Questions 15 and 16 are to be answered on the basis of the information given on the report forms pictured on the following page.

Chart I and Chart II are parts of the Field Patrol Sheets of two Parking Enforcement Agents. They show the number of violations issued on a particular day. Chart III is the Tally Sheet for that day prepared by the Senior Parking Enforcement Agent from the Field Patrol Sheets of the entire squad.

6 (#1)

CHART 1

Area or Post	TYPE OF VIOLATION											
	Mtrs	B/S	O/P	Hyd	N/S	N/Sp	Taxi	Curb	N/P	Alt	Other	Total
19	2	3	2	2	3	3	0	1	1	5	1	23
21	4	0	2	0	1	2	2	0	5	9	1	26
Totals	6	3	4	2	4	5	2	1	6	14	2	49

2/4   100   PEA Browne
Date   Badge   Signature

TCB-61

Checked By _____ Date _____

CHART II

Area or Post	TYPE OF VIOLATION											
	Mtrs	B/S	O/P	Hyd	N/S	N/Sp	Taxi	Curb	N/P	Alt	Other	Total
31	8	2	0	0	3	2	2	0	4	5	0	26
33	7	0	1	2	3	1	2	0	6	3	0	25
Totals	15	2	1	2	6	3	4	0	10	8	0	51

2/4   101   PEA Grey
Date   Badge   Signature

TCB-61

Checked By _____ Date _____

TRAFFIC CONTROL BUREAU SENIORS TALLY SHEET

Enf. 23A

Name	Mtrs Ptld	Mtrs	Bus Stop	Dble Park	Hyd	No Stand	No Stop	Taxi	Curb	No Park	Alt Park	Other	Total
Green		18	2	3	1	6	0	0	0	4	10	1	45
Browne		6	3	4	2	4	5	2	1	6	14	2	49
White		12	0	0	0	2	1	1	0	8	8	1	33
Black		20	5	2	3	8	7	5	1	5	4	0	60
Grey		15	2	1	2	9	3	4	0	10	8	0	50
Redding		17	0	1	3	7	5	3	0	8	6	0	50
TOTAL		88	12	11	11	36	21	15	2	41	50	4	288

15. The Senior Parking Enforcement Agent who prepared Chart III made an error in transferring the violation totals from the Field Patrol Sheets to the Seniors Tally Sheet
    Which one of the following PROPERLY describes the Tally Sheet entry if this error were corrected? Parking Enforcement Agent
    A. Browne's overall total of summonses issued would be 50.
    B. Browne's total of summonses issued for Double-Parking violations would be 3.
    C. Grey's total number of summonses issued for meter violations would be 6.
    D. Grey's total number of summonses issued for No Standing violations would be 6.

15.____

16. The parking enforcement agent who issued the MOST summonses for bus stop and taxi stand violations is
    A. Black   B. Redding   C. White   D. Browne

16.____

17. During a period of probation in which records were kept for 360 children fourteen to eighteen years of age, probation officers found that the group committed certain offenses, as shown in the following table:

I.Q.	No. of Offenders	No. of Offenses	Offenses Per Offender
61-80	125	338	2.7
81-100	160	448	2.8
101 & Over	75	217	2.9

According to the foregoing data,
   A. the more intelligent offenders are no more law-abiding than, and perhaps not so law-abiding as, the dull offenders
   B. brighter offenders present no more difficult problems than less intelligent offenders
   C. the majority of this probation group is found to be above the average in intelligence of a normal group of young persons within this age range
   D. the relationship between the effectiveness of probation work and the number of offenders is in inverse ratio

17.____

18.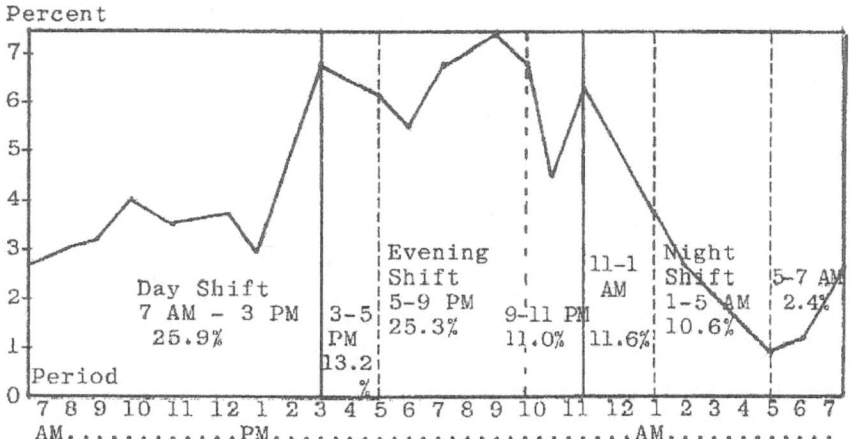

18.____

The percent for each hour is charted at the beginning of the hour. For example, 2.6% at the extreme left is for 7:00 A.M. to 7:59 A.M.
A certain police department has analyzed its need for police service and has computed the percentage distributions as shown on the chart on the preceding page. Despite good supervisory effort, there is a significant decrease in the amount of police service provided during the half-hour surrounding shift change. The police commander wishes to minimize this effect.
To accomplish its objective, taking into account the distribution of need for police services, which one of the following is the BEST time for this department to schedule its three principal shift changes? (Assume 8-hour shifts.)
   A. 4:00 A.M., Noon, 8:00 P.M.   B. 4:00 A.M., 1:00 P.M., 9:00 P.M.
   C. 6:00 A.M., 2:00 P.M., 10:00 P.M.   D. 7:00 A.M., 3:00 P.M., 11:00 P.M.

19. An inspector on a painting contract has to keep records on the progress of the work completed by a painting contractor.
The following is the progress of the work completed by a contractor at the end of 8 months.

Apartment Size	Estimated Number of Apartments	Number of Apartments Painted
3 rooms	120	100
4 rooms	160	140
5 rooms	120	40

The percentage of work completed on a room basis is MOST NEARLY
   A. 62%   B. 66%   C. 70%   D. 74%

20. Assume that an officer reported the following amounts of toll monies collected during each day of a five-day period:
    Tuesday $3,247.50
    Wednesday $2,992.50
    Thursday $3,917.50
    Friday $4,862.50
    Saturday $1,675.00

The TOTAL amount of toll money collected during this period was
   A. $15,702.50   B. $16,485.00   C. $16,695.00   D. $16,997.50

21. Suppose that during a two-hour period in a toll booth an officer collected the following:

Type of Money	Number of Bills
$20 bills	2
$10 bills	5
$5 bills	23
$1 bills	269

The TOTAL amount of money the officer collected was
   A. $299   B. $464   C. $474   D. $501

Questions 22-23.

DIRECTIONS: Questions 22 and 23 are to be answered SOLELY on the basis of the information shown below which indicates the charges for hospital services and physician services given in a hospital and a patient's annual income for each of four consecutive years.

Year	Patient's Annual Income	Charges for Hospital Services and Physician Services Given in a Hospital
2018	$45,000	$11,100
2019	$46,500	$11,970
2020	$64,500	$16,230
2021	$70,500	$17,325

22. A hospitalized patient may qualify for Medicaid benefits when the charges for hospital services and for physician services given in the hospital exceed 25 percent of the patient's annual income.
According to the information shown above, the one of the following that indicates ONLY those years in which the patient qualifies for Medicaid benefits is
   A. 2019, 2020
   B. 2018, 2019, 2021
   C. 2019, 2021
   D. 2019, 2020, 2021

23. The one of the following that is the patient's average annual income for the entire four-year period shown above is MOST NEARLY
   A. $48,375   B. $49,125   C. $56,025   D. $56,625

Questions 24-25.

DIRECTIONS: Questions 24 and 25 are to be answered SOLELY on the basis of the information shown below, which gives the hospital bill and the amount paid by an Insurance Plan for each of four patients.

Patient's Name	Hospital Bill	Amount Paid by the Insurance Plan Toward Hospital Bill
Mr. Harris	$8,753	$5,952
Mr. W. Smith	$4,504	$3,285
Mr. T. Jones	$7,211	$5,048
Mr. M. White	$12,255	$8,712

24. According to the information given above, which patient, when compared with the other three patients, had the HIGHEST percentage of his bill paid by the Insurance Plan?
   A. Mr. W. Smith   B. Mr. D. Harris   C. Mr. T. Jones   D. Mr. M. White

25. The average amount paid by the Insurance Plan toward the hospital bills of the four patients shown above is MOST NEARLY
    A. $5,269
    B. $5,499
    C. $5,749
    D. $5,766

KEY (CORRECT ANSWERS)

1.	D		11.	D
2.	C		12.	C
3.	A		13.	B
4.	B		14.	D
5.	D		15.	D
6.	B		16.	A
7.	A		17.	A
8.	B		18.	C
9.	C		19.	B
10.	A		20.	C

21. C
22. A
23. D
24. A
25. C

TEST 2

DIRECTIONS: Each question or incomplete statement is followed by several suggested answers or completions. Select the one that BEST answers the question or completes the statement. *PRINT THE LETTER OF THE CORRECT ANSWER IN THE SPACE AT THE RIGHT.*

Questions 1-2.

DIRECTIONS: Questions 1 and 2 are to be answered on the basis of the information contained in the following chart.

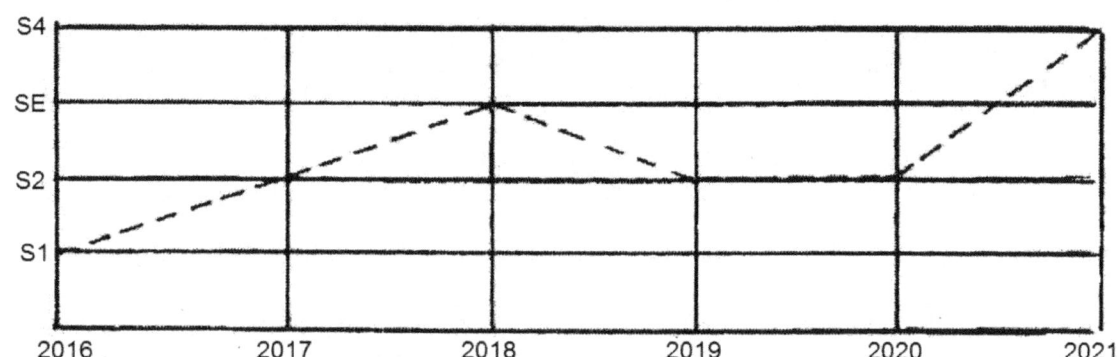

1. According to the above chart, the increase in the average price of the commodity from 2018 to 2021 was APPROXIMATELY   1.____
   A. 25%   B. 33 1/3%   C. 50%   D. 75%

2. According to the above chart, the increase in the average price of the commodity from 2016 to 2018 was APPROXIMATELY   2.____
   A. 20%   B. 30%   C. 200%   D. 300%

Questions 3-4.

DIRECTIONS: Questions 3 and 4 are to be answered SOLELY on the basis of the information contained in the chart below, which shows supply and demand of a commodity from January 1, 2017 to January 1, 2021.

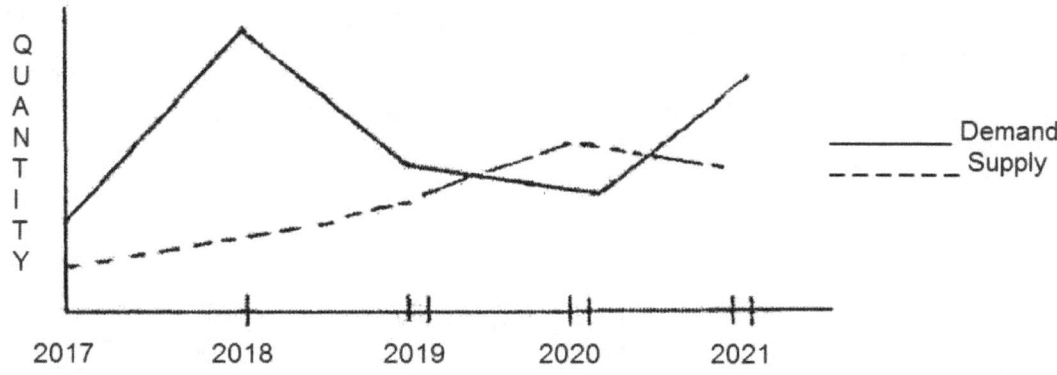

3. The above chart indicates that there was a seller's market during most of each of the following years EXCEPT
   A. 2017   B. 2018   C. 2019   D. 2020

4. According to the above chart, in the absence of price controls or other artificial or unusual circumstances, when would the price of the commodity have been the HIGHEST?
   A. 2017   B. 2018   C. 2019   D. 2020

5. In order to pay its employees, the Convex Company obtained bills and coins in the following denominations:

Denomination	$20	$10	$5	$1	$.50	$.25	$.10	$.05	$.01
Number	317	122	38	73	69	47	38	25	36

What was the TOTAL amount of cash obtained?
   A. $7,874.76   B. $7,878.00   C. $7,889.25   D. $7,924.35

6. Suppose that a business you are investigating presents the following figures:

Year	Net Income	Tax Rate on Net Income
2017	$55,000	20%
2018	$55,000	30%
2019	$65,000	20%
2020	$52,000	25%
2021	$62,000	30%
2022	$68,000	25%

According to these figures, it is MOST accurate to say that
   A. less tax was due in 2021 than in 2022
   B. more tax was due in 2017 than in 2020
   C. the same amount of tax was due in 2017 and 2018
   D. the same amount of tax was due in 2019 and 2020

7. The table below shows the total amount of money owed on the bills sent to each of four different accounts and the total amount of money which has been received from each of these accounts.

Name on Account	Amount Owed	Amount Received
Arnold	$55,989	$37,898
Barry	$97,276	$79,457
Carter	$62,736	$47,769
Daley	$77,463	$59,534

The balance of an account is determined by subtracting the amount received from the amount owed.

3 (#2)

Based on this method of determining a balance, the account with the LARGEST balance is
A. Arnold   B. Barry   C. Carter   D. Daley

8. A worksheet for a booth audit has the readings shown below for four turnstiles: 8.____

Turnstile No.	Opening Readings	Readings For Audit
1	26178	26291
2	65489	65752
3	72267	71312
4	45965	46199

With a fare of $1.00, what is the cash value of the TOTAL difference between the Opening Readings and the Readings for Audit for the four turnstiles?
A. $635   B. $653   C. $654   D. $675

Questions 9-10.

DIRECTIONS: Questions 9 and 10 are to be answered SOLELY on the basis of the information contained in the following table.

COMPARISON OF CUNY ATTRITION RATES FOR FALL 2021 DAY FRESHMEN THROUGH FALL 2022			
Colleges	Open Admissions (a)	Regular (b)	Overall
Senior	30%	14%	21%
Community	40%	34%	39%
Total	36%	20%	29%

a. Represents senior college students admitted with high school averages below 80 and community college students admitted wit high school averages below 75
b. Represents senior college students admitted with averages of 80 and above and community students admitted with averages of 75 and above

9. The category of students who remained in the City University in the GREATEST proportion were 9.____
   A. regular students in community colleges
   B. open admissions students in community colleges
   C. regular students in senior colleges
   D. open admissions students in senior colleges

10. Regular admission to a senior college was on the basis of an academic average 10.____
    A. above 70   B. of 80 or above
    C. above 75   D. above 85

Questions 11-12.

DIRECTIONS: Questions 11 and 12 are to be answered SOLELY on the basis of the information given below.

Time Scores	
Maximum qualifying time	15 minutes
Minimum qualifying time (subtract)	5 minutes
Range in qualifying time	10 minutes

Weighted Point Scores (Weight = 10)	
Maximum weighted score	10 points
Minimum qualifying score (subtract)	7 points
Range in weighted scores	3 points

From the foregoing, it is apparent that a simple conversion table can be prepared by giving the maximum qualifying time a minimum qualifying weighted core of 7 points and crediting three-tenths additional weighted points for each minute less than 15.

11. On the basis of the above paragraph, it is apparent that if the maximum *time* taken by any candidate on the task was 15 minutes, 11.____
    A. the test was too easy
    B. too much weight was given to the *time* portion
    C. less time should have been given for the task
    D. no one failed the *time* portion of the test

12. The BEST of the following interpretations of the above paragraph is that any candidate completing the task in 8 minutes would have received a weighted score for *time* of _____ points. 12.____
    A. 9.1   B. 8.5   C. 8.2   D. 7.9

Questions 13-14.

DIRECTIONS: Questions 13 and 14 are to be answered on the basis of the following illustration. Assume that the figures in the chart are cubes.

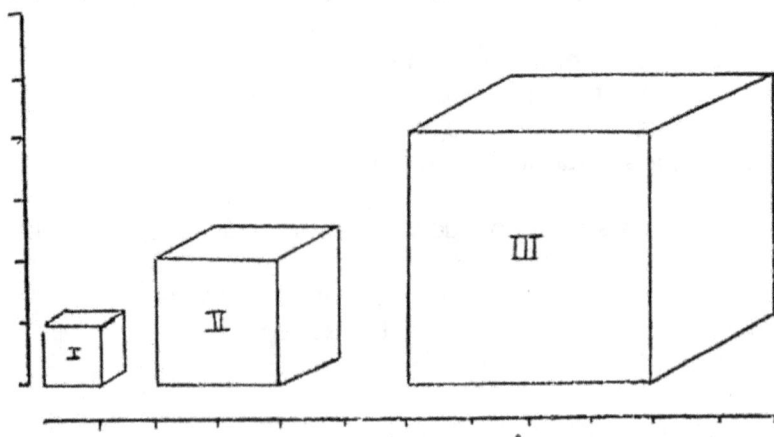

13. In the illustration above, how many times GREATER is the quantity represented by Figure III than the quantity represented by Figure II?
    A. 2   B. 4   C. 8   D. 16

13.____

14. The illustration above illustrates a progression in quantity BEST described as
    A. arithmetic   B. geometric   C. discrete   D. linear

14.____

Questions 15-16.

DIRECTIONS: Questions 15 and 16 are to be answered SOLELY on the basis of the following summary of salary increases applicable to a group of employees in a college office.

Hourly Rate 6/30/21	Increase 7/1/21	Increase 7/1/22
$10.20	$1.40/hr.	$1.40/hr.
$11.20	$1.20/hr.	$1.20/hr.
$12.20	$1.20/hr.	$1.20/hr.

Hourly Rate 6/30/21	Increase 7/1/21	Increase 7/1/2022
$13.20	$1.00/hr.	$1.00/hr.
$14.20	$1.00/hr.	$1.00/hr.
$15.20	$1.00/hr.	$1.00/hr.

15. A college office employee with an hourly salary of $14.20 as of June 30, 2021 worked for 32 hours during the week of April 16, 2022.
    Her gross salary for that week was
    A. $422.40   B. $454.40   C. $486.40   D. $518.40

15.____

16. A college office employee was earning an hourly salary of $12.20 in June of 2021.
    The percentage increase in her hourly salary as of July 2, 2022 will be MOST NEARLY
    A. 10%   B. 15%   C. 20%   D. 25%

16.____

17. An experiment was conducted to measure the error rate of typists. The results follow:

Typists	Percent of Total Output	Error Rate (in percent)
A	30	1.00
B	30	1.50
C	40	0.50

The error rate (in percent) for the three typists combined
A. is 0.95
B. is 1.00
C. is 3.00
D. cannot be calculated from the given data

17.____

Question 18.

DIRECTIONS: Question 18 is to be answered on the basis of the information given below.

At midnight on January 31, the following bodies were remaining.

Adults	Infants	Stillbirths	Amputations
37	23	40	21

On February 1st from 12:01 A.M. to 12:00 midnight, the following bodies were received:

Adults	Infants	Stillbirths	Amputations
24	13	18	8

In addition, the following bodies were claimed:

Adults	Infants	Stillbirths	Amputations
33	9	4	2

18. What is the number of cases remaining at midnight on February 1?

	Adults	Infants	Stillbirths	Amputations
A.	31	26	41	23
B.	28	27	54	27
C.	29	28	48	25
D.	27	29	62	28

Questions 19-25.

DIRECTIONS: Questions 19 through 25 are to be answered SOLELY on the basis of the following information.

ACCIDENTS

During one month, a certain division reported the number of accidents from various causes as follows:

Falls	6
Flying objects	5
Handling objects	4
Striking objects	3
Assaults	2
Stepping on objects	1

19. The GREATEST cause of accidents was
    A. striking objects
    B. handling objects
    C. flying objects
    D. falls

20. The accidents over which the injured person had LEAST control were those due to
    A. handling objects
    B. falls
    C. assaults
    D. flying objects

21. The accidents due to flying objects exceeded those due to striking objects by 21._____
    A. 2   B. 6   C. 3   D. 2

22. The TOTAL number of accidents as shown was 22._____
    A. 19   B. 20   C. 21   D. 22

23. The MOST likely cause for an accident to a station porter is 23._____
    A. stepping on objects   B. falls
    C. striking objects   D. assaults

24. The accidents which would MOST likely result in disciplinary action are those due to 24._____
    A. stepping on objects   B. assaults
    C. striking objects   D. falls

25. The TOTAL number of accidents involving objects was 25._____
    A. 8   B. 12   C. 13   D. 21

KEY (CORRECT ANSWERS)

1. B		11. D	
2. C		12. A	
3. C		13. C	
4. B		14. B	
5. A		15. C	
6. D		16. C	
7. A		17. A	
8. C		18. B	
9. C		19. D	
10. B		20. D	

21. D
22. C
23. B
24. B
25. C

INTERPRETING STATISTICAL DATA GRAPHS, CHARTS, AND TABLES

EXAMINATION SECTION

TEST 1

DIRECTIONS: Each question or incomplete statement is followed by several suggested answers or completions. Select the one that BEST answers the question or completes the statement. *PRINT THE LETTER OF THE CORRECT ANSWER IN THE SPACE AT THE RIGHT.*

Questions 1-12.

DIRECTIONS: Questions 1 through 12 are to be answered SOLELY on the basis of the information given in the graph and chart below.

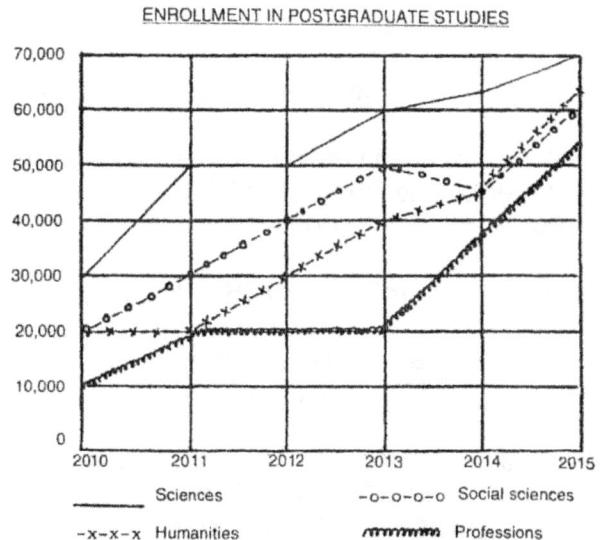

ENROLLMENT IN POSTGRADUATE STUDIES

——— Sciences −o−o−o−o Social sciences
−x−x−x Humanities ᴍᴍᴍᴍ Professions

Fields	Subdivisions	2014	2015
Sciences	Math	10,000	12,000
	Physical Science	22,000	24,000
	Behavioral Science	32,000	35,000
Humanities	Literature	26,000	34,000
	Philosophy	6,000	8,000
	Religion	4,000	6,000
	Arts	10,000	16,000
Social Services	History	36,000	46,000
	Sociology	8,000	14,000
Professions	Law	2,000	2,000
	Medicine	6,000	8,000
	Business	30,000	44,000

2 (#1)

1. The number of students enrolled in the social sciences and in the humanities was the same in
   A. 2012 and 2014
   B. 2010 and 2014
   C. 2014 and 2015
   D. 2011 and 2014

   1._____

2. A comparison of the enrollment of students in the various postgraduate studies shows that in every year from 2010 through 2015, there were MORE students enrolled in _____ than in the _____.
   A. professions; sciences
   B. humanities; professions
   C. social sciences, professions
   D. humanities; sciences

   2._____

3. The number of students enrolled in the humanities was GREATER than the number of students enrolled in the professions by the same amount in _____ of the years.
   A. two   B. three   C. four   D. five

   3._____

4. The one field of postgraduate study to show a DECREASE in enrollment in one year compared to the year immediately preceding is
   A. humanities
   B. sciences
   C. professions
   D. social sciences

   4._____

5. If the proportion of arts students to all humanities students was the same in 2012 as in 2015, then the number of arts students in 2012 was
   A. 7,500   B. 13,000   C. 15,000   D. 5,000

   5._____

6. In which field of postgraduate study did enrollment INCREASE by 20 percent from 2012 to 2013?
   A. Humanities
   B. Professions
   C. Sciences
   D. Social sciences

   6._____

7. The GREATEST increase in overall enrollment took place between
   A. 2010 and 2011
   B. 2012 and 2013
   C. 2013 and 2014
   D. 2013 and 2015

   7._____

8. Between 2012 and 2015, the combined enrollment of the sciences and social sciences INCREASED by
   A. 40,000   B. 48,000   C. 50,000   D. 54,000

   8._____

9. If the enrollment in the social sciences had decreased from 2014 to 2015 at the same rate as from 2013 to 2014, then the social science enrollment in 2015 would have differed from the humanities enrollment in 2015 MOST NEARLY by
   A. 6,000   B. 8,000   C. 12,000   D. 22,000

   9._____

10. In the humanities, the GREATEST percentage increase in enrollment from 2014 to 2015 was in
    A. literature   B. philosophy   C. religion   D. arts

    10._____

216

11. If the proportion of behavioral science students to the total number of students in the sciences was the same in 2011 as in 2014, then the increase in behavioral science enrollment from 2011 to 2015 was
    A. 5,000   B. 7,000   C. 10,000   D. 14,000

11.____

12. If enrollment in the professions increased at the same rate from 2015 to 2016 as from 2014 to 2015, the enrollment in the professions in 2001 would be MOST NEARLY
    A. 85,000   B. 75,000   C. 60,000   D. 55,000

12.____

KEY (CORRECT ANSWERS)

1.	B	7.	D
2.	C	8.	A
3.	B	9.	D
4.	D	10.	D
5.	A	11.	C
6.	C	12.	B

TEST 2

DIRECTIONS: Each question or incomplete statement is followed by several suggested answers or completions. Select the one that BEST answers the question or completes the statement. *PRINT THE LETTER OF THE CORRECT ANSWER IN THE SPACE AT THE RIGHT.*

Questions 1-5.

DIRECTIONS: Questions 1 through 5 involve calculations of annual grade averages for college students who have just completed their junior year. These averages are to be based on the following table showing the number of credit hours for each student during the year at each of the grade levels: A, B, C, D, and F. How these letter grades may be translated into numerical grades is indicated in the first column of the table.

Grade Value	Credit Hours – Junior Year					
	King	Lewis	Martin	Nonkin	Ottly	Perry
A = 95	12	23	9	15	6	3
B = 85	9	12	9	12	18	6
C = 75	6	6	9	3	3	21
D = 65	3	3	3	3	-	-
F = 0	-	-	3	-	-	-

Calculating a grade average for an individual student is a four-step process:
  I. Multiply each grade value by the number of credit hours for which the student received that grade.
  II. Add these multiplication products for each student.
  III. Add the student's total credit hours.
  IV. Divide the multiplication product total by the total number of credit hours.
  V. Round the result, if there is a decimal place, to the nearest whole number. A number ending in .5 would be rounded to the next higher number.

EXAMPLE:
Using student King's grades as an example, his grade average can be calculated by going through the following four steps:

  I. 95 × 12 = 1140
  II. 85 × 9 = 765
  III. 75 × 6 = 450
  IV. 65 × 3 = 195
  V. 0 × 0 = 0

  II. TOTAL = 2550

  III. 12
       9
       6
       3
       0
       30 TOTAL CREDIT HOURS

  IV. Divide 2550 by 30: $\frac{2550}{30} = 85$.

King's grade average is 85.

1. The grade average of Lewis is   1.____
   A. 83   B. 84   C. 85   D. 86

2. The grade average of Martin is
   A. 72   B. 73   C. 74   D. 75

3. The grade average of Nonkin is
   A. 85   B. 86   C. 87   D. 88

4. Student Ottly must attain a grade average of 90 in each of his years in college to be accepted into the graduate school of his choice.
   If, in summer school during his junior year, he takes two three-credit courses and receives a grade of 95 in each one, his grade average for his junior year will then be MOST NEARLY
   A. 87   B. 88   C. 89   D. 90

5. If Perry takes an additional three-credit course during the year and receives a grade of 95, his grade average will be increased to APPROXIMATELY
   A. 79   B. 80   C. 81   D. 82

KEY (CORRECT ANSWERS)

1. C
2. D
3. C
4. B
5. B

TEST 3

DIRECTIONS: Each question or incomplete statement is followed by several suggested answers or completions. Select the one that BEST answers the question or completes the statement. *PRINT THE LETTER OF THE CORRECT ANSWER IN THE SPACE AT THE RIGHT.*

Questions 1-5.

DIRECTIONS: Questions 1 through 5 are to be answered SOLELY on the basis of the following information and chart.

The following table gives pertinent data for six different applicants with regard to: Grade averages, which are expressed on a scale running from 0 (low) to 4 (high); Scores on qualifying test, which run from 200 (low) to 800 (high); Related work experience, which is expressed in number of months; Personal references, which are related from 1 (low) to 5 (high).

Applicant	Grade Average	Test Score	Work Experience	Reference
Jones	2.2	620	24	3
Perez	3.5	650	0	5
Lowitz	3.2	420	2	4
Uncker	2.1	710	15	2
Farrow	2.8	560	0	3
Shapiro	3.0	560	12	4

An administrative Assistant is in charge of the initial screening process for the program. This process requires classifying applicants into the following four groups:

A. SUPERIOR CANDIDATES: Unless the personal reference rating is lower than 3, all applicants with grade averages of 3.0 or higher and test scores of 600 or higher are classified as superior candidates.

B. GOOD CANDIDATES: Unless the personal reference rating is lower than 3, all applicants with one of the following combinations of grade averages and test scores are classified as good candidates:
   1. Grade average of 2.5 to 2.9 and test score of 600 or higher;
   2. Grade average of 3.0 or higher and test score of 550 to 599.

C. POSSIBLE CANDIDATES: Applicants with one of the following combinations of qualifications are classified as possible candidates:
   1. Grade average of 2.5 to 2.9 and test score of 550 to 599 and a personal reference rating of 3 or higher;
   2. Grade average of 2.0 to 2.4 and test score of 500 or higher and at least 21 months' work experience and a personal reference rating of 3 or higher;
   3. A combination of grade average and test score that would otherwise qualify as superior or good but a personal reference score lower than 3.

D. REJECTED CANDIDATES: Applicants who do not fall in any of the above groups are to be rejected.

EXAMPLE:
    Jones' grade average of 2.2 does not meet the standard for either a superior candidate (grade average must be 3.0 or higher) or a good candidate (grade average must be 2.5 to 2.9). Grade average of 2.2 does not qualify Jones as a possible candidate if Jones has a test score of 500 or higher, at least 21 months' work experience, and a personal reference rating of 3 or higher. Since Jones has a test score of 620, 24 months' work experience, and a reference rating of 3, Jones is a possible candidate. The answer is C.

Answer Questions 1 through 5 as explained above, indicating for each whether the applicant should be classified as a
  A. Superior candidate   B. Good candidate
  C. Possible candidate   D. Rejected candidate

1. Perez 1.____

2. Lowitz 2.____

3. Uncker 3.____

4. Farrow 4.____

5. Shapiro 5.____

KEY (CORRECT ANSWERS)

1. A
2. D
3. D
4. C
5. B

ARITHMETICAL REASONING
EXAMINATION SECTION
TEST 1

DIRECTIONS: Each question or incomplete statement is followed by several suggested answers or completions. Select the one that BEST answers the question or completes the statement. *PRINT THE LETTER OF THE CORRECT ANSWER IN THE SPACE AT THE RIGHT.*

1. The population of a city is, approximately, 7.85 million. The area is approximately 200 square miles. The number of thousand persons per square mile is
    A. 3.925	B. 39.25	C. 392.5	D. 39250

    1.____

2. The longest straight line that can be drawn to connect two points on the circumference of a circle whose radius is 9 inches is
    A. 9 inches	B. 18 inches	C. 28.2753 inches	D. 4.5 inches

    2.____

3. It is believed that every even number is the sum of two prime numbers. Two prime numbers whose sum is 32 are
    A. 7, 25	B. 22, 21	C. 13, 19	D. 17, 15

    3.____

4. To divide a number by 3000, we should *move* the decimal point 3 places to the
    A. right and divide by 3
    B. left and divide by 3
    C. right and multiply by 3
    D. left and multiply by 3

    4.____

5. The difference between the area of a rectangle 6 ft. by 4 ft. and the area of a square having the *same* perimeter is
    A. 1 sq. ft.	B. 2 sq. ft.	C. 4 sq. ft.	D. none of these

    5.____

6. The ratio of 1/4 to 3/8 is the *same* as the ratio of
    A. 1 to 3	B. 2 to 3	C. 3 to 2	D. 3 to 4

    6.____

7. If 7½ is divided by 1 1/5, the quotient is
    A. 6 1/4	B. 9	C. 7 1/10	D. 6 3/5

    7.____

8. A farmer has a cylindrical metal tank for watering his stock. It is 10 ft. in diameter and 3 ft. deep. If one cubic foot contains about 7.5 gallons, the *approximate* capacity of the tank in gallons is
    A. 12	B. 225	C. 4	D. 1707

    8.____

9. The fraction which fits in the following series, 1/2, 1/10, _____, 1/250, is
    A. 1/20	B. 1/100	C. 1/10	D. 1/50

    9.____

10. In two years, $200 with interest compounded semi-annually at 4% will amount to
    A. $216.48	B. $233.92	C. $208	D. $216

    10.____

SOLUTIONS TO ARITHMETICAL REASONING

1. Answer: (B) 39.25

   $$\frac{40,000}{20\overline{)8,000,000}}$$ (number of persons per square mile)(approximate population)

   Answer: 39.25 or (approximately) 40 (thousand persons per sq. mi.)

2. Answer: (B) 18 inches

   9" + 9" = 18 inches

3. Answer: (C) 13, 19
   A prime number is an integer which cannot be divided by itself and one integer; a whole number as opposed to a fraction or a decimal.

4. Answer: (B) 3 places to the left and divide by

   $$\frac{2}{3\overline{)6.000.}}$$

5. Answer: (A) 1 sq. ft.

   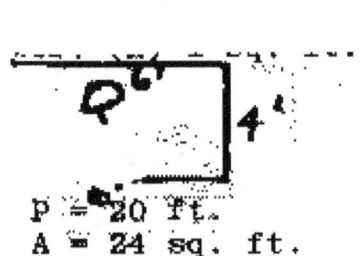   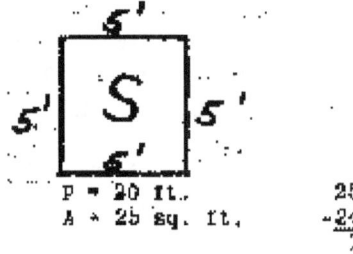

   P = 20 ft.   P = 20 ft.
   A = 24 sq.   A = 25 sq.

6. Answer: (B) 2 to 3

   $$\frac{1/4}{3/8} = 1/4 \div 3/8 = 1/4 \times 3/8 = 2/3$$

7. Answer: (A) 6 1/4

   $$\frac{7\ 1/2}{1\ 1/2} = \frac{15}{2} \div \frac{6}{5} = \frac{15}{2} \times \frac{5}{6} = \frac{25}{4} = 6\frac{1}{4} \quad \text{OR} \quad 1.2\overline{)7.5\ \tfrac{1}{4}} = 6\tfrac{3}{12}$$

8. Answer: (B) 225

$A = \pi R^2$
$= 3(5)^2$
$= 75$ sq. ft.

```
  225
 ×7.5
 1125
 1575    gal
1687.5
```

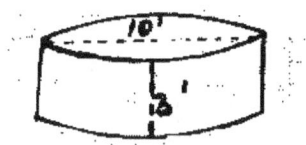

Volume of tank = 75 × 3 = 225 cu. ft.
(approximate capacity of tank in gallons)

9. Answer: (D) 1/50
A geometric series: each number is multiplied by the same number to get the succeeding number. (Multiply each number by 1/5). ½, 1/10, 1/50/$216, 1/250. The missing number if 1/50.

10 Answer: (A) $216.48
Compound Interest
4% a year compounded semi-annually is the same as 2% for a half year

A. $200 $200
   ×.02   × 4
   $4.00 Interest for 1st half yr. $204 Principal for 1st half yr.

B. $204 $204.00
   ×.02   × 4.08
   $4.08 Interest for 2nd half yr. $208.08 Principal for 1st half of 2nd yr.

C. $208.08 $208.08
   ×.02   × 4.16
   $4.1616 Interest for 1st half of 2nd yr. $212.24 Principal for 2nd half of 2nd yr.

D. $212.24 $212.24
   ×.02   × 4.24
   $4.2448 Interest for 2nd half of 2nd yr. $216.48 Principal at end of 2nd half of 2nd yr.

TEST 2

DIRECTIONS: Each question or incomplete statement is followed by several suggested answers or completions. Select the one that BEST answers the question or completes the statement. *PRINT THE LETTER OF THE CORRECT ANSWER IN THE SPACE AT THE RIGHT.*

1. With a *tax rate* of .0200, a tax bill of $1050 corresponds to an *assessed valuation* of 1.____
   A. $21,000 B. $52,500 C. $21 D. $1029

2. A sales agent, after deducting his commission of 6%, remits $2491 to his principal. The SALE amounted to 2.____
   A. $2809 B. $2640 C. $2650 D. $2341.54

3. The percent equivalent of .0295 is 3.____
   A. 2.95% B. 29.5% C. .295% D. 295%

4. An angle of 105 degrees is a _____ angle. 4.____
   A. straight B. acute C. obtuse D. reflex

5. A quart is approximately sixty cubic inches. A cu. ft. of water weighs approximately sixty pounds. Therefore, a quart of water weights *approximately* 5.____
   A. 2 lbs. B. 3 lbs. C. 4 lbs. D. 5 lbs.

6. If the *same* number is added to both the numerator and the denominator of a proper fraction, the 6.____
   A. value of the fraction is decreased
   B. value of the fraction is increased
   C. value of the fraction is unchanged
   D. effect of the operation depends on the original fraction

7. The *lease common multiple* of 3, 8, 9, 12 is 7.____
   A. 36 B. 72 C. 108 D. 144

8. On a bill of $100, the *difference* between a discount of 30% and 20% and a discount of 40% and 10% is 8.____
   A. nothing B. $2 C. $20 D. 20%

9. 1/3 percent of a number is 24. The NUMBER is 9.____
   A. 8 B. 72 C. 800 D. 7200

10. The cost of importing five dozen china dinner sets, billed at $32 per set, and paying a duty of 40% is 10.____
    A. $224 B. $2688 C. $768 D. $1344

SOLUTIONS TO ARITHMETICAL REASONING

1. Answer: (B) $52,500
   0200x = $1050   2x = $105,000
   200x = $10,500,000   x = $52,500 (assessed valuation)

2. Answer: (C) $2650
   $2491 + .06x = x
   x = 2491 + .06x

   1.00x - .06x = 2491

   Proof
   $2650 $2491
   × .06   + 159
   $159.00 $2650

   .94x = 2491
   .94x = 249,100

   $2,650
   94)249,100

3. Answer: (A) 2.95% [.0295 = 2.95%)

4. Answer: (C) obtuse angle
   An obtuse angle is an angle greater than 90°.

5. Answer: (A) 2 lbs.
   A quart = 60 cu. in.
   60 lbs. = 1 cu. ft. (or 1728 cu. in.) (12×12×12)
       (Keep like units of measure together)
   60 lbs. = 1728 cu. in.
   1 lb. = 1728/60 = approximately .29 cu. in.
   If 29 cu. in. weighs 1 lb., then 60 cu. in. weighs 2 lbs. (approximately). Therefore, a quart weighs 2 lbs. (approximately).

6. Answer: (B) the value of the fraction is increased

   (1) Start with the fraction 2/3

   (2) $\frac{2+2}{3+2} = \frac{4}{5}$ (Adding 2 to the numerator and the denominator)

   (3) $\frac{3}{2} = \frac{10}{15}$

   (4) $\frac{4}{5} = \frac{12}{15}$

7. Answer: (B) 72
   Common multiple can be evenly divided by all the numbers. Lease common multiple: the lowest of these numbers.

3 (#2)

8. Answer: (B) $2
   Formula: Step 1. Express percentages as decimals
              Step 2. Subtract each discount from *one*
              Step 3. Multiply all the results
              Step 4. Subtract the product from *one*

              Step 1. .3, .2 and .4, .1
              Step 2. .7, .8 and .6, .9
              Step 3. .7 × .8 = .56 (represents percent remaining after the discounts
                      .6 × .9 = .54 are taken)
              Step 4. 1.00   1.00
                       -.56   -.54
                        .44   .46

              Then, $100 × .02 = $2.00

9. Answer: (D) 7200

   $\frac{1}{300}x = 24;$ x = 24×300;   x = 7200

10. Answer: (B) $2688

    $32 $1920
    ×60   ×.40
    $1920 Cost of dinner sets before paying duty $768.00 Duty

    $1920
    + 768
    $2688 Cost of dinner sets *after* paying duty

TEST 3

DIRECTIONS: Each question or incomplete statement is followed by several suggested answers or completions. Select the one that BEST answers the question or completes the statement. *PRINT THE LETTER OF THE CORRECT ANSWER IN THE SPACE AT THE RIGHT.*

1. A motorist travels 120 miles to his destination at the average speed of 60 miles per hour and returns to the starting point at the average speed of 40 miles per hour. His *average speed* for the ENTIRE trip is _____ miles per hour.
   A. 53 B. 50 C. 48 D. 45

   1.____

2. A snapshot measures 2 1/2 inches by 1 7/8 inches. It is to be enlarged so that the longer dimension will be 4 inches. The length of the enlarged *shorter* dimension will be
   A. 2 1/2 inches B. 3 3/8 inches C. 3 inches D. none of these

   2.____

3. The approximate distance is, in feet, that an object falls in t seconds when dropped from a height is obtained by use of the formula $s = 16t^2$. In 8 seconds, the object will fall
   A. 15,384 feet B. 1,024 feet C. 256 feet D. none of these

   3.____

4. The PRODUCT of 75^3 and 75^7 is
   A. $(75)^{10}$ B. $(75)^{21}$ C. $(5,625)^{10}$ D. $(150)^{10}$

   4.____

5. The scale of a map is: 3/4 of an inch = 10 miles. If the distance on the map between two towns is 6 inches, the *actual* distance is
   A. 45 miles B. 60 miles C. 80 miles D. none of these

   5.____

6. If $d = m \dfrac{50}{m}$, and m is a positive number which increases in value, d
   A. increases in value B. decreases in value
   B. remains unchanged D. fluctuates up and down in value

   6.____

7. From a piece of tin in the shape of a square 6 inches on a side, the largest possible circle is cut out.
   Of the following, the ratio of the area of the circle to the area of the original square is *closest* in value to
   A. 4/5 B. 3/5 C. 2/3 D. 1/2

   7.____

8. A pound of water is evaporated from 6 pounds of sea water containing 4% salt. The percentage of salt in the *remaining* solution is
   A. 3 1/3 B. 4 C. 4 4/5 D. none of these

   8.____

9. If a cubic inch of a metal weighs 2 pounds, a cubic foot of the *same* metal weighs
   A. 8 pounds B. 24 pounds C. 288 pounds D. none of these

   9.____

10. Assume that, according to the Federal income tax law, if the taxable income in the case of a separate return is over $4,000, but not over $6,000, the tax is $840 + 26% of the excess over $4,000.
   If a taxpayer files a separate tax return and his taxable income is $5,500, the tax is

   A. $690   B. $1,230   C. $1,370   D. none of these

SOLUTIONS TO ARITHMETICAL REASONING

1. Answer: (C) 48 miles per hour
   120 miles = 2 hours (60 mph)
   120 miles = 3 hours (40 mph)
   240 miles = 5 hours = average of 48 mph

2. Answer: (C) 3 inches
   Change 2 1/2 to 20/8   Change 1 7/8 to 15/8
   Ratio is 20 to 15 or 4 to 3.
   If the longer dimension is 4 inches, then the shorter is 3 inches.

3. Answer: (B) 1,024 feet
   $s = 16 \times 8^2$ or 16×64 or 1024 feet

4. Answer: (A) $(75)^{10}$
   Because the 75 is constant, one needs only to add the exponents (7 and 3). Therefore, the product is 75^{10}.

5. Answer: (C) 80 miles
   $6 \div 3/4 = 6 \times 4/3 = 24/3$ or 8
   8×10 miles = 80 miles

6. Answer: (A) increases in value
   By increasing the value of my (by substituting numbers for letters), it is obvious that d increases in value.

7. Answer: (A) 4/5
   Area of square = 36 square inches
   Area of circle = π^2
   $\qquad = \pi 9 \ (3 \times 3)$
   $\qquad = 3 \ 1/7 \times 9$
   $\qquad = 28 \ 2/7$

   $$\frac{28 \ 2/7}{36} = \frac{198}{7} \times \frac{1}{36} = \frac{198}{252} \qquad \begin{array}{r} .78 = 78\% \\ 252 \overline{)198.00} \\ \underline{176\ 4} \\ 21\ 60 \\ \underline{20\ 16} \\ 1\ 44 \end{array}$$

   78% is closest to 4/5 (80%)

8. Answer: (C) 4 4/5
.04 × 6 = .24 lbs. of salt in 6 lbs. of salt water
When a pound of water is evaporated, the salt content remains the same.

```
    .24
 5).24
    .04  4/5 = 4 4/5%
```

9. Answer: (D) none of these
1728 cubic inches   = 1 cubic foot
1 cubic inch   = 2 pounds
1728 cubic inches   = 3,456 pounds

10. Answer: (B) $1,230

$5,500
-4,000
$1,500   (excess over 4000)

$1500 × 25% = $390.00
              +840.00
              $1230.00 (tax)

TEST 4

DIRECTIONS: Each question or incomplete statement is followed by several suggested answers or completions. Select the one that BEST answers the question or completes the statement. *PRINT THE LETTER OF THE CORRECT ANSWER IN THE SPACE AT THE RIGHT.*

1. If the number of square inches in the area of a circle is equal to the number of inches in its circumference, the DIAMETER of the circle is
   A. 4 inches   B. 3 inches   C. 1 inch   D. none of these

   1._____

2. The *least common multiple* of 20, 24, 32 is
   A. 900   B. 1,920   C. 15,360   D. none of these

   2._____

3. Six quarts of a 20% solution of alcohol in water are mixed with 4 quarts of a 60% solution of alcohol in water. The *alcoholic* strength of the mixture is
   A. 80%   B. 50%   C. 36%   D. none of these

   3._____

4. To find the radius of a circle whose circumference is 60 inches,
   A. multiply 60 by π
   B. divide 60 by 2π
   C. divide 30 by 2π
   D. divide 60 by π and extract the square root of the result

   4._____

5. A micromillimeter is defined as one millionth of a millimeter. A length of 17 micromillimeters may be represented by
   A. .00017 mm.   B. 0000017 mm.
   C. .000017 mm.   D. .00000017 mm.

   5._____

6. If 9x + 5 = 23, the numerical value of 18x + 5 is
   A. 46   B. 41   C. 32   D. 23 + 9x

   6._____

7. When the fractions 2/3, 5/7, 8/11 and 9/13 are arranged in ascending order of size, the result is
   A. 8/11, 5/7, 9/13, 2/3   B. 5/7, 8/11, 2/3, 9/13
   C. 2/3, 8/11, 5/7, 9/13   D. 2/3, 9/13, 5/7, 8/11

   7._____

8. If the outer diameter of a metal pipe is 2.84 inches and the inner diameter is 1.94 inches, the *thickness* of the metal is
   A. .45 of an inch   B. .90 of an inch   C. 1.94 inches   D. 2.39 inches

   8._____

9. An office manager employs 3 typists at $450 per week, 2 general clerks at $400 per week, and a messenger at $320 per week. The *average* weekly wage of these part-time employees is
   A. $372.50   B. $390.00   C. $411.70   D. none of these

   9._____

10. A rectangular bin 4 feet long, 3 feet wide, and 2 feet high is solidly packed with bricks whose dimensions are 8 inches, 4 inches, and 2 inches. The *number* of bricks in the bin is
    A. 54   B. 648   C. 1,298   D. none of these

    10._____

SOLUTIONS TO ARITHMETICAL REASONING

1. Answer: (A) 4 inches
   Assume there are 100 square inches in the area of a circle and 100 inches in its circumference.
   A = 1/2Cr
   100 = 1/2 × Xr
   50r = 100
   r = 2
   d = 4

2. Answer: (D) none of these
   2)20 – 24 - 32
   2)10 – 12 – 16
   2)20 – 24 – 32
      5 – 3 – 4

   $2 \times 2 \times 2 \times 5 \times 3 \times 4 = 480$

3. Answer: (C) 36%
   6 quarts × 20%   =   120%
   4 quarts × 60%   =   240%
   10 quarts   =   360%
   1 quart   =   36%

4. Answer: (B) divide 60 by 2

   C = 2r

   $2\pi r = 60$

   $2r = \dfrac{60}{\pi}$

   $r = \dfrac{60}{\pi} \times \dfrac{1}{2}$

   $r = \dfrac{60}{2\pi}$

5. Answer: (C) .000017 mm.
   1 micromillimeter   =   .000001 mm.
   17 micromillimeters =   .000017 mm.

6. Answer: (B) 41
   9x + 5 = 23
   9x = 23 – 5 or 9x = 18
   x = 2
   18x + 5 = 36 + 5 or 41

7. Answer: (D) 2/3, 9/13, 5/7, 8/11
   Find the least common denominator = 3003

   $\dfrac{2}{3} = \dfrac{2002}{3003}$ $\dfrac{9}{13} = \dfrac{2079}{3003}$ $\dfrac{5}{7} = \dfrac{2145}{3003}$ $\dfrac{8}{11} = \dfrac{2184}{3003}$

   Correct order is 2/3, 9/13, 5/7, 8/11

3 (#4)

8. Answer: (A) .45 of an inch
   2.84 inches = outer diameter
   1.94 inches = inner diameter
    .90 inches = thickness (both sides)
    .45 inches = thickness (one side)

9. Answer: (C) $41.17
   3 × 45 = $135
   2 × 40 = 80

   $\frac{1}{6}$ × 32 = $\frac{32}{\$247}$

   $247 ÷ 6 = $41 1/6 or $41.17

10. Answer: (B) 648

    There are 1728 cu. inches in 1 cu. ft. (12 × 12 × 12)
    4 × 3 × 2 = 24 cu.ft. × 1728 = 41472 cu. in. ÷ 64 (8 × 4 × 2) = 648 bricks

TEST 5

DIRECTIONS: Each question or incomplete statement is followed by several suggested answers or completions. Select the one that BEST answers the question or completes the statement. *PRINT THE LETTER OF THE CORRECT ANSWER IN THE SPACE AT THE RIGHT.*

1. If x is less than 10, and y is less than 5, it follows that
    A. x is greater than y
    B. x = 2y
    C. x-y = 5
    D. x+y is less than 15

    1._____

2. A dealer sells an article at a loss of 50% of the cost. Based on the selling price, the *loss* is
    A. 25%
    B. 50%
    C. 100%
    D. none of these

    2._____

3. If 8 men get together at a reunion and each man shakes hands once with each of the others, the *total number* of handshakes is
    A. 49
    B. 56
    C. 64
    D. 28

    3._____

4. The world record for cycling a stretch of 20 kilometers is 26 minutes. This corresponds to an average speed of, *approximately*,
    A. 29 miles per hour
    B. 46 miles per hour
    C. 32 miles per hour
    D. none of these

    4._____

5. The sum, s, of n consecutive integers beginning with 1 can be found by use of the formula $s = \frac{n(n+1)}{2}$. The sum of the *first 100 consecutive integers* is
    A. 5,001
    B. 5,050
    C. 10,000
    D. 10,100

    5._____

6. Of the following, the value of $\frac{\sqrt[3]{64.32}}{\sqrt{.041}}$ is closest to
    A. 400
    B. 200
    C. 20
    D. 16

    6._____

7. If each edge of a cube is increased by 2 inches, the
    A. volume is increased by 8 cubic inches
    B. area of each face is increased by 4 square inches
    C. diagonal of each face is increased by 2 inches
    D. sum of the edges is increased by 24 inches

    7._____

8. In a school in which 40% of the enrolled students are boys, 80% of the boys are present on a certain day. If 1,152 boys are present, the total school enrollment is
    A. 1,440
    B. 2,880
    C. 3,600
    D. none of these

    8._____

9. An agent received a commission of d% of the selling price of a house. If the commission amounted to $600, the selling price, in dollars, was 9.____

   A. $\frac{60,000}{d}$ B. 600/d   C. 6d   D. 600d

10. A ship sails due north from a position 5 28' South Latitude to a position 6 43' North Latitude. Given that one minute of latitude is equivalent to 1 nautical mile, the ship has sailed a distance of _____ nautical miles 10.____
    A. 75   B. 371   C. 731   D. 1,211

SOLUTIONS TO ARITHMETICAL REASONING

1. Answer: (D) x + y is less than 15
   If x is less than 10 and y is less than 5, then x + y MUST be less than 15. None of the others is possible.

2. Answer: (C) 100%
   Based on selling price, the formula is written:
   Cost – Loss = Selling Price
   100% - 50% = 50%
   Loss = 100% of the Selling Price (loss equal to Selling Price)

3. Answer: (D) 28
   A shakes hands with the other 7
   B shakes hands with the other 6 (has already shaken A's)
   and so on....... Thus 7, 6, 5, 4, 3, 2, 1 = 28 handshakes

4. Answer: (A) 29 miles per hour
   1 kilometer = 5/8 of a mile
   20 kilometers = 20 × 5/8 = 12 1/2 miles
   12 1/2 miles : 26 minutes = x : 60 minutes
   $26x = 750$
   $x = 28+$ or 29 miles per hour

5. Answer: (B) 5,050

   $s = \dfrac{n(n+1)}{2} \qquad s = \dfrac{100(100+1)}{2} \qquad s = \dfrac{10,100}{2} \qquad s = 5,050$

6. Answer: (C) 2

   $\sqrt[3]{64.32} = 4.01 \qquad \dfrac{4}{.2} = 4 \times \dfrac{10}{2} = 20$

   $\sqrt{.041} = .202$

7. Answer: (D) the sum of the edges is increased by 24 inches. Since there are 12 edges to a cube and each edge is increased by 2 inches, the total increase is 24 inches.

8. Answer: (C) 3,600

   $1152 \div \dfrac{8}{10} = 1440 = 1440$ boys enrolled (1152 × 10/8)

   $1440 \div \dfrac{4}{10} = 1440 \times \dfrac{10}{4}$ (total school enrollment)

9. Answer: (A) $\dfrac{60,000}{d}$

4 (#5)

$$600 \div d = 600 \times \frac{100}{d} = \frac{60{,}000}{d}$$

10. Answer: (C) 731 nautical miles

    5° 28'   1° = 60'
    6° 43'   11° = 660'
  11° 71'   + 71'
                                    731'

1' = 1 nautical mile
731' = 731 nautical miles

MATHEMATICS PROBLEM SOLVING

EXAMINATION SECTION
TEST 1

DIRECTIONS: Each question or incomplete statement is followed by several sug-gested answers or completions. Select the one that BEST answers the question or completes the statement. *PRINT THE LETTER OF THE CORRECT ANSWER IN THE SPACE AT THE RIGHT.*

1. Mr. Marsh left an estate amounting to $24,000. By his will, 10% was to be given to a col-   1.____
lege, 15% to a church, and the remainder was to be divided equally among 3 nieces.
How much money did *each* niece receive?

    A. $6120   B. $2000   C. $6333.33
    D. $6000   E.   *None of these answers*

2. After selling one third of his apple crop, a farmer sold the remainder at the same price   2.____
per bushel for $600. What was the *value* of the crop?

    A. $1000   B. $1200   C. $1800   D. $800
    E.   *None of these answers*

3. A village has an assessed valuation of $2,400,000. The rate for school taxes is 80¢ per   3.____
$100 valuation. If all but 2% of the taxes are collected, how many dollars remain *uncol-
lected*?

    A. $18,816   B. $48,000   C. $384   D. $600
    E.   *None of these answers*

4. When $a = 2$, $c = 1$, and $d = 0$, what is the value of the ex-pression $4a + 2c^2 - 3d^2$?   4.____

    A.   7   B.   9   C.   12   D.   15
    E.   *None of these answers*

5. The difference between one half of a number and one fifth of it is 561. Find the number.   5.____

    A.   168   B.   2805   C.   1870   D.   5610
    E.   *None of these answers*

6. Two triangles of the same shape are *always*   6.____

    A.   similar   B.   equilateral   C.   congruent
    D.   symmetrical   E.   equal

7. Which of the following is the BEST illustration of con-gruence?   7.____

    A.   A pair of shoes
    B.   Two dinner plates from the same set of dishes
    C.   Any two tables
    D.   A can of fruit and a cylinder
    E.   A slide and its projection on a screen

8. On the average, 5 oranges will give 3 cupfuls of juice. If 2 cupfuls make a pint, how many oranges must be used to make 3 gallons of juice?
   A. 16   B. 20   C. 80
   D. 40   E. None of the above

   8.____

9. What is the difference in cost to a purchaser between an article listed at $500 less 10% and 20% and one listed at $490 less 20%?
   A. $18   B. $42   C. $58
   D. $48   E. None of the above

   9.____

10. A salesman receives a monthly salary of $80, a 2% commission on all monthly sales over $2,000 and an additional 1% commission on all sales over $11,000 a month.
    If his total sales for January came to $13,500, how much did he earn that month?
    A. 355   B. 365   C. 385
    D. 405   E. 415

    10.____

KEY (CORRECT ANSWERS)

1. CORRECT ANSWER: D ($6,000)
   Since Mr. Marsh left 10% to a college and 15% to a church, 75% of his estate was to be equally divided among the three nieces, that is, 25% each. ¼ × $24,000 = $6,000.

2. CORRECT ANSWER: E (None of the above)
   Let x = the value of the crop. 2/3x = $600, x = $900.

3. CORRECT ANSWER: C ($384)
   Divide $2,400,000 by 100 to obtain the number of hundreds. The number is 24,000. 24,000 × .80 = $19,200 (total taxes to be collected) and $19,200 × .02 = $384 (taxes uncollected).

4. CORRECT ANSWER: E (None of the above)
   $4a + 2c^2 - 3d^2$ $4 \times 2 + 2 \times 1^2 - 30 \times 0^2 = 8 + 2 - 0 = 10$

5. CORRECT ANSWER: C (1,870)
   If x = the number, then the numbers are x/2 and x/5 (given).
   ∴ x/2 − x/5 = 561 or 3x = 5,610, x = 1,870

6. CORRECT ANSWER: A (Similar)
   By definition

7. CORRECT ANSWER: B (Two dinner plates from the same set of dishes)
   By definition, congruent figures agree in size and shape. Statement B appears to answer this requirement.

8. CORRECT ANSWER: C (80)
   Table: 2 pints = 1 quart and 4 quarts = 1 gallon. Since 8 pints = 1 gallon and 2 cupfuls = 1 pint, there are 48 cupfuls in 3 gallons. Let x − the number of oranges needed to make 3 gallons of juice. Then, 5(oranges)/3(cupfuls) = x(oranges)/48(cupfuls) or 3x = 240x = 80.

9. CORRECT ANSWER: E (None of the above)
   1. $550 × .10 = $50; $500 - $50 = $450
      $450 × .20 = $90; $450 - $90 = $360
   2. $490 × .20 = $98; $490 - $98 = $392
      $392 - $360 = $32.

10. CORRECT ANSWER: A ($355)
    Basic salary: $80 a month
    .02 × $11,500 ($13,500 - $2,000) = $230
    .01 × $2,500 ($13,500 - $11,000) = $25
    ∴ $80 + $230 + $25 = $335 (total monthly earnings)

TEST 2

DIRECTIONS: Each question or incomplete statement is followed by several suggested answers or completions. Select the one that BEST answers the question or completes the statement. *PRINT THE LETTER OF THE CORRECT ANSWER IN THE SPACE AT THE RIGHT.*

1. How much longer does it take an automobile to travel one mile at 20 miles per hour than at 30 miles per hour?
   A. 1 minute
   B. 10 minutes
   C. 20 minute
   D. 40 minutes
   E. None of the above

   1.____

2. A man wishes to construct a poultry house 12 feet long in which to keep 20 hens.
   If each hen requires 4 square feet of floor space, how wide should he construct the poultry house?
   A. 28 feet
   B. 80 feet
   C. 5 feet
   D. 6 feet 8 inches
   E. None of the above

   2.____

3. Aluminum bronze consists of copper and aluminum, usually in the ratio of 10:1 by weight.
   If a machine made of this alloy weighs 66 pounds, how many pounds of aluminum does it contain?
   A. 660
   B. 60
   C. 6.6
   D. 59.4
   E. None of the above

   3.____

4. Mr. Brown owned a house, which he rented for $600 a month. The house was assessed at $90,000. In 2005 the rate of taxation was increased from $250 to $280 per $10,000 assessed valuation.
   By what amount should the monthly rent have been RAISED to absorb the increase in that year's taxes?
   A. $72.00
   B. $22.50
   C. $30.00
   D. $210
   E. None of the above

   4.____

5. A dealer bought 3 gross of pencils at $3.80 a dozen. He sold the pencils at $.50 each.
   How much was his profit per gross?
   A. $79.20
   B. $26.40
   C. $2.20
   D. $6.60
   E. None of the above

   5.____

6. How many cubic yards of earth had to be removed to make an excavation 30 feet long, 21 feet wide, and 6 feet deep?
   A. 1,260
   B. 3,780
   C. 140
   D. 420
   E. None of the above

   6.____

7. By what number is the area of a circle MULTIPLIED if its radius is doubled?
   A. $2\pi r$
   B. 2
   C. 3.1416
   D. 4
   E. None of the above

   7.____

244

8. The State tax rate on 2003 incomes was 2% on the first $10,000 of income subject to tax and 3% on the next $20,000 or any part thereof. By special law, the State allowed a deduction of ¼ of the tax computed on the above schedule. In 2003, $18,000 of Mr. Brown's income was subject to tax.
   What was the amount of his tax?
   - A. $110
   - B. $270
   - C. $330
   - D. $90
   - E. None of the above

   8.____

9. A baseball team won *w* games and lost 1 game. What fractional part of its games did it win?
   - A. 1/W
   - B. W/1
   - C. W – 1/W
   - D. W + 1/W
   - E. None of the above

   9.____

10. A pole is held upright by 3 guy wires, each fastened to the pole 12 feet above the ground. The other ends of these wires are fastened to stakes 16 feet from the foot of the pole.
    Find the number of feet of wire required if 2 feet are added to each guy wire for making connections.
    - A. 18 feet
    - B. 66 feet
    - C. 90 feet
    - D. 54 feet
    - E. None of the above

    10.____

KEY (CORRECT ANSWERS)

1. **CORRECT ANSWER: A (1 minute)**
   1. Since the automobile travels 1 mile at 20 miles per hour, it covers 20 miles in 1 hour or 1 mile in 3 minutes (60/20).
   2. Since the automobile travels 1 mile at 30 miles per hour, it covers 30 miles in 1 hour or 1 mile in 2 minutes (60/30)
   3. ∴ it takes automobile (1) 1 minute more than automobile (2) (3 minutes − 2 minutes = 1 minute)

2. **CORRECT ANSWER: D (6 feet 8 inches)**
   Total area of poultry house = 4 sq. ft. × 2 hens = 80 sq. ft.
   Formula: length × width = area
   Since the length, 12 ft., is given, we may represent the width by w.
   ∴ 12 × w = 80, w = 6 $^2/_3$ ft. = 6 feet 8 inches

3. **CORRECT ANSWER: E (None of the above)**
   In other words, 1 lb. of every 11 pounds of aluminum bronze is aluminum
   ∴ 1/11 × 66 lbs. = 6 lbs.

4. **CORRECT ANSWER: B ($22.50)**
   First rate of taxation: $90,000 (assessment) × .25 ($250 per $10,000)
   = $2,250 (total taxes)
   Second rate of taxation (2005): $90,000 (assessment) × .28 ($280 per $10,000)
   = $2,520 (total taxes)
   The increase in taxes = $270 per year ($2,520 - $2,250);
   ∴ the monthly rent should have been raised $22.50 ($270/12).

5. **CORRECT ANSWER: B ($26.40)**
   Since the selling price per dozen = $6.00 (.5 × 12) and the cost = $3.80 (given) per dozen, the profit per dozen = $2.20 ($6.00 - $3.80).
   ∴ the profit per gross (= 12 doz.) = $2.20 × 12 = $26.40

6. **CORRECT ANSWER: C (140)**
   Change the feet to yards since we are to deal with cubic yards.
   Formula: Volume = length × width × depth.
   By substitution, volume = 10 yds. × 7 yds. × 2 yds. = 140 cu. yds.

7. **CORRECT ANSWER: D (4)**
   Formula: Area of a circle = π^2
   If x = radius of original circle, then 2x = radius of new circle.
   Area of original circle $\pi \times 2$; area of new circle = $\pi(2x)^2 = 4\pi x^2$
   ∴ the area of the original circle has been multiplied by 4.

4 (#2)

8. CORRECT ANSWER: C ($330
   $10,000 × .02 = $200 (2% tax on the first $10,000)
   $8,000 × .03 = $240 (3% tax on the next $20,000, in this case $18,000, or $8,000).
   Total tax computed = $440; deduction = $110 (1/4 × $440).
   ∴ $440 - $110 = $330 (Mr. Brown's tax).

9. CORRECT ANSWER: E (None of the above)
   Formula: won/played = fractional part of games won.
   Games won = w; games played = w + 1
   ∴ w/w + 1 = fraction part of games won.

10. CORRECT ANSWER: B (66 feet)
    A right triangle is formed.
    Let x = the length of each guy wire.
    ∴ $x^2 = 12^2 + 16^2$ or $x^2 = 400$; x = 20 ft.; 20 ft. + 2 ft. = total length of each guy wire for making connections = 22 ft.
    ∴ 22 ft. × 3 = 66 ft. (total amount of wire needed for all 3 guy wires).

TEST 3

DIRECTIONS: Each question or incomplete statement is followed by several suggested answers or completions. Select the one that BEST answers the question or completes the statement. *PRINT THE LETTER OF THE CORRECT ANSWER IN THE SPACE AT THE RIGHT.*

1. What is the number of feet traversed in 1 second by an automobile that is traveling 30 miles an hour?
   A. 176
   B. 2
   C. 2,640
   D. 44
   E. None of the above

   1.____

2. The Jonesville Construction Company borrowed $225,000 for five years at 3 ½%.
   What was the ANNUAL charge for interest?
   A. $1,575
   B. $1,555
   C. $7,875
   D. $39,375
   E. None of the above

   2.____

3. The stock that Mr. Ames bought cost him $80 a share. The par value of the stock is $100.
   If the stock pays $6 a year in dividends, what rate of interest is Mr. Ames getting on his money?
   A. 16 $2/3$%
   B. 7 ½%
   C. 3%
   D. 6%
   E. None of the above

   3.____

4. The figure shown at the right represents a rectangle whose dimensions are l and w, surmounted by a semicircle whose radius is r. Express the area of this figure in terms of l, w, r and π.
   A. $wl + \pi r^2/2$
   B. $lw + \pi r^2$
   C. $lw + \pi r$
   D. $\pi/2 - r^2 lw$
   E. None of the above

   4.____

5. If one machine can do a piece of work in 10 hours and a second machine can do the same work in 15 hours, how many hours will it take BOTH machines working simultaneously to do the work?
   A. 12 ½
   B. 25
   C. 5
   D. 6
   E. None of the above

   5.____

6. A baseball diamond is a square 90 feet on a side. Find, correct to the nearest foot, the distance from third base to first base.
   A. 180 feet
   B. 135 feet
   C. 127 feet
   D. 90 feet
   E. None of the above

   6.____

7. A painted wooden cube whose edge is 3 inches is cut into 27 one-inch cubes. How many of these small cubes have just two painted sides?
   A. 12
   B. 18
   C. 8
   D. 9
   E. None of the above

8. A certain lending library charges a cents for the first week that a book is loaned and b cents for each day over one week.
   Write the formula for C, the cost in cents, of taking a book for d days from this library, (d > 7).
   A. C = a + bd
   B. C = a + b(d-7)
   C. C + ad
   D. C = 7a + b(d-7)
   E. None of the above

9. How many gallons of water must be added to 20 gallons of a 10% solution of salt and water to REDUCE it to an 8% solution?
   A. 10
   B. 2
   C. 16
   D. 4
   E. None of the above

10. The net profit of the ABC Company dropped from 34 million dollars in 2014 to 33 million in 2015.
    What percent of decrease does this represent? (Give answer correct to the nearest tenth of a percent)
    A. 97.0
    B. 2.9
    C. 3.0
    D. 97.1
    E. None of the above

KEY (CORRECT ANSWERS)

1. CORRECT ANSWER: D (44)
   If the auto is traveling 30 miles an hour, this means that the auto covers 30 miles in one hour, or ½ mile in one minute (30 miles = 60 min.). To convert to seconds, as the answer calls for, divide ½ by 60 sec., viz, 1/2/60 = 1/120 mile in one second.
   Then, 120/x × 5,280 ft. (= 1 mile) = 44 ft. in one second.

2. CORRECT ANSWER: C ($7,875)
   Formula: Principal × rate × time = interest $225,000 × .035 × 1 yr. = $7,875.

3. CORRECT ANSWER: B (7 ½%)
   Formula: Principal × rate = interest (or dividend). Let x = rate of interest.
   By substitution, $80 × $6 or x = 6/80, x = .075 or 7 ½%

4. CORRECT ANSWER: A (wl + $\pi r^2/2$)
   This figure represents both a rectangle and a semicircle.
   Formulas: Area of rectangle = l (length) ×w (width) or lw or wl
   Area of semicircle: $\pi r^2 2$
   Area of this figure = wl + $\pi r^2/2$

5. CORRECT ANSWER: D (6)
   Formula: Time worked/Time required = Part of job completed
   Let x = number of hours it will take both machines together to do work.
   Then, x/10 = work of one machine and x/15 = work of second machine.
   We now form the equation: x/10 + x/15 = 1 (the entire job) or 15x + 10x = 150, or 25x = 150, x = 6.

6. CORRECT ANSWER: C (127 feet)
   A right triangle is formed when a line, x, is drawn from third base to first base.
   ∴ $x^2 = 90^2 + 90^2$ or $x^2 = 16,200x$,
   x = 127.2 ft. or 127 ft. (to the nearest foot).

   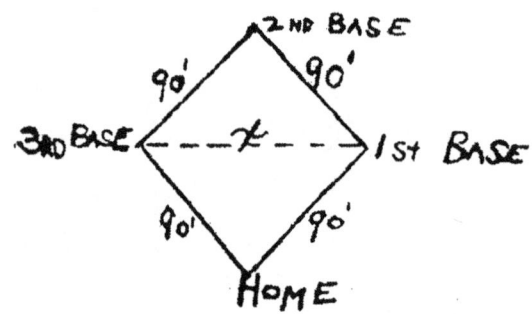

7. CORRECT ANSWER: A (12)
   By inspection

8. CORRECT ANSWER: B (C = a + b(d-7)
   a = cents charged for first week
   b = cents charged for each day over one week
   d-7 = extra days beyond the first week (given: d > 7)
   ∴ C = a + b(d-7)

4 (#3)

9. CORRECT ANSWER: E (None of the above)
Let x = number of gallons of water that must be added.
Then, 20 + x = quantity of solution after water is added.
10% × 20 gal. = 2 gal. salt in the first solution.
8% × (20+x) = amount of salt in second solution.
∴ 2 gal. (amount of salt in first solution) = .08(20+x) (amount of salt in the second solution)
or 2 = 1.60 + .08x or 8x = 40, x = 5 gal.

10. CORRECT ANSWER: B (2.9)
The drop in profit = one million dollars (34 million – 33 million)
∴ 1/34 = .0293 = 2.9% (to the nearest tenth of a percent).

TEST 4

DIRECTIONS: Each question or incomplete statement is followed by several suggested answers or completions. Select the one that BEST answers the question or completes the statement. *PRINT THE LETTER OF THE CORRECT ANSWER IN THE SPACE AT THE RIGHT.*

1. One manufacturing plant built 150 tanks in the last six months in 2005. This was an increase of 150% over the number built in the preceding six months. Find the number of tanks built in the preceding six months. 1.____
   A. 100 B. 50 C. 0
   D. 60 E. None of the above

2. What is the difference between the area of a rectangle 10 feet by 6 feet and the area of a square having the same perimeter? 2.____
   A. 165 sq.ft. B. 8 sq.ft. C. No difference
   D. 4 sq.ft. E. None of the above

3. How many cubic yards of concrete are needed to make 1,200 square concrete posts 9 inches by 6 feet? 3.____
   A. 150 B. 194,400 C. 5,400
   D. 4,050 E. None of the above

4. Find, correct to the nearest tenth of a foot, the diameter of the largest circular mirror that will pass through a doorway 7 feet high and 3 feet wide. (Neglect thickness of mirror.) 4.____
   A. 6.9 feet B. 7.0 feet C. 3.0 feet
   D. 7.6 feet E. None of the above

5. What is the GREATEST number of pictures, each 2½ inches by 3½ inches, that a photographer can print on an 8-inch by 10-inch piece of sensitized paper? 5.____
   A. 9 B. 6 C. 3
   D. 8 E. None of the above

6. The net profits of the ABC Company dropped from 35 million dollars in 2004 to 28 million in 2005.
   What percent decrease does this represent? 6.____
   A. 7% B. 20% C. 25%
   D. 80% E. None of the above

7. If 12 gallons of gas drove one car a distance of 188.4 miles and the same amount of gas took another car a distance of 202.8 miles, how much BETTER mileage per gallon has the second car than the first? 7.____
   A. 1.7 B. 5 C. 12
   D. 14.4 E. None of the above

8. The length of a rectangle is 12 inches and its width is 8 inches. Let the length of the rectangle be increased by 3 inches and the width be decreased by 3 inches.
Which of the following statements is TRUE?
   A. The area of the rectangle remains the same.
   B. The area is increased by 9 square inches.
   C. The perimeter remains the same.
   D. The perimeter is increased by 6 inches.
   E. Both the perimeter and the area remain the same.

8.____

9. Approximately how many tons of coal will a bin 10 feet by 6 feet by 5 feet hold if 1 ton fills 38 cubic feet of space? (Find the answer correct to the nearest ton.)
   A. 1
   B. 7
   C. 3
   D. 8
   E. None of the above

9.____

10. The gauge on a 10-gallon oil tank indicates that exactly 3/8 of the oil remains in the tank.
How many gallons will it require to fill the tank?
   A. 2¼
   B. 3¾
   C. 6½
   D. 7¼
   E. None of the above

10.____

KEY (CORRECT ANSWERS)

1. **CORRECT ANSWER: D (60)**
   Let x = number of tanks built first half of 2005
   Let 1.5x (150%x) = increase in number of tanks built last half of 2005.
   x + 1.5x = number of tanks built last half of 2005.
   ∴ x + 1.5x = 150 or 25x = 1500, x = 60

2. **CORRECT ANSWER: D (4 sq. ft.)**
   Area of rectangle = length × width = 10 × 6 = 60 sq. ft.; perimeter of rectangle = 2.
   (length +width) = 2(10+6) = 32 ft.
   Perimeter of square = 32 ft. (given, same as that of rectangle)
   One side of square = 8 ft. (¼ of perimeter)
   Area of square = (side)2 = 82 = 64 sq. ft.
   ∴ 64 sq. ft. (area of square) – 60 sq. ft. (area of rectangle) = 4 sq. ft.

3. **CORRECT ANSWER: A (150)**
   First convert the inches and feet to yards since the answer calls for cubic yards, viz.,
   9 in. = ¼ yd. and 6 ft. = 2 yds.
   Formula: Volume (of a post) = length × width × height
   Volume (of 1200 posts) = 1200 × ¼ × ¼ × 2 = 150 cu. yds.

4. **CORRECT ANSWER: D (7.6 feet)**
   By drawing the diagonal (or diameter) AD, a right triangle
   is formed.
   Designate the diagonal by x.
   ∴ $x^2 = 3^2 + 7^2$ or $x^2 = 58$, x = 7.6 ft. (to the nearest
   tenth of a foot)

   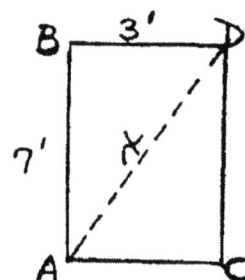

5. **CORRECT ANSWER: D (8)**
   This problem is solved by sketches of the only two possible ways of securing the greatest
   number of pictures, shown below.

   SKETCH 1   SKETCH 2

   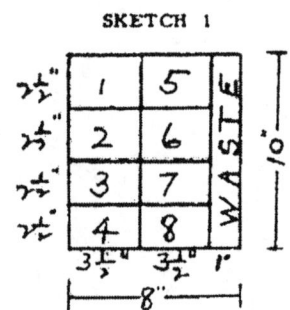 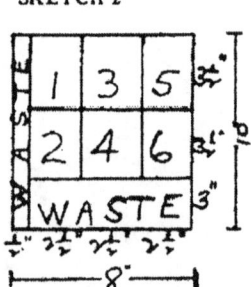

   8 pictures are secured when the 2½ in. side is cut along the 10 in. side of the sensitized
   paper and only 6 pictures are obtained when the 2½ in. side is cut along the 8i in. side of
   the sensitized paper.

4 (#4)

6. CORRECT ANSWER: B (20%)

$$\frac{7 \text{ (drop in net profits)(in millions of dollars)}}{35 \text{ (profit in 2004)(in millions of dollars)}} = \frac{1}{5} = 20\%$$

7. CORRECT ANSWER: E (None of the above)
The problem may be solved as follows:

Formula: $\frac{\text{distance}}{\text{gallons used}}$ = mileage

Mileage of car 1: by substitution, $\frac{188.4 \text{ miles}}{12 \text{ gal}}$ = 15.7 miles per gal.

Mileage of car 2: by substitution, $\frac{202.8 \text{ miles}}{12 \text{ gal}}$ = 16.9 miles per gal.

∴ car 2 exceeds car 1 in mileage by 1.2 miles per gal.

8. CORRECT ANSWER: C (The perimeter remains the same.)
Since the area of a rectangle = length × width, the area of the original triangle = 96 sq. in. (12" × 8") and the area of the newly-formed triangle = 75 sq. in. (15" × 5"). Using this information, we find that all of the statements, except C, are false. To prove statement C is true, we use the formula: perimeter = 2 (length+width).
By substitution, we find that the perimeter of the original rectangle = 40 in. (2(12+8)), and the perimeter of the newly-formed rectangle = 40 in. (2(15+5)).

9. CORRECT ANSWER: D (8)
Formula: volume = length × width × height
By substitution, the volume of the bin = 10 × 6 × 5 = 300 cu. ft.
Let x = no. of tons of coal that the above bin will hold.
We form the proportion: 1 ton : 38 cu. ft. = x : 300 cu. ft. or 38x = 300, x = 7.8 tons or 8 tons (to the nearest ton).

10. CORRECT ANSWER: E (None of the above)
Since 3/8 of the oil is left in the tank, 5/8 more is needed to fill it.
∴ 5/8 × 10 (capacity:given) = 6¼ gal.

TEST 5

DIRECTIONS: Each question or incomplete statement is followed by several suggested answers or completions. Select the one that BEST answers the question or completes the statement. *PRINT THE LETTER OF THE CORRECT ANSWER IN THE SPACE AT THE RIGHT.*

1. A pile of steel plates is 2.75 feet high. If the plates are .375 inch thick, how many are there in the pile?
   A. 7
   B. 8
   C. 14
   D. 88
   E. None of the above

   1._____

2. At the rate of $1.50 per 6-oz. bar of chocolate, how much would a pound of chocolate cost?
   A. $3.00
   B. $3.40
   C. $3.90
   D. $4.50
   E. None of the above

   2._____

3. A man walks diagonally from one corner of a rectangular lot to the opposite corner.
   If he walks at the rate of 5 feet a second, and the lot is 50 feet by 120 feet, how many seconds will he save by walking diagonally instead of walking along the perimeter of the lot?
   A. 8
   B. 10
   C. 17
   D. 34
   E. None of the above

   3._____

4. The afternoon classes in a school begin at 1 P.M. and end at 3:52 P.M. There are 4 class periods with 4 minutes between classes.
   How many minutes are there in each class period?
   A. 39
   B. 40
   C. 59
   D. 60
   E. None of the above

   4._____

5. A snapshot measures $1^7/_8$" × $2^1/_2$". It is to be enlarged so that the longer dimension will be 4".
   What will be the length of the SHORTER dimension?
   A. $2^3/_8$"
   B. $2^1/_2$"
   C. 3"
   D. $3^3/_8$"
   E. None of the above

   5._____

6. The minimum temperatures at Jonesville for each day of one week were as follows: +7°, +13°, +5°, -4°, 0°, +3°.
   Find, to the nearest degree, the AVERAGE minimum temperature.
   A. 6°
   B. 2°
   C. 16°
   D. 4°
   E. None of the above

   6._____

7. If the outer diameter of an iron pipe is 14.38 inches and the inner diameter is 12.50 inches, what is the thickness of the pipe?
   A. 94"
   B. 1.88"
   C. 16.88"
   D. 26.88"
   E. None of the above

   7._____

8. In the fall of 2012, a store charged $4.40 a pound for chuck steak. In February 2013, the same store had increased by 50% the price of that grade of steak. Later, the government announced a ceiling of $5.50 a pound.
What percent reduction did the store have to make in its February 2013 price in order to comply with the government ruling?
   A. $11\frac{1}{9}\%$
   B. $16\frac{2}{3}\%$
   C. 20%
   D. 25%
   E. None of the above

   8.____

9. A certain whole number has 10 digits. If the square root of this number is taken, how many digits will there be in the integral part of the answer?
   A. 1
   B. 5
   C. 9
   D. 100
   E. None of the above

   9.____

10. Four tractors working together can plow a field in 12 hours.
How long will it take 6 tractors to plow a field of the same size if all tractors work at the same rate?
   A. 6 hr.
   B. 9 hr.
   C. 10 hr.
   D. 18 hr.
   E. None of the above

   10.____

KEY (CORRECT ANSWERS)

1. CORRECT ANSWER: D (88)
   Convert 2.75 ft. to inches by multiplying by 12 = 33 in.
   Then, 33/.375 = 88

2. CORRECT ANSWER: E (None of the above)
   $1.50 is the price of a 6 oz. bar of chocolate.
   Since 1 lb. = 16 oz., the cost of 1 lb. of chocolate = $4.00 (16 × 2½).

3. CORRECT ANSWER: A (8)
   First, we must figure the number of feet that the man walks diagonally (AC in the diagram), and then we must find the number of feet that he will walk by going along the perimeter of the lot (from C to A by way of D, or CD + AD).
   Since the diagonal represented by x forms a right triangle, we have the equation:
   $x^2 = 50^2 + 120^2$ or $x^2 = 16,900$ x = 130 ft. (AC). CD + AD (walking along the perimeter) = 170 ft. (50+120).
   ∴ the man saves 4 ft. by walking diagonally (170-130); and since he walks at the rate of 5 ft. a second, he saves 8 sec. (40/5).

   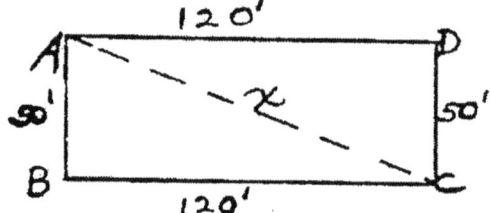

4. CORRECT ANSWER: B (40)
   Total time = 2 hours 52 min. or 172 min. (3:52 P.M. – 1 P.M.). Since there are 4 class periods, there are 3 intervals of 4 min. each (12 min. in all) between these periods.
   ∴ 172 – 12 = 160 min. (total time for the class periods) and 160/4 = 40 min. (time in each class period).

5. CORRECT ANSWER: C (3")
   Let x = length of the shorter dimension.
   ∴ $1^7/_8$: x = 2½ : 4 or
   5/2x = 60/8 or 40x = 120, x = 3"

6. CORRECT ANSWER: B (2°)
   The sum of the temperatures given = 16; the number of readings is 7.
   ∴ 16°/7 = $2^2/_7$° or 2° (to the nearest degree)

7. CORRECT ANSWER: A (.94")
   Since the diameter of a circle is twice the radius, the outer radius is 7.19" (14.38"/2), and the inner radius is 6.25" (12.5÷2).
   ∴ the thickness of the pipe = .94" (7.19 – 6.25).

4 (#5)

8. CORRECT ANSWER: B ($16^2/_3\%$)
   $4.40 + .50($4.40) = $6.60 (price as of February 2013).
   Since the ceiling price was announced as $5.50, a reduction of $1.10 was necessary ($6.60 - $5.50).
   $\therefore \$1.10 \div \$6.60 = \dfrac{1}{6} = 16^2/_3\%$.

9. CORRECT ANSWER: B (5)
   In computing square root, we group the digits by two's, beginning with the decimal point and moving by two's to the left. Since there are 5 groups of two, each of which will have 1 digit in the answer, there will be 5 digits.

10. CORRECT ANSWER: E (None of the above)
    Let x = time required for 6 tractors
    $\therefore$ 4:6 (tractors) = x:12 (time) or
    6x = 48, x = 8 hours

EXAMINATION SECTION
TEST 1

DIRECTIONS: Each question or incomplete statement is followed by several suggested answers or completions. Select the one that BEST answers the question or completes the statement. *PRINT THE LETTER OF THE CORRECT ANSWER IN THE SPACE AT THE RIGHT.*

1. At 7:00 A.M., a student leaves his home in his automobile to drive to school 28 miles away. He averages 50 mph until 7:30 A.M., when his car breaks down. The student has to walk and run the rest of the way.
   If he wants to arrive at school at 8:00 A.M., how fast, in mph, must he travel on foot?
   A. 3   B. 4   C. 5   D. 6   E. 7

2. Express $1 + \dfrac{\frac{1}{2+1}}{1+\frac{1}{4}}$ in simplest terms.
   A. 27/28   B. 30/43   C. 1 1/9   D. 1 1/27   E. 1 13/30

3. A theater charges $5.00 admission for adults and $2.50 for children. At one showing, 240 admissions brought in a total of $800.
   How many adults attended the showing?
   A. 40   B. 80   C. 120   D. 160   E. 266

4. $\sqrt{25+?} = 5 + 8$
   A. 8   B. 12   C. 64   D. 144   E. 169

5. The perimeter of a square is 20.
   Which of the following represents the area?
   A. 5   B. 10   C. 20   D. 25   E. 100

6. Evaluate the expression $\dfrac{1}{4} + \dfrac{3}{8} - \dfrac{6}{16} - \dfrac{8}{32}$
   A. 7/16   B. 1/32   C. 1/8   D. 1/4   E. 0

7. Bill spent 20% of the money he initially had in his wallet on groceries and 25% on gas. He had $66.00 left.
   How much money did he have before he shopped?
   A. $85   B. $100   C. $110   D. $111   E. $120

8. Express the product $(2x+5y)^2$ in simplest form.
   A. $4x^2 + 25y^2$ B. $4x^2 + 20xy + 25y^2$ C. $4x^2 + 10y + 25y^2$
   D. $4x^2 - 20xy + 25y^2$ E. $4x + 25y$

9. A student received test grades of 83, 90, and 88.
   What was her grade on a fourth test if the average for the four tests is 84?
   A. 85   B. 80   C. 75   D. 70   E. 65

10. A rectangular room is 3 meters wide, 4 meters long, and 2 meters high. How far is it from the northeast corner at the floor to the southwest corner at the ceiling?
 _____ meters.
 A. $\sqrt{29}$ B. $\sqrt{11}$ C. $\sqrt{9}$ D. 9   E. 5

11. If an electron has a mass of 9.109×10^{-31} kg and a proton has a mass of 1.672×10^{-27} kg, approximately how many electrons are required to have the same mass as one proton?
 A. 150,000
 B. 1,800
 C. 5.4×10^{4}
 D. 5.4×10^{-4}
 E. 15×10^{-58}

12. The introduction of a new manufacturing process will affect a saving of $1,450 per week over the initial 8-week production period. New equipment, however, will cost 1/4 of the total savings.
 How much did the equipment cost?
 A. $11.600.00
 B. $2,900.00
 C. $725.00
 D. $362.50
 E. $181.25

13. If P dollars is invested at r percent compounded annually, at the end of n years it will have grown to $A = P(1+r)^n$. An investment made at 16% compounded annually. It grows to $1,740 at the end of one year.
 How much was originally invested?
 A. $150
 B. $278.40
 C. $1,461.60
 D. $1,500
 E. $1,700

14. What is 1/4% of 200?
 A. 0.05   B. 0.5   C. 5   D. 12.5   E. 50

15. Which of the following is .5% of .95?
 A. .000475   B. .00475   C. .0475   D. .475   E. 4.75

16. What is the value of (5 lbs. 1 oz.)/(3 lbs. 6 oz.) in ounces?
 A. 22   B. 1.66   C. 1.5   D. 0.66   E. 0.28

17. If 1 inch = 2.56 centimeters, 3/8 centimeter equals which of the following in inches?
 A. 6.77   B. .95   C. .39   D. .38   E. .15

18. If $2x + y = 7$ and $x - 4y = 4$, then x equals which of the following?
 A. -15/9   B. -1/9   C. 7/15   D. 11/9   E. 32/9

19. What part of an hour is 6 seconds?
 A. 1/600   B. 1/10   C. 1/360   D. 1/60   E. 1/5

20. If $1/3 + 5(x-1) = 8$, then which of the following is the value of x?
 A. 8/13   B. 8/5   C. 38/25   D. 38/15   E. 38

21. Which line is perpendicular to the x-axis?
    A. x = 3   B. y = 3   C. x = y   D. x = y/3   E. y = x/3

22. If a dental hygienist at a certain office is paid H dollars a week, the dental assistant works 36 hours a week at A dollars per hour, and the receptionist works 40 hours a week and receives R dollars every other week, which of the following represents the weekly payroll for these three employees?
    A. H/3 + 36A + 40R/3
    B. H + 36A + R/2
    C. H/3 + 12A + R/6
    D. 5H + 36 + 20R
    E. H/3 + 12A + 40R

23. Company A ordered five units of anesthetic at $12.00 per unit. Company B ordered 10 units at $13.00 per unit, and Company C ordered 4 at $10.00 per unit. Since all these companies were at one address, the three orders were put on one bill.
    Approximately what percent of the total bill did Company A have to pay?
    A. 5   B. 18   C. 26   D. 36   E. 55

24. Which of the following is the value of A, if 50(A/100) = 2A²?
    A. 25   B. 1   C. 5/2   D. 1/4   E. 1/2

25. Five-eighths of the employees in the company are single males.
    What percentage of the employees in the company are single males?
    A. 12.5   B. 20.0   C. 25.0   D. 32.0   E. 62.5

26. If x = 20% of y, and z = 35% of x, then z = _____% of y.
    A. 70   B. 57   C. 7   D. 1.75   E. .07

27. Which of the following is the value of the expression $\frac{|14-3|-|7-16|}{3|(-2)+1}$?
    A. -20/3   B. -2/3   C. 0   D. 23   E. 20/3

28. A tank can be filled by a pipe in 30 minutes and emptied by another pipe in 50 minutes.
    How many minutes will it take to fill the tank if both pipes are open?
    A. 45   B. 60   C. 75   D. 80   E. 100

29. If (4/5)x = (2/5)y, then which of the following is equal to y/x?
    A. 1/2   B. 2/5   C. 25/8   D. 2   E. 3

30. Which of the following would NOT result in a straight line? x =
    A. 1/y   B. 2y + 5   C. (y+6)/(2)   D. 5 − y   E. 4(x+3y)

31. $\frac{5}{4} + \frac{4}{5} + \frac{3}{2} -$ _____ = a positive integer.
    A. 10/20   B. 11/20   C. 71/20   D. 3/20   E. 4/20

32. If $\frac{2}{x} + \frac{3}{5} = \frac{4}{3}$, then which of the following is the value of x?
    A. 30/11   B. 30/29   C. 11/30   D. -11/6   E. -5/2

33. Optometry school applicants decreased by 25% during a 4-year period. During the same time, the number of first-year openings in optometry school increased by 12%.
    If the ratio of applicants to first-year student openings had been 3 to 1, then which of the following would be the APPROXIMATE ratio at the end of the 4-year period?
    A. 1.5 to 1   B. 2 to 1   C. 3 to 2   D. 4 to 3   E. 6 to 5

34. If then which of the following is the value of x?
    A. 4   B. 27   C. 29   D. 40   E. 729

35. Two cars start at the same point and travel north and west at the rate of 24 and 32 mph, respectively.
    How far apart are they at the end of 2 hours?
    A. 63   B. 80   C. 112   D. 116   E. 100

36. Right triangle ABC with right angle C and AB = 6, BC = 3, find AC.
    A. 3   B. 6   C. 27   D. 33   E. $3\sqrt{3}$

37. When each of the sides of a square is increased by 1 yard, the area of the new square is 53 square yards more than that of the original square.
    What is the length of the sides of the original square?
    A. 25   B. 26   C. 27   D. 52   E. 54

38. Evaluate: $3(2)^2 + \sqrt{25} - (-2)^3$.
    A. 9   B. 24   C. 25   D. 33   E. 76

39. Which of the following is the length of the line segment BC if AB = 14, AD = 5, and angle BAD = 30°?
    A. $\sqrt{221}$
    B. $\sqrt{171}$
    C. $7\sqrt{3}$
    D. 7
    E. 9

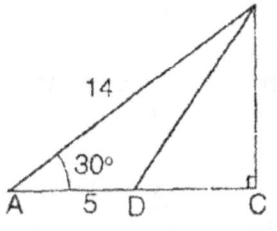

40. A bowl contains 7 green and 3 red marbles.
    What is the probability that two marbles selected at random from this bowl without replacement are both red?
    A. 1/15   B. 9/100   C. 21/100   D. 47/90   E. 6/10

41. If x pens cost 75 cents and y pencils cost 57 cents, then which equation below can be used to find the cost of 2 pens and 3 pencils?
    A. 2(75/x) + 3(57/y)   B. 3x/75 + 2y/57   C. 75/2x + 57/3y
    D. 2(x/75) + 3(y/57)   E. 3(75/x) + 2(57/y)

42. Maria has a number of dimes and quarters whose total value is less than $9.00. There are twice as many dimes as quarters.
    At most, how many quarters could she have?
    A. 14   B. 15   C. 19   D. 20   E. 35

43. The number (1, 2, 3, 6) have an average (arithmetic mean) of 3 and a variance of 3.5.
    What is the average (arithmetic mean) and variance of the set of numbers (3, 6, 9, 18)?
    A. 9, 31.5   B. 3, 10.5   C. 3, 31.5   D. 6, 7.5   E. 9, 27.5

44. A fence encloses a triangular-shaped region whose sides are 20 feet, 20 feet, and 10 feet in length.
    If the number of inches between fence posts (centers) is 30 inches, how many posts will be needed?
    A. 17   B. 20   C. 21   D. 22   E. 23

45. A ceiling 6 feet by 7 feet can be painted for $52.
    Find the cost of painting a ceiling 18 feet by 21 feet, all things equal except the dimensions.
    A. $104   B. $126   C. $156   D. $378   E. $468

46. Three consecutive odd numbers have a sum of 51.
    What is the LARGEST of these numbers?
    A. 15   B. 17   C. 18   D. 19   E. 21

47. It takes 5 hours for a qualified typist to complete a report. Coffee break begins at 10:15 A.M. It is now 9:55 A.M.
    How much of the task can the typist be expected to complete by coffee break?
    A. 1/8   B. 1/25   C. 1/3   D. 1/6   E. 1/15

48. A container in the form of a rectangular solid is 10 feet long, 9 feet wide, and 2 feet deep. The container is filled with a liquid weighing 100 pounds per cubic foot.
    A. 90   B. 180   C. 1,800   D. 9,000   E. 18,000

49. The value of cost $(\pi/3)$ equals the value of
    A. $-\cos(2\pi/3)$ B. $\cos(2\pi/3)$ C. $\cos(6\pi/3)$
    D. $-\cos(5\pi/3)$ E. $\cos(4\pi/3)$

50. If $5 \leq x \leq 12$ and -2y9, then is as large as possible when x = _____ and y = _____.
    A. 12; 9   B. 12; 0   C. 12; -2   D. 0; 0   E. 0; 0

KEY (CORRECT ANSWERS)

1. D	11. B	21. A	31. B	41. A
2. E	12. B	22. B	32. A	42. C
3. B	13. D	23. C	33. B	43. A
4. D	14. B	24. D	34. C	44. B
5. D	15. B	25. A	35. B	45. E
6. E	16. C	26. C	36. E	46. D
7. E	17. E	27. D	37. B	47. E
8. B	18. E	28. C	38. C	48. E
9. C	19. A	29. D	39. D	49. A
10. A	20. D	30. A	40. A	50. B

SOLUTIONS TO PROBLEMS

1. Let x = rate of walking/running. Then, (50)(1/2) + (x)(1/2) = 28. Simplifying, 1/2x = 3. Solving, x = 6.

2. $3 + \frac{1}{4} = 3\frac{1}{4}$, $1/3\frac{1}{4} = \frac{4}{13}$, $2 + \frac{4}{13} = 2\frac{4}{13}$, $1/2\frac{4}{13} = \frac{13}{30}$
Finally, $1 + \frac{13}{30} = 1\frac{13}{30}$

3. Let x = number of adults, 240-x = number of children.
Then, 5x + 2.50(240-x) = 800. Simplifying, we get 5x + 600 – 2.50x = 800. This reduces to 2.50x = 200. Solving, x = 800

4. $\sqrt{25 + x}$ = 13 squaring both sides, 25 + x = 169. So, x = 144.

5. If the perimeter of a square is 20, each side must be 5. The area is 5^2 = 25.

6. Changing to a denominator of 32, we get 8/32 + 12/32 + 12/32 − 12/32 − 8/32 = 0/32 = 0

7. Let x = original amount. 100% - 20% - 25% = 55%. Then, $66 = .55x. Solving, x = $120

8. $(2x+5y)^2 = 4x^2 + 10xy + 25y^2 = 4x^2 + 20xy + 25y^2$

9. Let x = grade on her 4th test. Then, (83+90+88+x)/4 = 84. This becomes (261+x)/4 = 84. Further reduction leads to 261 + x = 336, so x – 75.

10. The required distance is $\sqrt{3^2 + 4^2 + 2^2} = \sqrt{9 + 16 + 4} = \sqrt{29}$

11. $(1.672 \times 10^{-27}) \div (9.1109 \times 10^{-31})$. $1836 \times 10^4 \approx 1800$

12. Total savings is $1450)(8) = $11,600. Equipment costs (1/4)($11,600) = $2900.

13. $1740 = P(I+.16)'. Then, P = $1740 ÷ 1.16 = $1500.

14. 1/4% of 200 is (.0025)(200) = .5

15. .5% of .95 is (.005)(.95) = .00475

16. 5 lbs. 1 oz. = 81 oz. and 3 lbs. 6 oz. = 54 oz. Then, 81 oz. ÷ 54 oz. = 1.5

17. 3/8 cm = 3/8 ÷ 2.54 = .375 ÷ 2.54 ≈ .1476 ≈ .15 inch.

18. From equation 1, y = 7 – 2x. Substituting into equation 2, x – 4(7-2x) = 4. Simplifying, x – 28 + 8x = 4. This reduces to 9x = 32, so x = 32/9

19. Since there are 3600 seconds in 1 hour, 6 seconds would represent 6/3600 = 1/600 of an hour.

20. $1/3 + 5(x-1) = 8$. Simplify to $1/3 + 5x - 5 = 8$. This will reduce to $5x = 12\ 2/3$, so $x = 38/15$.

21. A line perpendicular to the x-axis must have an undefined slope. The equation must be x = constant. The only choice fitting this format is $x = 3$.

22. The receptionist works 40 hours at R/2 dollars per week. Thus, the weekly payroll for all three workers is $H + 36A + R/2$. (The 40 hours is not used in computing.)

23. The total bill was $(5)(\$12) + (10)(\$13) + (4)(\$20) = \$230$. Company A's bill was $60. Thus, $\$60/\$230 \approx 26.1\% \approx 26\%$.

24. $50(A/100) = 2A^2$ becomes $A/2 = 2A^2$. Simplifying further, we get $A = 4A^2$. Simplifying further, we get $A = 4A^2$ or $A(4A-1) = 0$. The two values of A are 0 and 1/4.

25. The number of single males is represented as $(5/8)(1/5)(100)\% = 12.5\%$

26. $z = .35x$ and $x = .20y$. Thus, $z = (.35)(.20)y = .07y$.

27. The numerator is $|11| - |-9| = 11 - 9 = 2$. The denominator is $3|-1| = 3$. Thus, the fraction = 2/3.

28. Let x = required number of minutes. Then, $1/30x - 1/50x = 1$. Multiplying by 150, $5x - 3x = 150$. Solving, $x = 75$.

29. $\frac{4}{5}x = \frac{2}{5}y$. Then, $\frac{y}{x} = \frac{4}{5} \div \frac{2}{5} = 2$

30. $x = \frac{1}{y}$ becomes $xy = 1$, which represents a hyperbola.

31. $\frac{5}{4} + \frac{4}{5} + \frac{3}{2} = (25+16+30)/20 = 71/20$. If $71/20 - x$ = a positive integer, then the only correct values of x are 11/20, 31/20, 51/20.

32. Multiplying the equation by 15x, we get $30 + 9x = 20x$. Then, $30 = 11x$, so $x = 30/11$.

33. Let 3x = number of applicants, x = 1st year student openings. Over the 4-year period, the number of applicants dropped to $.75(3x) = 2.25x$ and the number of openings rose to $1.12x$. Now, $2.25x \div 1.12x \approx 2$ to 1.

34. $\sqrt{x - 25} = 2$. Squaring both sides, $x - 25 = 4$, so $x = 29$.

35. At the end of 2 hours, their individual <u>distances</u> are 48 miles and 64 miles. Their distance apart is = 80 miles.

36. $AC^2 + 3^2 = 6^2$. This simplifies to $AC^2 = 27$. Thus, $AC = \sqrt{27} = 3\sqrt{3}$

37. Let x = original length of each side, so that x + 1 = new length of each side of the square. Then, $(x+1)^2 - x^2 + 53$. This simplifies to $x^2 + 2x + 1 = x^2 + 53$. Then, $2x + 1 = 53$, so x = 26.

38. $3(2)^2 + \sqrt{25} - (-2)^3 = 12 + 5 + 8 = 25$.

39. Sine 30° = BC/14 1/2 = BC/14, so BC = 7.

40. Probability of 2 red marbles being drawn without replacement is (3/10)(2/9) = 1/15.

41. Each pen costs 75/x cents and each pencil costs 57/y cents. Then, 2 pens and 3 pencils cost 2(75/x) + 3(57/y).

42. Let x = number of quarters, 2x = number of dimes. Then, .25x + .10(2x) < 9.00. Solving, x < 20, so x = 19.

43. The new set of numbers is 3 times as large as the original set. Therefore, the mean is 3 times as big, which is 9, and the variance is 3^2 or 9 times as big, which is (9)(3.5)= 31.5.

44. Using the diagram shown at the right, for the fence $\overline{BC}$, we'll need 5 posts whose distance from each other is 12 1/2'. (This includes a post at B and a post at C.) Now along $\overline{AB}$, since AB = 20' and $20 \div 2\frac{1}{2} = 8$, we'll need 8 posts (including a post at A). Finally, starting at A and ending at C, we need to place only 20 ÷ 2 1/2 – 1 = 7 posts since a post already exists at A and at C. Thus, the total number of posts is 5 + 8 + 7 = 20.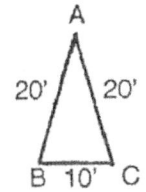

45. (6')(7') = 42 square feet costing $52, which means $52/$42 or $(26/21) per square foot. Now a ceiling 18 ft. by 21 ft. is 378 square feet and will cost (26/21)(378) = $468.

46. Let x, x+2, x+4 represent the three odd numbers. Then, x + x+2 + x+4 = 51. This reduces to 3x + 6 = 51, from which x = 15. The three numbers are 15,17, 19 and so the largest is 19.

47. From 9:55 A.M. to 10:15 A.M. represents 20 minutes. Then, 20 minutes/5 hours = 20 minutes/300 minutes, which reduces to 1/15.

48. Volume is (10)(9)(2) = 180 cu. ft. The weight of the liquid is (100)(180) = 18,000 lbs.

49. Cosine $\frac{\pi}{3}$ = .5, which is also the value of -Cosine $\frac{2\pi}{3}$.

50. To make (3x-4)(4+5y²) as large as possible, we maximize the numerator and minimize the denominator. Given the restriction $5 \leq x \leq 12$, use x = 12. Given the restriction use y = 0. (Note carefully that y = 0 yields a smaller value of 4 + 5y² than y = -2)

MATHEMATICS

EXAMINATION SECTION
TEST 1

DIRECTIONS: Each question or incomplete statement is followed by several suggested answers or completions. Select the one that *BEST* answers the question or completes the statement. *PRINT THE LETTER OF THE CORRECT ANSWER IN THE SPACE AT THE RIGHT.*

1. If $r + q = s$ and $r + q + s = w$, what does w equal in terms of r and q? 1.____

   A. $2r + q$ B. $2q + r$ C. $2r + 2q$
   D. $r + q + s$ E. $2s + 2r + q$

2. In a circle a chord is cut off so that it equals the radius. How many degrees are there in the central angle formed by two radii and this chord? 2.____

   A. 50   B. 52   C. 54   D. 57   E. 60

3. Find the shaded area formed by 4 overlapping squares, each having a 3" side and a 1" overlap.

   A. 36
   B. 32
   C. 30
   D. 24
   E. 22

   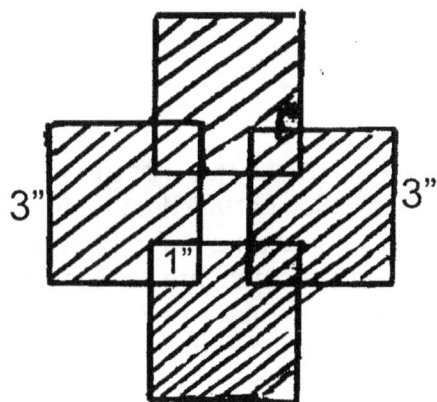

4. $(x+y)^2 - x^2 - y^2 = (?)$ 4.____

   A. $2xy$ B. xy C. 0   D. $2x^2 + 2y^2$ E. y^2

5. If $x-2 = x-2$, what does x equal numerically? 5.____

   A. Only 0   B. Any number   C. 7
   D. 2   E. 5

6. What approximate percent of 72 is 43? 6.____

   A. 56   B. 57   C. 58   D. 60   E. 61

7. What is the area of the shaded triangle?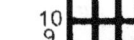

   A. 9 1/2
   B. 10
   C. 10 1/2
   D. 11
   E. 12

   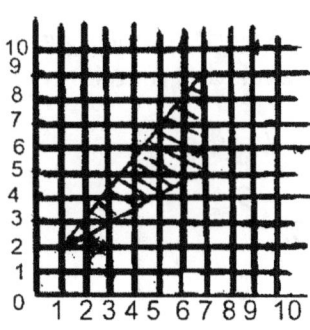

8. In a marine base 12% of the men are from California and 4% of these marines are from Anaheim. What percent of the men are from Anaheim?

   A. 48 B. 4.8 C. .48 D. .048 E. .0048

9. A book shelf is 4 feet long. How many books will fit on the shelf if each book is 3 1/3 inches thick?

   A. 11 B. 12 C. 13 D. 14 E. 15

10. The areas of the complete circles are x, y, and z. The areas of the portions of the circles are r, s, t, u and w. What is the area of x + y - z?

    A. r + t + w
    B. r + 2t + w
    C. s + t + u
    D. r + s + w
    E. s + u + w

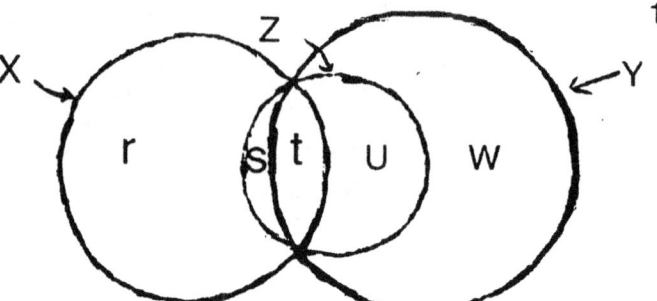

Questions 11-15.

DIRECTIONS: Each of the questions below is followed by two statements, labeled (1) and (2), in which certain data are given. In these questions you do not actually have to compute an answer, but rather you have to decide whether the data given in the statement are *sufficient* for answering the question. Using the data given in the statements *plus* your knowledge of mathematics and everyday facts, you are to print in the space at the right the letter

   A. if statement (1) ALONE is sufficient but statement (2) alone is not sufficient to answer the question asked;
   B. if statement (2) ALONE is sufficient but statement (1) alone is not sufficient to answer the question asked;
   C. if BOTH statements (1) and (2) TOGETHER are sufficient to answer the question asked, but NEITHER statement ALONE is sufficient;
   D. if EACH statement is sufficient by itself to answer the question asked;
   E. if statements (1) and (2) TOGETHER are NOT sufficient to answer the question asked and additional data specific to the problem are needed.

11. The distance to John's house is 40 miles from his college. John went to school Friday but then returned home. *How long* did the entire trip take?

    (1) If John went 40 miles per hour faster it would have taken him half the time.
    (2) He traveled at a uniform rate, both going and coming, of 40 miles per hour.

12. 4x - 8y = 4. y = ?

    (1) x - 2y = 0
    (2) x = 5

13. There are 75 people in the town that attend either meeting x or meeting y or both. How many attend each meeting?   13._____

    (1) 30 people attend meeting x *only*
    (2) 45 people attend meeting y

14. In triangle RST, how many degrees is angle R if   14._____

    (1) RS/ST = 1 (2) RS/TR = 1
    angle R = 60 degrees

15. In triangle RST, angle S is 90 degrees and SR = ST. Find the area of triangle RST.   15._____

    (1) SR = 5
    (2) RT = $5\sqrt{2}$

KEY (CORRECT ANSWERS)

1. C   6. D
2. E   7. E
3. B   8. C
4. A   9. D
5. B   10. A

11. D
12. B
13. E
14. C
15. D

SOLUTIONS TO PROBLEMS

1. Since $r + q = s$ and $r + q + s = w$, we get $r + q + r + q = w$. Simplified, $w = 2r + 2q$

2. In a circle with center O, if chord equals the radius, that $\triangle$ AOB is equilateral. Then, the central angle = $60°$.

3. By adding up the areas of the 4 large squares, each little square has been added twice. The shaded area will be $(4)(3^2) - 4(1^2) = 32$ sq.in.

4. $(x + y)^2 - x^2 - y^2 = x^2 + 2xy + y^2 - x^2 - y^2 = 2xy$

5. Since $x - 2 = x - 2$ is an identity, x can equal any number.

6. $43/72 = .597 \approx 60\%$

7. Area = $(1/2)(base)(height) = (1/2)(4)(6) = 12$

8. The percent of men from Anaheim is $(.04)(.12) = .0048 = .48\%$

9. 4 ft. = 48 in. Then, $48 \div 3\frac{1}{3} = 14.4$. So, 14 books will fit on the shelf.

10. $x + y - z = (r+s+t) + (t+u+w) - (s+t+u) = r + t + w$

11. Let x = rate. Statement 1 alone is sufficient, since we could solve $40/(x + 40) = 1/2(40/x)$, yielding $x = 40$.
    Thus, time = 1 hour. Statement 2 alone is also sufficient since letting x = time we get x =40/40= 1 hour.

12. Statement 1 alone will not be sufficient to solve for y, since substituting $x = 2y$ into the given equation yields $4(2y) - 8y = 4$ which has no solution. Statement 2 alone would be sufficient.
    If $x = 5$, $(4)(5) - 8y = 4$, so $y = 2$.

13. Statement 1 alone would not be sufficient because we don't know how many people attended meeting y only and how many attended both x and y. Statement 2 alone is not sufficient because we don't know how many of the 45 attended both x and y, versus how many attended only y. Finally, the two statements together are still insufficient.

14. Each of statements 1 and 2 separately is not sufficient to find $\angle R$, but together they imply that RS = ST = TR. So, $\angle R = 60°$.

15. Statement 1 alone is sufficient because ST = SR = 5. Then, the area of the triangle is $(1/2)(5)(5) = 12.5$. Statement 2 alone is also sufficient because given RT = $5\sqrt{2}$ and SR = ST, we let SR = x. Then, $x^2 + x^2 = (5\sqrt{2})^2$. Solving, $x = 5$. Area of triangle = $(1/2)(5)(5) = 12.5$.

TEST 2

DIRECTIONS: Each question or incomplete statement is followed by several suggested answers or completions. Select the one that *BEST* answers the question or completes the statement. *PRINT THE LETTER OF THE CORRECT ANSWER IN THE SPACE AT THE RIGHT.*

1. A man runs 220 yards in 20.7 seconds. The first 90 yards he runs in 11.8 seconds. In approximately *how many* seconds does he run the first 100 yards if he runs the last 130 yards at a uniform rate?

    A. 12.0   B. 12.2   C. 12.5   D. 12.7   E. 13.0

2. The symbol $\begin{vmatrix} a & b \\ c & d \end{vmatrix}$ is called the *determinant* of the quantities a, b, c, d. The value of the determinant is (ad-bc). Find the value of the determinant $\begin{vmatrix} 2 & 3 \\ 3 & 1 \end{vmatrix}$

    A. 3   B. -7   C. 5   D. 7   E. -5

3. In the figure, angle B is obtuse, AP = 8, BP = 5, and Q is any point on AB. Which of the following expresses possible values of the length of PQ?

    A. 8 > PQ > 5
    B. 8 > 5 > PQ
    C. 5 > PQ > 8
    D. PQ > 8 > 5
    E. None of these

4. If a man buys several articles for n cents per dozen and sells them for n/9 cents per article, *what* is his profit, in cents, on each article?

    A. n/36   B. n/12   C. 3n/4   D. 4n/3   E. n/18

5. Five billion dozen eggs are used in the United States each year. If every twelfth egg is made into powder, *how many* billion eggs per year are powdered?

    A. 2   B. 2 1/2   C. 3   D. 4   E. 5

6. The symbols ° and * designate two different mathematical operations. If a° (b*c) = a°b*a°c, then the operation is said to be *distributive* with respect to the operation *. If ° represents the operation of multiplication (x), then * may represent which of the following operations:

    I. +   II. -   III. ÷

    The *CORRECT* answer is:

    A. I only
    B. II only
    C. I and II only
    D. I, II, and III
    E. None of these

7. If the *additive inverse* of a number a is termed (-a) in the real number system, find the additive inverse of -7/2

    A. 2/2   B. 2/7   C. -7   D. -2   E. 7/2

275

8. If x = ay, where y does not equal zero, express a in terms of x and y.

   A. -y/x B. x/y C. xy D. x+y E. x-y

9. Which of the following has *no* finite value that can be determined?

   A. 0/3 B. 3 x 0 C. 0 - 3
   D. 3/0 E. None of these

10. The coordinates of P_1 are (1,4). What are the coordinates of P_2?

    A. (2,3)
    B. (1,2)
    C. (5,2)
    D. (2,2)
    E. (5,3)

Questions 11-15.

DIRECTIONS: Each of the data sufficiency problems below consists of a question and two statements, labeled (1) and (2), in which certain data are given. You have to decide whether the data given in the statements are *sufficient* for answering the question. Using the data given in the statements *plus* your knowledge of mathematics and everyday facts, you are to print in the space at the right the letter

   A. if statement (1) *ALONE* is sufficient, but statement (2) alone is not sufficient to answer the question asked;
   B. if statement (2) *ALONE* is sufficient, but statement (1) alone is not sufficient to answer the question asked;
   C. if *BOTH* statements (1) and (2) *TOGETHER* are sufficient to answer the question asked, but *NEITHER* statement *ALONE* is sufficient;
   D. if *EACH* statement *ALONE* is sufficient to answer the question asked;
   E. if statements (1) and (2) *TOGETHER* are *NOT* sufficient to answer the question asked, and additional data specific to the problem are needed.

11. Given triangle ABC. How many degrees in angle A?

    (1) AB = AC
    (2) Angle B = 40 degrees

12. There are 24 pencils in a box. How many have both erasers and dull points?

    (1) 21 have erasers
    (2) 3 have dull points

13. Given equilateral triangle ABC and hexagon DEFGHI formed as in the figure. What is the ratio of the area of the hexagon to the area of triangle ABC?

    (1) Triangles ADE, BFG and CHI are all equilateral
    (2) AD = CH = BF

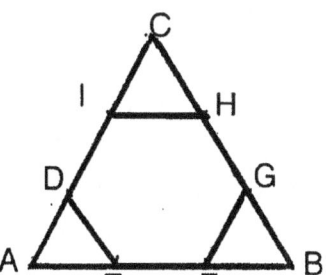

14. A and B go on a 300-mile trip by car. They take turns driving, each driving for eight hours. Find the average rate of each.

    (1) A drove 48 miles more than B
    (2) A averaged 6 miles an hour faster than B

15. A table is 30 inches long and 9 inches wide. It is covered by three overlapping napkins each 9 inches wide. *How long* is each of the napkins?

    (1) All three napkins are of equal length
    (2) If the table were 1 1/2 times as long as it is now, the napkins would just cover the table without overlapping.

KEY (CORRECT ANSWERS)

1. C
2. B
3. A
4. A
5. E
6. C
7. E
8. B
9. D
10. D
11. C
12. E
13. E
14. D
15. C

SOLUTIONS TO PROBLEMS

1. $(220 - 90) \div (20.7 - 11.8) \approx 14.6$ yds. per second for the last 130 yards. The time needed to run the 10 yards from the 90-yard marker to the 100-yard marker $10 \div 14.6 \approx .7$ sec. = Since he ran the first 90 yards in 11.8 seconds, his time, in seconds, for the first 100 yards = $11.8 + .7 = 12.5$.

2. $\begin{vmatrix} 2 & 3 \\ 3 & 1 \end{vmatrix} = (2)(1) - (3)(3) = -7$

3. In $\triangle PQB$, $\overline{PQ}$ must be the longest side since $\angle B$ is obtuse. Then, $PQ > 5$. In $\triangle APQ$ $\angle Q$ is obtuse, so $AP = 8$ must be the longest side. This implies $PQ < 8$. Finally, $8 > PQ > 5$.

4. n cents per dozen articles means n/12 cents per article. His profit in cents on each article = $n/9 - n/12 = n/36$.

5. Five billion dozen ÷ 1 dozen = 5 billion.

6. Only statements I and II are correct since $a \cdot (b+c) = a \cdot b + a \cdot c$ and $a \cdot (b-c) = a \cdot b - a \cdot c$.

7. The additive inverse of $-7/2 = -(-7/2) = +7/2$

8. If $x = ay$, dividing by y yields $a = x/y$

9. 3/0 has no finite value since division by zero has no meaning.

10. Since P_2 lies 1 unit to the right and 2 units below P_1, the coordinates of P_2 are (2,2).

11. If $AB = AC$, then $\angle B = \angle C$, but we cannot determine the measurement of $\angle A$. If $\angle B$ is known to be 40°, $\angle A + \angle C$ must equal 180°, but we could not determine $\angle A$. These two statements together would be sufficient to determine $\angle A$. Since $\angle B = 40°$, $\angle C = 40°$. Then, $\angle A = 180° - 40° - 40° = 100°$.

12. The two statements together are insufficient. For example, we might have 21 pencils with erasers and no dull points along with 3 pencils with dull points but no erasers. Another possibility is 20 pencils with erasers and no dull points, 3 pencils with dull points and no erasers, 1 pencil with both an eraser and a dull point, and 1 pencil with no eraser and no dull point.

13. Statement 1 alone is not sufficient to determine the sides of the hexagon. Statement 2 alone is not sufficient since we do not know if $\triangle$ ADE, $\triangle$ BFG, $\triangle$ CIH are equilateral. So the sides of the hexagon are still unknown. Together, statements 1 and 2 are still not sufficient. (The required information would be: $\triangle$ ADE, $\triangle$ BFG, $\triangle$ CHI are equilateral and AD = DI = IC.)

5 (#2)

14. Statement 1 alone is sufficient. Let x = distance driven by B and x + 48 = distance driven by A. Then, x + x + 48 = 300, so x = 126, x + 48 = 174. The average rates of A and B are 174/8 = 21.75 and 126/8 = 15.75. Using statement 2 alone, let x = average rate for B and x + 6 = average rate for A. Then, (x+6)(8) + 8x = 300. Thus, x = 15.75, x + 6 = 21.75.

15. Each statement alone is not sufficient, but taken together let x = each napkin's length. Then, 3x = (30)(1 1/2) = 45.
Thus, x = 15.

TEST 3

DIRECTIONS: Each question or incomplete statement is followed by several suggested answers or completions. Select the one that BEST answers the question or completes the statement. PRINT THE LETTER OF THE CORRECT ANSWER IN THE SPACE AT THE RIGHT.

Questions 1-10.

DIRECTIONS: In each of the problems below, do *not solve the problem,* but simply indicate one of the following choices:
- A. if not enough information is given to solve the problem;
- B. if just enough information is given to solve the problem;
- C. if statement (1) is needed to solve the problem, but not statement (2);
- D. if statement (2) is needed to solve the problem, but not statement (1);
- E. if neither statement (1) nor (2) is needed to solve the problem.

1. The bases of an isosceles trapezoid are 6 and 10. Find the area of the trapezoid. 1.___

   (1) The diagonals of the trapezoid are 9.
   (2) The lower base angles are acute.

2. How far is A from C? 2.___

   (1) A is 10 miles from B.
   (2) B is 15 miles from C.

3. A cylindrical glass 6 inches high is full of water. How many lbs. of water does the glass contain? 3.___

   (1) A cubic foot of water weighs 62.5 pounds.
   (2) The diameter of the glass is 4 inches.

4. Find the height of the flagpole. 4.___

   (1) The shadow of a yardstick is 4 ft. long.
   (2) At the same time and place the shadow of a flagpole is 36 ft.

5. A man has 18 coins consisting of nickles and dimes. HOW many of each are there? 5.___

   (1) The total value is $1.20.
   (2) There are twice as many nickles as dimes.

6. Find each number. 6.___

   (1) Three numbers are in the ratio 5:7:9.
   (2) The middle number is equal to half the sum of the first and third numbers.

7. How many pounds of each does he use? 7.___

   (1) A dealer mixes coffee worth $1.80 a pound with coffee worth $2.10 a pound.
   (2) The mixture sells for $1.98 a pound.

8. The area of a square is 36 square inches. Find the side of the square. 8.____

   (1) A rectangle is formed equal in area to the square.
   (2) The length of the rectangle is 3 inches more than a side of the square.

9. Find the number of dollars invested at each rate, 9.____

   (1) A man invests a certain amount of money, part at 6% and the rest at 8%.
   (2) The total annual income from the two investments is $290.

10. Find each integer. 10.____

    (1) The sum of three consecutive integers is 33.
    (2) The largest of the three integers is 2 more than the smallest.

KEY (CORRECT ANSWERS)

1. C	6. A
2. A	7. A
3. B	8. E
4. B	9. A
5. D	10. C

SOLUTIONS TO PROBLEMS

1. 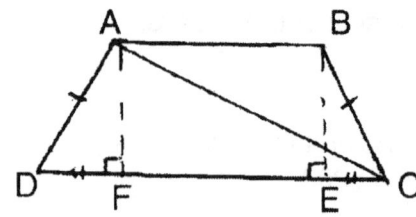 Let AB = 6, DC = 10. Using statement 1, in right triangle AFC, FC = 6 + 2 = 8, AC = 9, so The area of the trapezoid $\frac{1}{2}(\sqrt{17})(6 + 10)$ or $8\sqrt{17}$. This means statement 2 will not be needed.

2. There is insufficient information to find the distance from A to C. (Note that AC = 25 ONLY if points A, B, C are collinear.)

3. Using both statements together, the volume of the glass is Since a cubic foot of water weighs 62.5 pounds, the weight of water in the glass = $(62.5)(\frac{2}{3}\pi) = 41\frac{2}{3}\pi$ pounds.

4. Using both statements together, let x = height of the flagpole. Then, x/36 = 3/4. Thus, x = 27 ft.

5. Statement 1 is not needed. With statement 2 alone, let x = number of dimes, 2x = number of nickels. Then, x + 2x = 18, so x = 6. There are 6 dimes and 12 nickels.

6. Let the three numbers be represented as 5x, 7x, 9x. Since 7x = 1/2(5x + 9x) anyway, statement 2 is not needed. We now conclude that there is insufficient information to find each number.

7. There is insufficient information to find the number of pounds of each type of coffee. The only conclusion we can reach is that UNEQUAL number of pounds of each type is used since 1.98 ≠ (1.80 + 2.10) / 2.

8. From the given information, each side of the square Neither of statements 1 nor 2 is needed.

9. Let x = amount invested at 6%, y = amount invested at 8%. Then, .06x + .08y = 290, if we use both statements. This is still insufficient to find x or y.

10. From statement 1, x, x + 1, x + 2 could represent the integers. Then, x + x + 1+ x + 2 = 33. Solving, the numbers are 10, 11, and 12. This means statement 2 will not be needed.

TEST 4

DIRECTIONS: Each question or incomplete statement is followed by several suggested answers or completions. Select the one that *BEST* answers the question or completes the statement. *PRINT THE LETTER OF THE CORRECT ANSWER IN THE SPACE AT THE RIGHT.*

Questions 1-5.

DIRECTIONS: Each of the data sufficiency problems below consists of a question and two statements, labeled (1) and (2), in which certain data are given. You have to decide whether the data given in the statements are *sufficient* for answering the question. Using the data given in the statements *plus* your knowledge of mathematics and everyday facts (such as the number of days in June or the meaning of *counterclockwise*), you are to print in the space at the right of the letter:

A. if statement (1) *ALONE* is sufficient, but statement (2) alone is not sufficient to answer the question asked;
B. if statement (2) *ALONE* is sufficient, but statement (1) alone is not sufficient to answer the question asked;
C. if *BOTH* statements (1) and (2) *TOGETHER* are sufficient to answer the question asked, but *NEITHER* statement *ALONE* is sufficient;
D. if *EACH* statement *ALONE* is sufficient to answer the question asked;
E. if statements (1) and (2) *TOGETHER* are *NOT* sufficient to answer the question asked, and additional data specific to the problem are needed.

1. Which side of $\triangle$ RST is the longest?   1.____

   (1) < S = 54 degrees, < T = 36 degrees
   (2) < R is a right angle

2. Is the sum of the three integers, x, y, and z, odd?   2.____

   (1) xyz = 105
   (2) The sum and the difference of any two of the numbers are each even, and y is odd.

3. What is the two-digit number Q?   3.____

   (1) The sum of its digits is 13 and the product of its digits is 36.
   (2) If it were multiplied by 2, the result would still be a two-digit number. .

4. If x and y are integers, is x+y odd?   4.____

   (1) xy = 6
   (2) x-y is odd.

5. x + y + z = (?)   5.____

   (1) x + y = 3
   (2) x + z = 5

6. Two variables in a scientific experiment are such that their product is always 1. If, for a certain time, one variable is greater than zero, less than 1, and decreasing, then which of the following describes the second variable?

   A. Greater than 1 and increasing
   B. Greater than 1 and decreasing
   C. Not changing
   D. Less than 1 and increasing
   E. Less than 1 and decreasing

7. If x, y, z, and w are all real numbers and none of them is zero, which of the following expressions can equal zero?

   I. $x+y+z+w$
   II. $x^2 + y^2 + z^2 + w^2$
   III. $x^3 + y^3 + z^3 + w^3$
   IV. $x^4 + y^4 + z^4 + w^4$

   The CORRECT answer is:

   A. I only
   B. III only
   C. II and IV only
   D. I and III only
   E. I, II, III, and IV

8. If x(x-y) = 0 and if y does not equal zero, which of the following is true?

   A. x = 0
   B. Either x = 0 or x = y
   C. x = y
   D. $x^2 = y$
   E. Both x = 0 and x - y = 0

9. If n is an integer and if the following are arranged in order, which integer is in the middle?

   A. n+3
   B. n-9
   C. n-4
   D. n+6
   E. n-1

10. If ϕ is an operation on the positive numbers, for which of the following definitions of is $x \phi y = y \phi x$?

    A. $x \phi y = x/y$
    B. $x \phi y = x - y$
    C. $x \phi y = x(x + y)$
    D. $x \phi y = \dfrac{yx}{y+x}$
    E. $x \phi y = x^2 + xy^2 + y^4$

11. In the figure to the right, a card is covering part of the left number which is known to be in the hundred thousands. Which of the following is the only number that could possibly be the above product?

    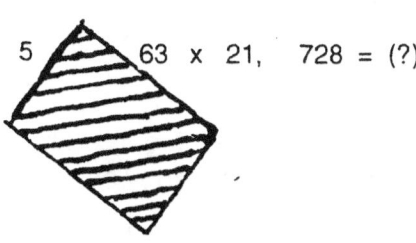

    5 ⟨ 63 x 21, 728 = (?)

    A. 1, 107, 130, 464
    B. 1, 107, 130, 466
    C. 11, 076, 130, 444
    D. 11, 076, 130, 464
    E. 11, 076, 130, 466

12. If $x^2 + 2xy + y^2 = k$, where x and y are positive integers and x is odd and y is even, which of the following statements is true?

    A. k is odd and a perfect square
    B. k is even and a perfect square
    C. k is odd and not a perfect square
    D. k is even and not a perfect square
    E. None of these

13. If the average of 13 consecutive whole numbers is odd, then the product of the first and last of these numbers must necessarily be

    A. odd
    B. even
    C. a multiple of 7
    D. a multiple of 13
    E. a multiple of the average of the 13 numbers

14. How many of the numbers between 100 and 300 begin or end with 2?

    A. 20   B. 40   C. 180   D. 100   E. 110

15. A prime number is a number that can be divided only by itself and one. Which of the following is NOT a prime number?

    A. 101   B. 93   C. 53   D. 47   E. 17

16. If $2x + 2 > 8$, x must be

    A. < 8   B. < 5   C. > 3   D. > 4   E. > 6

17. Which one of the following must be excluded so that the remaining four are consistent?

    A. a > b   B. a > d   C. b > c   D. c > a   E. d > c

18. The sides of a triangle are 9, 12, and x. What are all the values of x for which the triangle will be acute?

    A. x < 21
    B. x > 3
    C. 3 < x < 21
    D. x < 15
    E. $3\sqrt{7} < x > 15$

19. The fraction a/b(a and b positive) will have a value greater than 2 if

   A. 2a = 2b
   B. a > b
   C. a > 2
   D. a > 2b
   E. 2b > a

20. If Tom knows that x is an integer > 3 but < 8 and Charley knows that x is an integer > 6 but < 11, then Tom and Charley can *correctly* conclude that

   A. x can be exactly determined
   B. x may be either of 2 values
   C. x may be any of 3 values
   D. x may be any of 4 values
   E. there is no value of x satisfying these conditions

KEY (CORRECT ANSWERS)

1. D
2. D
3. C
4. D
5. E
6. A
7. D
8. B
9. E
10. D
11. D
12. A
13. A
14. E
15. B
16. C
17. D
18. E
19. D
20. A

SOLUTIONS TO PROBLEMS

1. From statement 1, ∠S = 54°, ∠T = 36°, so ∠R = 90°. Then the hypotenuse $\overline{ST}$ of this right triangle must be the longest. From statement 2, $\overline{ST}$ must be the hypotenuse, and so must be the longest side. Each of statements 1 and 2 is sufficient to find the longest side of △RST.

2. From statement 1, if xyz = 105, then all three numbers must be odd. This implies x + y + z is odd. From statement 2, y is odd and since |x-y|, |x-z|, |z-y| must each be even, we know that x and z must also be odd. Thus, x + y + z must be odd. Each of statements 1 and 2 is sufficient.

3. Let 10x + y represent Q. From statement 1 alone, x + y = 13 and xy = 36. Solving this system of equations, x = 9 and y = 4 or x = 4 and y = 9. Q = 49 or 94. Now using statement 2, we have 2(10x + y) < 100. With both statements 1 and 2, Q must be 49 since 2(94) exceeds 100.

4. From statement 1, if xy = 6, one of x,y is odd and the other is even. So, x + y must be odd. From statement 2, x - y is odd would mean that one of x, y is odd and the other is even. Again, x + y must be odd. Each of statements 1 and 2 is sufficient.

5. Using both statements together, we could determine only that z - y = 2. This would still be insufficient to determine the value of x + y + z.

6. If 0 < x < 1, xy = 1, and x is decreasing, then y must be increasing and y > 1. For example, if x = .5 and y = 2, when x decreases to .25, y = 4.

7. x + y + z + w could be zero. (For example, x = 1, y = -1, z = 2, w = 2.) Those same values would also make $x^3 + y^3 + z^3 + w^3 = 0$. But $x^2 + y^2 + z^2 + w^2 > 0$ and $x^4 + y^4 + z^4 + w^4 > 0$. Only statements I and III could be zero.

8. Given x(x-y) = 0 and y ≠ 0, then x = 0 or x-y = 0.
   This means x = 0 or x = y.

9. The 5 selections arranged in ascending order are: n-9, n-4, n-1, n+3, n+6. Thus, n-1 is the middle integer.

10. If $x \phi y = \dfrac{xy}{x+y}$, then $y \phi x = \dfrac{yx}{y+x}$, which is equivalent to $\dfrac{xy}{x+y}$. Thus, $x \phi y = y \phi x$.

11. Since 500,000 x 21,728 > 11,000,000,000, only choices C, D, E are possible. Since the last digits of each factor are 3 and 8, respectively, the product must end in 4. We now eliminate choice E. Consider the first line of the multiplication. 8 x 3 = 4 with a carry of 2 and 8 x 6 + 2 = 0 digit in the ten's column. Another contribution to the ten's column will be the result of multiplying 3 (from the unknown number) by 2 (from 21,728) to get a 6 digit. The answer must now have a digit of 0 + 6 = 6 in the ten's column. Only choice D is possible. Note: 11,076,130,464 ÷ 21,728 = 509,763.

12. $x^2 + 2xy + y^2 = (x+y)^2 = k$. Since x is odd and y is even, x + y is odd and so is $(x+y)^2$ an odd number. This means that k is odd and a perfect square.

13. The average of 13 consecutive whole numbers must be the 7th number. If this 7th number is odd, then both the first and last numbers must also be odd. Consequently, their product must be odd.

14. There are 10 numbers between 100 and 200 (non-inclusive) which end with a 2, namely 102, 112, 122,..., 182, 192. Between 200 and 300 (inclusive), there are 100 numbers beginning with a 2 (and some ending with a 2 as well), namely, 200, 201, 202,..., 298, 299. The total of numbers satisfying the given requirements = 100 + 10 = 110.

15. 93 is not a prime number since it has factors other than 1 and 93, namely 3 and 31.

16. If $2x + 2 > 8$, then $2x > 6$, so $x > 3$.

17. By excluding choice D, there is consistency among the others, so that a > b or d and b or d > c.

18. If x is the largest side, then $x^2 = 9^2 + 12^2$ will result in a right triangle. Solving, $x = 15$. This would mean if $x \geq 15$, this will not be an acute triangle. (If $x \geq 15$, this will be an obtuse triangle.) Now suppose x is the smallest side. The largest angle will lie opposite the side which is 12. We know that $12^2 = 9^2 + x^2 - (2)(9)(x) \cdot \cos$ (angle opposite 12). To maintain an acute triangle, cos (any angle) must be positive. To insure this, $12^2 - 9^2 - x^2$ must be negative. This leads to $x^2 > 144 - 81 = 63$, so $x > \sqrt{63} = 3\sqrt{7}$. Finally, the restrictions on x are $3\sqrt{7} < x > 15$.

19. If $a/b > 2$, then $a > 2b$. (Both a, b > 0.)

20. If x fulfills both $3 < x < 8$ and $6 < x < 11$, then $x = 7$ (if x must be an integer).

QUANTITATIVE COMPARISON COMMENTARY

The item-type designated as *QUANTITATIVE COMPARISON* is a novel form of mathematics problem stressing the finest and highest types of conceptualizing, reasoning, and evaluating.

The examinee is directed to compare two quantities and to decide, on the basis of the information given, which, if either, is greater.

For example, if you were requested to compare 5/8 X 1/4 X 1/5 X 1/6 with 3/7 X 1/4 X 1/5 X 1/6, it would NOT be necessary to compute *each* product. It would suffice, *preferably,* to see at once that 1/4 X 1/5 X 1/6 is common to both items and, immediately, to appreciate that 5/8 > 3/7. Therefore, 5/8 X 1/4 X 1/5 X 1/6 must be, of course, the greater quantity.

Fundamental to the quantitative-comparison question are the concepts *greater than, less than,* and *equal to,* and the meaning and use of the symbols, > ("greater than"), and < ("less than"), which should be overlearned since these symbols appear or are implied in practically every question.

It would be wise to review the basic principles and concepts of algebra and geometry as a necessary preparation for this question-type. However, the candidate is advised that advanced mathematics is *not* required in the solution or interpretation of any of these problems.

Following are the directions in detail for the quantitative-comparison question:

DIRECTIONS: Each question in this section consists of two quantities, one in Column A and one in Column B. You are to compare the two quantities and, on the answer sheet, blacken space
  (A) if the quantity in Column A is the greater;
  (B) if the quantity in Column B is the greater;
  (C) if the two quantities are equal;
  (D) if the relationship cannot be determined from the information given.

DIAGRAMS
Position of points, angles, regions, etc., can be assumed to be in the order shown.

Figures are NOT NECESSARILY drawn to scale and may NOT agree to measure shown unless a note states that the figure is drawn to scale,
Lines shown as straight can be assumed to be straight.
Figures are assumed to lie in the plane unless otherwise indicated,

Note: All numbers used are real numbers, In a question, information concerning one or both of the quantities to be compared is centered above the two columns, A symbol that appears in both columns represents the same thing in Column A as it does in Column B.

Definitions of symbols:

< is less than   ≤ is less than or equal to
> is greater than   ≥ is greater than or equal to
⊥ is perpendicular to   ∥ is parallel to
        ≠ is not equal to

SAMPLE QUESTIONS

DIRECTIONS: See page 1.

1.   Column A   Column B
    2 X 6   2 + 6

The correct answer is A, since, obviously, 2 *times* a number is patently greater than 2 *more than* that same number.

Questions 2-4.

DIRECTIONS: Questions 2-4 refer to △ PQR.

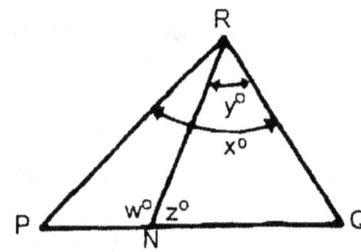

2.   Column A   Column B
     PN   NQ

The correct answer is D, since nothing can be assumed about measures from the figure.

3.   Column A   Column B
     Y   X

The correct answer is B, since N is between P and Q.

4.   Column A   Column B
    w + z   180

The correct answer is C, since PQ is a straight line.

EXAMINATION SECTION
TEST 1

DIRECTIONS: Each question in this section consists of two quantities, one in Column A and one in Column B. You are to compare the two quantities and, on the answer sheet, blacken space
- (A) if the quantity in Column A is the greater;
- (B) if the quantity in Column B is the greater;
- (C) if the two quantities are equal;
- (D) if the relationship cannot be determined from the information given.

1. | Column A | Column B | 1._____ |

BA ⊥ AD
x° = y°
AE ⊥ BD

| BE | ED |

2. | Column A | Column B | 2._____ |

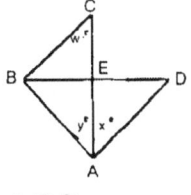

BA ⊥ BC
BA = BC
AC ⊥ BD

| W° | X° |

3. | Column A | Column B | 3._____ |

e ⊥ d
e ⊥ b
a ∥ c

| a | c |

4. | Column A | Column B | 4._____ |

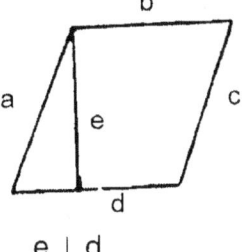

e ⊥ d
e ⊥

| b | d |

2 (#1)

5. | Column A | | Column B | 5.____
	$a \times b \geq c \times d$	
	$a > d$	
b		c

6. | Column A | | | Column B | 6.____
	$a > b < c$	$a > 0$	
	$a < c$	$b > 0$	
		$c > 0$	
c - b			c - a

7. | Column A | | Column B | 7.____
   | | $a \leq 0$ | |
   | a^2 | | $a - a$ |

8. | Column A | | Column B | 8.____
   | | $\sqrt{x^2 + 16} = x + 4$ | |
   | x | | zero |

9. Column A — Column B — 9.____

Given: Steel melts at 2800° F at the constant rate of 1 cubic inch per half hour

Time needed to melt a solid rectangular steel object, 1 foot wide, 2 feet high, 6 inches deep

One month

10. Column A — Column B — 10.____

Circle has center P

[Diagram: Circle with center P, diameter 8", angle 9° at P, points X and Z on circle, segment of length 6]

Area of given circle $\sqrt{2500}$ sq. in.

KEY (CORRECT ANSWERS)

1. C
2. D
3. C
4. D
5. D

6. A
7. D
8. C
9. A
10. A

TEST 2

DIRECTIONS: Each question in this section consists of two quantities, one in Column A and one in Column B. You are to compare the two quantities and, on the answer sheet, blacken space

    (A) if the quantity in Column A is the greater;
    (B) if the quantity in Column B is the greater;
    (C) if the two quantities are equal;
    (D) if the relationship cannot be determined from the information given.

Questions 1-2.

DIRECTIONS: Questions 1-2 are based upon the description given below.

A line is drawn from P (center of given circle) to X (point outside circle). Another line is drawn from P to Z (a point on the circle). Another line connects X and Z and is tangent to the circle at A.

1. Column A — Line PZ
   Column B — Line PX

2. Column A — Angle a°
   Column B — Angle b°

3. Column A — 7/2
   Column B — $\sqrt{10}$

4. Column A — Number of one-inch links in a 12-foot chain
   Column B — Number of one-foot links in a 45-yard chain

5. Column A — The number of sides in a pentagon
   Column B — The cube root of 343 minus the cube root of 27

6. Column A — 9/16 x 4/3 x 3 x 1/2 x 8
   Column B — 8/16 x 3/4 x 11 x 4 x 5/8

7. | Column A | Column B | 7.____

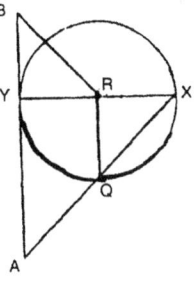

AY∥QR

QR ⊥ YX

BR>AQ

AX AB

8. | Column A | Column B | 8.____

$3x=4y$

$4x=x^2+4$

7x 9y+1

Questions 9-10.

DIRECTIONS: Questions 9-10 are based on the diagram of a circle appearing below.

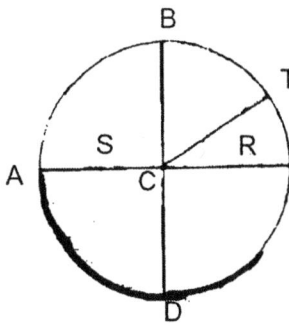

9. Column A | Column B | 9.____
Area ABC | Area ADC

10. Column A | Column B | 10.____
AC | CT

KEY (CORRECT ANSWERS)

1. B
2. B
3. A
4. A
5. A

6. B
7. D
8. B
9. D
10. D

TEST 3

DIRECTIONS: Each question in this section consists of two quantities, one in Column A and one in Column B. You are to compare the two quantities and, on the answer sheet, blacken space
- (A) if the quantity in Column A is the greater;
- (B) if the quantity in Column B is the greater;
- (C) if the two quantities are equal;
- (D) if the relationship cannot be determined from the information given.

1. | Column A | | Column B | 1.____ |
   |---|---|---|---|
   | | CE∥FH | | |
   | | GF=GB=FB | | |
   | ∡CDG | | 1/2 of ∡BOH | |

2. | Column A | | Column B | 2.____ |
   |---|---|---|---|
   | ∡ADC + ∡FGB | CE∥FH | The total of all angles of a right triangle | |

3. Column A   Column B   3.____

   CE∥FH

   ∡FGB   ∡ADE

4. | Column A | | Column B | 4.____ |
   |---|---|---|---|
   | | $a \leq 0$ | | |
   | | $b \leq 0$ | | |
   | | $a \neq b$ | | |
   | b-a | | b+a | |

5. | Column A | Column B | 5.____ |
   |---|---|---|
   | 9 X 8 X 283 | 283 X 6 X 12 | |

2 (#3)

6. | Column A | Column B | 6.___
   | The average number of leaves shed per day by tree X during November if tree X shed all 300 of its leaves that month | 10 |

7. | Column A | | Column B | 7.___
   | | 0 > a | |
   | $a^3 + 1$ | | 0 |

8. | Column A | | Column B | 8.___
	a < 0	
	b < 0	
a - b		a + b

9. Column A   Column B   9.___

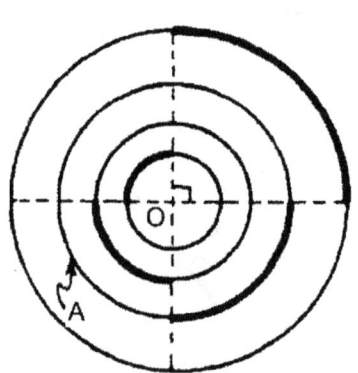

All circles have center O.
The diameter of the largest circle is 2d and the diameter of each other circle is 1/2 the diameter of the next larger circle.

Total length of darkened areas   Circumference of Circle A

10. | Column A | Column B | 10.___
    | | $2x \frac{<x-4}{2}$ | |
    | x | x^3 |

KEY (CORRECT ANSWERS)

1. C
2. C
3. C
4. D
5. C
6. B
7. D
8. B
9. B
10. A

TEST 4

DIRECTIONS: Each question in this section consists of two quantities, one in Column A and one in Column B. You are to compare the two quantities and, on the answer sheet, blacken space
  (A) if the quantity in Column A is the greater;
  (B) if the quantity in Column B is the greater;
  (C) if the two quantities are equal;
  (D) if the relationship cannot be determined from the information given.

Questions 1-3.

DIRECTIONS: Questions 1-3 refer to the diagram below.

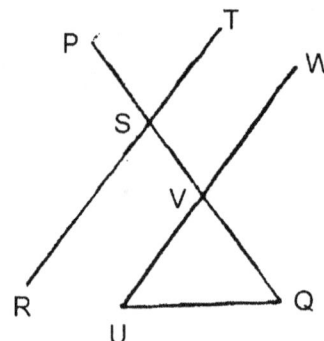

1. Column A   RT∥ UW   Column B
   ∡ UVQ   ∡ PST

2. Column A   Column B
                        RT ∥ UW
   ∡FSR+ ∡UVQ   180°

3. Column A   Column B
                        RT ∥ UW

                      UV = VQ = UQ
   ∡ RSV   1/2 of ∡WVQ

4. Column A.   Column B
   $5/2$ $\sqrt{6}$
   $5/2$

Questions 5-7.

2 (#4)

DIRECTIONS: Questions 5-7 refer to the diagram below:

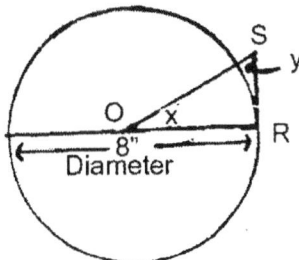

5.	Column A Area of circle	Column B 500 sq. in.	5.____
6.	Colunm A OR	Column B OS	6.____
7.	Column A ∡X	Column B ∡Y	7.____
8.	Column A	Column B	8.____

$$2a < \frac{a}{2} - 2$$

a a^3

Questions 9-10.

DIRECTIONS: Questions 9 and 10 refer to the diagram below:

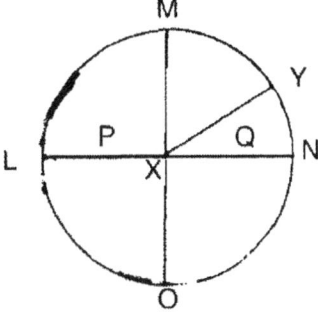

Point X bisects line LN
MO ⊥ LN

9.	Column A Area LMX	Column B Area LXO	9.____
10.	Column A LX	Column B XY	10.____

301

KEY (CORRECT ANSWERS)

1. C
2. C
3. C
4. A
5. A

6. B
7. D
8. A
9. D
10. D

———

ESSAY WRITING

THE WRITING PROCESS

Under ideal conditions, writing involves a series of steps:

1. Pre-writing activities which facilitate understanding the purpose and the audience for a particular piece of writing and which might include generating ideas through brainstorming, notes, reflection, research, or discussion;

2. Focusing the material generated in step one by framing a thesis (controlling idea) and a direction (organization);

3. Getting the first draft on paper, using standard grammar, correct mechanics, and accurate spelling;

4. Assessing the success of the first draft by yourself or in consultation with a reliable reader;

5. Revising the draft by clarifying the thesis, topic sentences, supporting detail, and word choice; and

6. Proofreading for mistakes in grammar and spelling.

Ideal conditions do not always exist in the real world. Often you have to write under pressure and produce a clear statement. This is the case in a test situation. You must streamline the writing process to compose an acceptable essay in approximately one hour. This section will help you to practice necessary strategies by describing how you might do the following:

1. Turn the directions into a purpose statement.
2. Brainstorm for material to put in the essay.
3. Group and focus your ideas.
4. Compose your essay with clear signals for the reader.
5. Proofread for word choice, grammar, and mechanics.

TURN DIRECTIONS INTO PURPOSE STATEMENTS

For each of the following sets of essays, the directions specify a topic, an audience, and some possible ways to develop the essay. You have some choice about how to develop the essay, but you must stick to the topic given and a style appropriate to the audience. The directions consist of four sentences which give

1. an indication of audience,
2. a description of audience,
3. suggestions for development, and
4. a restatement of the topic.

You can distinguish the sentences that suggest development because they contain words which give options rather than commands; for example, the sentences that give you commands about the topic will look like this:

In writing, tell the panel why you are considering teaching as a career.

On the other hand, sentences that suggest development will look like this:
The reasons may include…
You might want to consider…
The experiences could be…

Your first step, then, is to sort out the essential commands in the directions and convert them into a clear purpose statement such as *I will explain my reasons for choosing teaching as a career.* The purpose statement must cover all the essential parts of the assignment.

EXERCISE B

For each of the following sets of directions, underline the sentences that give you commands about the topic and write a purpose statement, using your own words if possible.

Prompt 1
A committee of teachers and administrators is reviewing your qualifications for a scholarship. In writing, tell the committee about a special activity you engage in, either in school or outside of school. It could be a job, an organization you belong to, a hobby or sport you participate in, or something you do with your family. Tell the committee what your special activity is and explain why this activity is important to you.

Prompt 2
A superintendent of schools has reviewed your application for a teaching position. Before holding a formal interview with you, the superintendent wants you to provide a writing sample that tells what motivated you to choose teaching as a profession. You might want to discuss a special learning experience you had or your interest in a chosen field or subject. Tell the superintendent what your motivation is and explain why your learning experience or your interest in a special field or subject is important to you.

Prompt 3
Your college advisor has just notified you that the college has instituted an open curriculum. As a result, you may choose any three courses or activities you wish to take next semester. You will be given equal course credit for academic subjects and activities such as sports, cultural

activities (music, theater, art), school newspaper or literary magazine activities, fraternities, sororities, community projects, or any other activity whose importance you can justify. In writing, indicate what three courses you would select and how each one would make you a better person.

Prompt 4
You have just been given the opportunity to write a letter of application to the Director of Admissions at the college of your choice. Imagine that cost is not a concern to you; you may choose a college that offers a traditional liberal arts curriculum or one that allows you to study only those courses that relate to your field of interest. In your essay, tell the Director of Admissions the type of college you are choosing and identify the reasons for your choice.

Prompt 5
A committee of teachers is reviewing your application for admission into the teacher education program of your choice. The committee has asked you to write an essay that describes a book that made the most lasting impression on you or from which you believe you learned some valuable lesson. The book may be on any subject, fiction or nonfiction, that is meaningful to you. The book need not be something you read for a course. Explain to the committee what your impression or lesson is and why it is important to you.

BRAINSTORM FOR MATERIAL TO PUT IN THE ESSAY

The directions on the subtest often contains suggestions for areas to explore. The sample directions which ask for an essay on your reasons for choosing a teaching career suggest that you consider *examples set by other people, benefits you expect from a teaching career, or the challenges you think teaching offers.* Remember that these suggestions are only suggestions. Before you respond to them, you should think about how you would accomplish the writing task if the suggestions had not been made. To be convincing, the material in your essay must come from your own experiences and knowledge. Brainstorming can help you accomplish this.

There are different ways to brainstorm. Some people prefer to write freely for 5-10 minutes. Others like to make lists or sketches. Others mull over ideas and ask themselves questions before jotting down a few key words. If you have a method that works for you, stick with it. If you don't, try one of the three approaches just mentioned.

EXERCISE C

1. Think about your reasons for wanting to teach and jot down a list of those reasons.

2. Compare your list with the suggestions given for considering teaching as a career: (examples, benefits, and challenges).

3. Which reasons fit the category of the rewards of teaching?

4. Which reasons could be labeled challenges of teaching?

5. Which reasons are related to examples set by other people?

6. What labels or categories do your other reasons fall under?

7. Are some of your reasons related to experiences that you have had as a learner or teacher (e.g., sports, scouting, 4-H, religious classes)?

8. Are some of your reasons related to your interest in a particular subject such as mathematics or art?

9. Are some of your reasons related to particular qualities you possess such as patience, enthusiasm, or tolerance?

LISTEN TO YOUR INNER VOICE

The purpose of brainstorming is to come up with enough detail or elaboration to satisfy the evaluation requirements. You should aim to produce enough material for an introduction and at least three additional paragraphs. Once you list a few initial ideas, the best way to generate more detail is to imagine a voice saying, *Tell me more about that.* Let's suppose that your initial list of reasons for wanting to teach looked like this.

- I like kids.
- Summers off.
- Make a contribution to society.
- Encouragement from teachers.

Responding to that imaginary voice saying, *Tell me more*, might help you elaborate the first reason as follows:

I like kids...
  because they all have some undeveloped potential.
  because their responses aren't always predictable.
  because they get so excited when they learn something new.

Another way to elaborate on the first reason is through examples:

- The two boys I used to babysit.
- The girl I helped to get over her fear of water.
- The special education student who was my *little brother*.

Imagine the voice asking for more information until you believe you have enough for a satisfactory essay. Not every statement will give you as much room for development as others, but you can expand upon all of the statements. Each time you elaborate, your writing becomes more specific. Including specific detail makes your ideas concrete and your writing more convincing. Specific detail is one of the criteria for evaluating your essay.

EXERCISE D

1. Go back to the list of purpose statements that you developed in Exercise C, and brainstorm for material you might include in an essay.

2. Go back to your list of reasons for wanting to teach and elaborate as much as you can on each one.

GROUP AND FOCUS YOUR IDEAS

A good essay is unified by a controlling idea or thesis which dictates a pattern of organization. The thesis should be stated in one or two sentences. The words you choose to write the thesis statement should repeat or echo the directions for the essay. This strategy will ensure that you state the topic clearly. One way to write a thesis is to do one of the following:

1. Look at your purpose statement.
   Example 1: I must explain my reasons for choosing teaching as a career.
   Example 2: I must explain how a learning experience motivated me to go into teaching.

2. Look at the list of ideas you generated by brainstorming and try to sum up the ideas in a sentence or two:
   Sample Thesis 1: I have chosen teaching as a career because I enjoy young children, particularly those who have a learning disability. Teaching is a career that will enable me to make a contribution to society.
   Sample Thesis 2: The experience that I had as a *big brother* to a special education student helped me to realize that everyone has the potential to learn. This experience strengthened my interest in teaching as a career.

The thesis prepares the reader for what is to follow. It is a promise that you will discuss certain ideas and not others.

You will not always use all the material you generated during the brainstorming step. In the sample that we have been discussing, you might have decided not to use material related to summers off or the encouragement of teachers. However, if you decide that there is some material you want to include in the body of your essay material which is not indicated by the thesis, you need to revise the thesis. Suppose you decide to include the information about summers off and the encouragement of teachers, how could you revise the thesis? Here is one possibility:

Revised Thesis: There are many reasons why I have chosen teaching as a career. The pleasure of working with children, the opportunity to make a contribution to society, the encouragement of teachers, and time during the summer to continue my own education and interests are a few of them.

You should understand that it is not necessary or advisable to give every reason why you would like to teach. Be selective. Choose reasons on which you can elaborate and ones you feel strongly about. This will make a more convincing essay.

OUTLINING

There are different ways of grouping brainstorming ideas. The traditional format is the outline. Here is one example, based on the thesis we have been discussing.

<u>Thesis:</u> There are many reasons why I have chosen teaching as a career; some of them are the pleasure of working with children, the opportunity to make a contribution to society, the encouragement of teachers, and time during the summer to continue my own education and interests.

I. I enjoy working with children.
   A. All children have potential.
   B. Their responses are unpredictable.
   C. They are excited when they learn something.

II. I will make a contribution to society.
   A. Many jobs have questionable social value even if they have high salaries.
   B. Teachers can help children develop a good self-image and give them necessary skills.

III. Teachers have encouraged me.
   A. They say I can express myself clearly.
   B. They see that I am enthusiastic about learning.

IV. Summers will be time to continue my education and interests.
   A. Teachers must be lifelong learners.
   B. Intensity of teaching requires time for pursuing other interests.

CLUSTERING

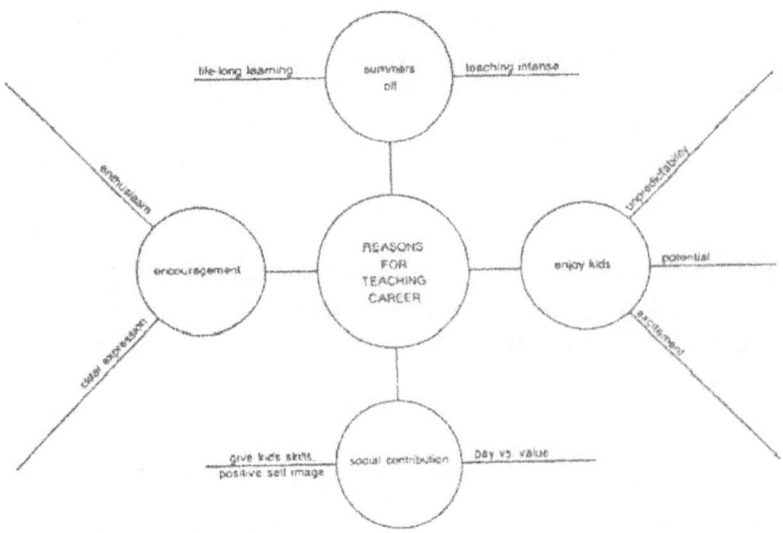

FLOW CHARTS

Still another way to map ideas is with the help of a flow chart. The main idea is placed in a box at the top, and other categories branch off below.

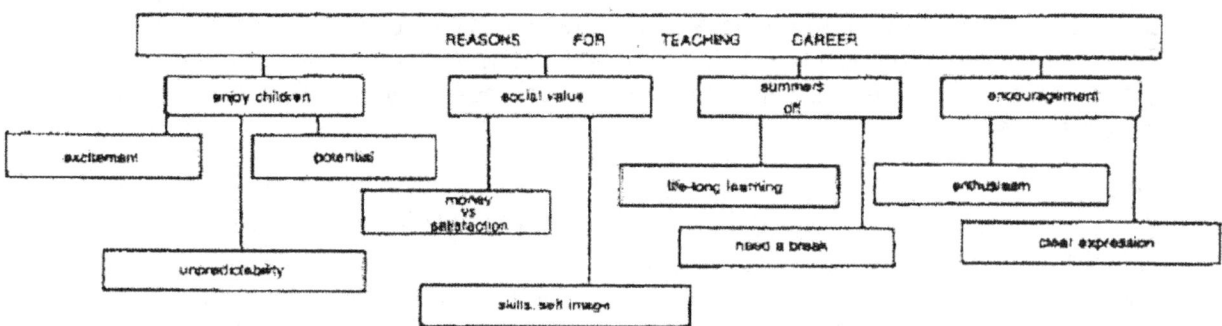

INFORMAL LISTS

An informal list is an easy way to group ideas.

My Reasons:

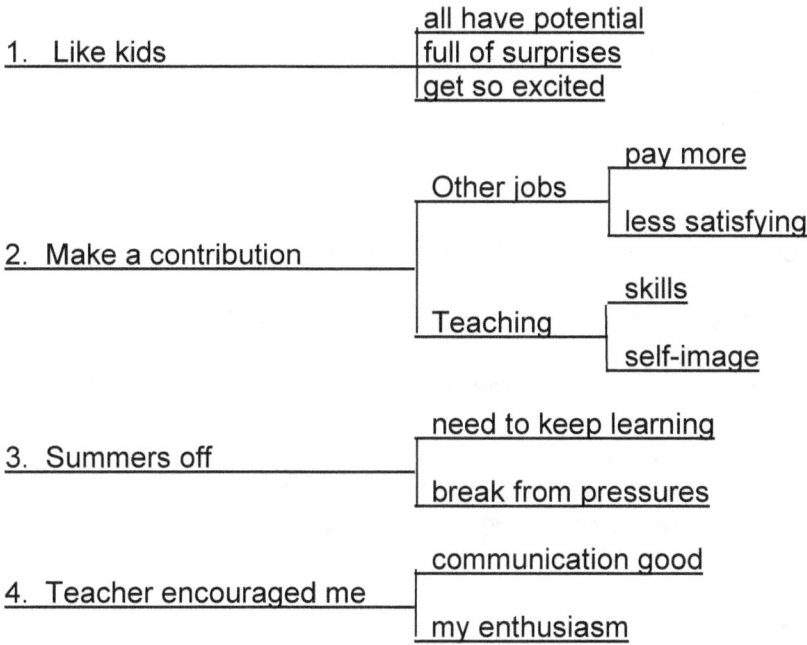

Regardless of which method you use to group your ideas, the goal is to pull together related bits of information and sketch the paragraph structure for your essay before you actually start writing your essay in the test booklet.

EXERCISE E

1. Go back to the material that you produced through brainstorming in Exercise D.2 and group the ideas by using one of the formulas illustrated.

2. Using one of the strategies mentioned previously, group the ideas given below in each set. For each set, read through the ideas in the set and identify or create a thesis statement; group related sentences; and find or create a sentence or phrase that will hold each group of sentences together.

SET A.
1. TV cartoons show characters recovering quickly from serious injury.
2. Mr. Rogers never loses his temper.
3. Ads associate happiness and good times with possession of a product.
4. The ads show cereal boxes opening by themselves and dancing on the table.
5. TV gives children a distorted sense of reality.
6. Mr. Rogers always takes off his shoes when he comes inside.
7. A character falls off a mountain top, shakes his head, and gets up.
8. Positive role models, like Mr. Rogers, are unlike any real-life adult.
9. Mr. Rogers never raises his voice.
10. The ads are deceptive and manipulative.
11. Characters who smash into walls are never badly hurt.

SET B.
1. I felt welcome when I went to see my math teacher during his office hours.
2. The activity fair during orientation week had something to offer everyone.
3. The counselors were helpful.
4. Many teachers ask if students need help rather than wait for the students to get in trouble.
5. The counselors helped with course selection.
6. Resident advisors counsel students about adjustment problems.
7. The counselors provided placement testing.
8. Teachers talk to students after class rather than just rushing off.
9. Students on campus are friendly.
10. My experience at Winona College has been good, and I would recommend it to others.
11. Teachers go over sample tests before you take the first test.
12. The dorm council plans activities and projects to bring students together.
13. The counselors offer minicourses on taking notes and tests.

SET C.
1. I don't belong to any organizations.
2. I'm not involved in any special activities.
3. I go to classes, work at the store, and see my friends on weekends.
4. My job isn't special.
5. I work at a supermarket.
6. I need the job for spending money and college expenses.

7. I have learned some things from working.
8. It's not like school.
9. You have to be there to get paid.
10. The boss isn't always fair.
11. Sometimes she is impatient.
12. As a lowly clerk, you don't get any respect.
13. The boss seemed annoyed when I brought back the shopping carts.
14. There were long lines at the registers.
15. She told me to help bag groceries.
16. There's a pecking order in most companies.
17. My boss is under pressure from the manager.
18. I'm trying to stay on top of the situation rather than just reacting.
19. I ask the boss how things have been going.
20. I try to anticipate what she'll ask me to do and offer to do it first.
21. Sometimes I feel frustrated about being low on the totem pole.
22. The manager doesn't even know who I am.
23. There's not much incentive to do good work.
24. You can always be replaced by another minimum wage worker.

SET D.
1. DEATH OF A SALESMAN is a book that influenced me because of the connections between the play and my own life.
2. Each time I had a different reaction.
3. I read the play once in high school, again in college, and then saw it on TV.
4. In high school, Biff was a good-looking football hero.
5. The play is about a salesman named Willy, his wife, and two sons, Biff and Happy.
6. Happy was just an ordinary kid, living in his brother's shadow.
7. When Biff learned that his father was not perfect, he began to drift around.
8. I realized I was only hurting myself.
9. I had an older brother who was a star.
10. I was always trying to get my parents' attention.
11. I even tried to get their attention by doing poorly in school.
12. At first, I identified with Happy.
13. Biff had a big ego because of all the attention he received.
14. Biff became a bum because of all the attention he received as a teenager.
15. When I read the play in college, I sympathized with Willy.
16. He never received any respect from his boss.
17. I have been working at a supermarket.
18. Clerks are a dime a dozen, just like salespeople.
19. I want a career where a paycheck is not the only satisfaction you receive.
20. The TV version made me admire the mother.
21. She held the family together.
22. She was completely loyal to Willy.
23. We all want someone to stick by us like she did.

SET E.
1. Earning credit for my choice of courses and activities will give me a chance to integrate course work and real experience.
2. Reading Methods is a required course.
3. I'll learn how to assess a student's reading level.
4. I'll learn about various methods for teaching reading skills.
5. I plan to work as a literacy volunteer.
6. I want to know why people don't learn to read.
7. I'll learn about methods for teaching adults.
8. I'll learn how illiteracy affects a person's life.
9. I'll realize what's at stake if the education system fails.
10. I want to take either an advanced composition course or an independent study in composition.
11. I would like to keep a journal of my experience as a literacy volunteer.
12. I would like to write about the connections I see between the methods course and my tutoring experience.
13. I would like to write some feature stories about illiteracy for the college newspaper.

COMPOSE YOUR ESSAY WITH CLEAR SIGNALS FOR THE READER

Your essay is judged on how well the essay communicates a whole message. If you keep the reader in mind, your essay is likely to communicate more effectively. The most important signals to use are topic sentences to state the main idea of each paragraph and transitions to link sentences within the paragraphs. One basic pattern you might use in composing your paragraphs is the five paragraph essay. Here is one example of such an essay written in response to Prompt 1, Exercise B. Study the way in which the topic sentences give the reader a preview of what will be discussed.

Paragraph I.   Lead and thesis statement.

Lead   Some students may have time for sports, clubs, or volunteer organizations. Unfortunately, my schedule of classes and part-time work does not give me much time to devote to other activities. However, my job has been quite a learning experience.

Thesis   <u>Although I am just a supermarket clerk, I have gained insight into the demands of a job, the behavior of supervisors, and my ability to influence a situation.</u>

Paragraph II   Topic sentence developed with sufficient detail.

Topic Sentence   <u>I realized that the demands of a job re not always like the demands of school.</u> Maybe that is something that other people know from the start, but it did not work that way for me. In fact, I can remember how the equation between work and pay dawned on me; if I missed an afternoon of work, I missed an equivalent amount of money in my paycheck. The connection between work and rewards is not quite so clear in school. A student can study hard for a test and do poorly. On the other hand, a student can sometimes bluff through a test and get a good grade.

Paragraph III.	Another topic sentence with supporting detail.
Topic Sentence	<u>I did not work for very long before I also realized that bosses can be difficult.</u> At first, my supervisor seemed like a nice enough person. However, I had a look at her other side one day when I returned to the store, pushing a long line of shopping carts which she had told me to gather from the parking lot. Lines had formed at all the registers, and she snapped at me to bag for one of the cashiers. It was as if it my fault that she had sent two of the cashiers out for supper just as it was getting busy in the store.
Paragraph IV.	Another topic sentence followed by detail.
Topic sentence	<u>After my initial anger at the boss's behavior, I decided to try to influence the situation rather than just reacting to it.</u> I realized this approach might work as I was bagging groceries. I saw the store manager peering down at my box from her office window. My boss had a boss who had a boss who had a boss. She was part of the pecking order just like me. Now I try to make small talk with her, ask how things have been going, and so forth. Also, I try to anticipate what she might ask me to do and then offer to do it first. This gives me the feeling that I can be an actor rather than just a puppet.
Paragraph V.	Conclusion with restatement of thesis.
Thesis Restated	Sometimes I still get frustrated at work. As a lowly clerk, I do not get much respect in a large, impersonal company. <u>However, my job has shown me that even the most ordinary parts of my life can give me an opportunity to learn something about myself and other people.</u>

Topic sentences do not always occur at the beginning of paragraphs. In fact, at times it seems stilted to put the topic sentence at the start of a paragraph. You may need a sentence or two that makes a bridge with the preceding paragraph. For example, the fourth paragraph in the sample essay above might have been written more chronologically, following the sequence of events more closely.

Example:	After my initial anger, I noticed the store manager peering down at my boss from the upstairs office window. I realized that my boss had a boss who had a boss;
Thesis Statement	She was just a part of the pecking order like me. <u>I decided to try to influence the situation instead of just reacting to it.</u>

Placing the topic sentence at the start of a paragraph gives the clearest signal to a reader, but it is not always essential to place the topic sentence at the beginning. It is important, however, to have a sentence that holds the rest of the paragraph together. It can come at the beginning, the middle, or the end of the paragraph. Here is a paragraph without a topic sentence:

Ms. Rodriquez always had a word of encouragement on each test she handed back. Furthermore, she taught me the difference between an intelligent mistake and a dumb one. An intelligent mistake occurs when a learner applies a rule or procedure to a special situation where it does not apply. For example, if a young child says, "I taked the book," she is applying the rule to use a "d" sound for a past action. Ms. Rodriguez also had a way of making math problems exciting mysteries. We watched her solve equations on the board like Sherlock Holmes in pursuit of a suspect. The work was never easy, but she always made us feel that it was possible to succeed if we put in enough time.

One way to phrase a topic sentence for the paragraph above would be:
<u>Ms. Rodriguez was one of the best teachers I ever had.</u>

Even if you think that the point of the paragraph is perfectly clear without a topic sentence, put one in. You are now writing this essay for a sophisticated magazine; you are taking a test to show that you can get an idea across clearly to a reader.

EXERCISE F.

1. Each paragraph below lacks a topic sentence. Create a topic sentence for each paragraph and decide where best to place it.

   a. I would be happy if I could make some difference in the lives of the students I will teach. It might just mean making them more curious about the world or more accepting of themselves. I realize that it is difficult to reach each student, but that does not mean that I will not try.
   b. Mr. Wright began every class by putting the homework on the board. Then he would announce what we were going to do that day. Usually, we went over the homework problems first. Students were asked to put their solutions on the board. After discussing them and making necessary corrections, Mr. Wright would turn to the new material. Using three or four pieces of colored chalk, he illustrated and commented on the examples in the book. Finally, if we finished all of the scheduled lesson, there was time at the end of class to start on the homework.
   c. Every teacher spends a minimum of 35 hours in school. In addition, teachers must often supervise activities such as the drama club or school newspaper. Conferences with parents, staff meetings, and required professional development activities also add to the total hours required. A teacher usually has three different course-related preparations, each of which may take an hour or more, depending on the teacher's experience. English teachers who have 25 to 30 students per class may assign a short piece of writing each week, and may spend 4 to 5 minutes reading each paper. This may add 13 hours of additional work per week.

2. Go back to the material that you brainstormed and organized in Exercise D. Pick at least one batch of material and turn it into an essay following the pattern of the five-paragraph essay described previously.

TRANSITIONS

Transitions are signals to your reader about how your ideas are connected. Certain words and phrases prepare the reader for what is to follow. Examples of important transitions to use in your essay are:

1. Words that indicate sequence of events or ideas: first, second (etc.), finally, last, ultimately, eventually, later, meanwhile, afterwards;

2. Words that indicate examples: for instance, for example, specifically, in particular;

3. Words that indicate addition of similar ideas: and, also, furthermore, moreover, similarly, equally important, another;

4. Words that indicate addition of contrasting ideas: however, but, on the other hand, on the contrary, still, yet, in contrast, nevertheless.

Transitions between sentences can also be achieved by repeating key words, using synonyms, or using pronouns.

1. Example of a repeated key word: *Literacy* is not just a matter of learning the ABC's, *Literacy* means having sufficient control of the language to function in one's society.

2. Example of use of a synonym: *Literacy* is not just a matter of learning the ABC's. One's ability to read and write must be equal to the demands of one's society.

3. Example use of a pronoun: *Literacy* is not just a matter of learning the ABC's. It means having sufficient control of the language to function in your society.

EXERCISE G.

1. Look at the paragraphs you wrote in Exercise F and underline all the transitions.

2. Go back to the essay you wrote in Exercise F. Underline any transitions you used. Find places where you might insert additional transitions.

PROOFREAD FOR WORD CHOICE, GRAMMAR, AND MECHANICS

Under ideal conditions, you would complete a first draft and then evaluate it for content and structure. However, a subtest, lasting approximately one hour, does not allow time for true revision. You may want to think of your brainstorming as a type of first draft and your focusing as a type of revision. As you focus and compose your essay, you will do a certain amount of revision, deciding to change the order of paragraphs, inserting or deleting details, trying out sentences in your head before you put them down on paper. Once you have completed the essay, you need to proofread to make sure you have used words correctly and avoid errors that will detract from your essay and subsequently from the score you receive for your essay.

WORD CHOICE

In choosing words to express your ideas, keep in mind that the directions on the examination writing subtest are likely to specify an audience that requires you to use a professional tone. You should avoid slang and cliches. On the other hand, don't go overboard and complicate your essay with fancy terms and inflated language. Aim for a clear and direct expression of your ideas.

Here are a few examples of the kinds of words and expressions to avoid:

1. One activity that I've really *gotten into* lately is sailing. (Substitute *became involved in, become interested in, become enthusiastic about*).

2. The person sitting behind me talked *a lot* during the class. (Try to be as specific as possible about what *a lot* means in the sentence where you are tempted to use it. Here, you might use *continuously* or *incessantly*, but at other times, you might want to substitute *a great deal* or *often*.)

3. My first class was *awful*. (General words such as *awful, perfect, beautiful*, etc. are acceptable if you are going to follow up with more specific description. However, it is almost always better to use specific language. In what respect was the experience or the person awful, perfect, or beautiful? In the example above, was the class dull, disorganized, too demanding?)

4. I was faced with a *number of alternatives*. (Strictly defined, an alternative is a choice between two things. If you mean more than two, use *options* or *choices*.)

5. Computers are a *new innovation* in the classroom. (Innovation means *new*; therefore, the phrase is redundant. The same would be true of expressions such as *personal friend* and *advance planning*.)

Our language is constantly changing. At any period in history, some words and expressions are considered suitable for formal writing while others are considered colloquial and appropriate only for informal settings. As you prepare for the writing subtest, you might want to use a dictionary or a glossary of usage in a handbook. These references will provide guidance in currently acceptable choices. You might also want to keep in mind that no references will be available during the test. Therefore, if you have any doubt about the appropriateness of a word or phrase, you might want to avoid using it, and choose words about which you feel more confident.

Excess words are as much a problem as inexact words. When people don't know what to write, they often try to pad the paragraphs with sentences that say the same thing in slightly different words or fill up the sentences with empty phrases. Superfluous words and sentences may bore, frustrate, or even confuse your reader. You will be spared these problems if you practice brainstorming for relevant and interesting details before you compose your essay. Here are some examples of padded writing:

Wordy: Education faces a crisis today. At the present time, a number of problems are troubling concerned citizens. Not a day goes by that you do not hear about one problem or another.

To the Point: Many problems in education call for our attention.

Wordy: Due to the fact that a problem arose concerning the time our committee should meet, we decided in the final analysis that it would be best to postpone our decision until the new chairperson took over.

To the Point: Unable to agree on a meeting time, our committee postponed the decision until the new chairperson took over.

EXERCISE H

1. Find places in your own writing where you could eliminate words without losing meaning.

2. Trim unnecessary words from the following sentences and rewrite.

   a. The aspects of teaching that I imagine I will most enjoy are the diversity of students and the freedom to organize my own classes.

   b. The problem that I foresee causing the most difficulty in the future is that a few years from now we are going to have even more non-native English speaking students than we do now and people don't understand the need for bilingual education.

   c. In conclusion, the final point that I want to make is to say that the productivity of our economic system will decline unless we do something to tackle the problem of illiteracy among the many people who can't read at all or who can barely read.

EXERCISE I

There are a number of commonly confused words. Use a dictionary or handbook to check the correct choice for each of the sentences that follow.

1. I _____ your invitation to the party. (accept, except, expect)
2. I _____ to do well on my math exam. (accept, except, expect)
3. Everyone is going _____ Susan. (accept, except, expect)
4. I went to my guidance teacher for some good _____. (advise, advice)
5. I always _____ my students to take French literature. (advise, advice)
6. The _____ of the hurricane was horrendous. (affect, effect)
7. Does this test _____ my grade? (affect, effect)
8. _____ never too late to try. (Its, It's)
9. The committee reported _____ decision. (its, it's)
10. Please place the books over _____. (there, they're, their)
11. _____ my brother's friends. (There, They're, Their)
12. The boys have lost _____ shoes. (there, they're, their)

13. Most of the students could not choose _____ the four answers. (between, among)
14. Mary is trying to decide _____ two majors: History and French. (between, among)
15. John arrived at the game, _____. (to, too, two)
16. Please place _____ books on this corner. (to, two, too)
17. David gave the ball _____ Mark. (to, two, too)
18. Peter ran the mile _____. (bad, badly)
19. I feel _____ when it rains. (bad, badly)
20. Teachers often have to _____ packaged materials to the special needs of their students. (adopt, adapt)
21. Our school would like to _____ a dress code for all students. (adopt, adapt)
22. This corner will be the _____ for the reading materials. (site, cite)
23. Students must learn how to _____ source materials in a research paper. (site, cite)
24. Individualized activities are needed to _____ group activities. (compliment, complement)
25. Teachers should _____ children often on the work that they successfully complete. (compliment, complement)

GRAMMAR AND MECHANICS

An occasional error in grammar or mechanics in an essay written without access to a dictionary will not result in failing the writing portion of the exam. However, frequent errors will detract from the effectiveness of your message and can cause failure. There are so many possible errors, that they cannot be covered in this brief guide. A discussion of the most serious errors will be followed by a set of sentences you can use to test your proofreading skills.

1. <u>Sentence Boundaries</u>: Running two or more independent clauses together without linking words or proper punctuation violates basic rules. A grammatically incomplete sentence is equally distracting.

    a. Run-on, fused sentence, or comma splice: Teaching is not an easy field, the rewards aren't always there. (A comma is not sufficient to separate two independent clauses. Substitute a period, a semi-colon, or a linking word, such as *because* for the comma.)

    b. Fragment: The best example being the difference between the way we see a character on TV and the way we visualize a character in a story. (The *ing* form of the verb creates a fragment. Substitute *is* for *being* to correct the sentence.)

2. <u>Agreement of Sentence Elements</u>: Verbs must agree with their subjects; pronouns with the nouns to which they refer. Similar elements must have parallel structure. Parts of the sentence must fit together grammatically.

    a. Lack of subject-verb agreement: The problems that young readers have seems to come partly from the environment. (*problems* calls for the verb form *seem* not *seems*. In sentences where several words come between subject and verb, it is easy to lose track of the elements.)

b. Lack of pronoun agreement: Everyone wants to achieve their potential. (*Everyone* is singular and calls for *his/her*, not *their*.)

c. Lack of parallel structure: I learned to operate the computer, write some simple programs, and the fundamentals of word processing. (*Operate* and *write* set up a pattern which calls for a similar word. Therefore, the last part of the sentence should be rephrased to include a verb; for example, *...and use the fundamentals of word processing*.)

d. Lack of grammatical fit: While taking an elective course in design my freshman year sparked my interest in art. (The introductory phrase, *While taking an elective course*, calls for a subject to come before the verb. This sentence could be revised in at least two ways:
While taking an elective course in design my freshman year, I became interested in art.
Taking an elective course in design my freshman year sparked my interest in art.

SELECTED CAPITALIZATION RULES

A few of the rules governing capitalization are reviewed below. Consult a dictionary or handbook for more complete coverage of this topic.

1. Capitalize proper nouns and adjectives.
   Example: Capitalize: *Judy Blume* and *Southington High School*.
   Do not capitalize *the author* or *my high school*.

2. Capitalize titles when they precede proper names, but not when they follow proper names or are used alone.
   Example: Professor Kent Curtis
   Kent Curtis, professor of history
   the history professor

3. Do not capitalize the names of academic years or terms.
   Example: spring semester
   my sophomore year

4. Capitalize the names of specific courses, but not fields of study unless they are languages.
   Example: Capitalize *English, Spanish,* and *Math 101*
   Do not capitalize *math, physics,* or *education*.

5. Capitalize the important words in titles of books and underline the titles.
   Example: Catcher in the Rye
   Grapes of Wrath

PUNCTUATION

Punctuation is another area that you should review with the help of a good handbook or dictionary. One simple rule to remember is: Do not use the dash as a substitute for the proper punctuation. Example of a punctuation error: Although I took up swimming—the doctors said it would be good exercise—but I found that I did not have the ability to make the team

(The problem with relying on dashes is that, as in the example, dependence can lead to sloppy sentence construction. The sentence above should be revised: I took up swimming because the doctors said it would be good exercise, but I found that I did not have the ability to make the team.)

EXERCISE J

1. Proofread the following essay to identify errors in grammar, mechanics, and word use. Underline or cross out all errors.

2. Rewrite the essay, using correct grammar, mechanics, and wording.

   The extent of illiteracy in the Country is documented in Illiterate America—a book by Jonathan Kozol. When I read this book and realized the extent of illiteracy gave me a shock. Kozol claims that 25 million people can not red warning labels or a simple news story, another 35 million do not read well enough to survive in the Modern Age—Like being able to follow printed instructions. For someone who can't read and has to support himself or a family could be a real disadvantage.

   The problem of illiteracy will be difficult to solve. There being many causes that go deep into our society. Schools have failed to halt the problem and may be contributing to it. My parents say that the problem with schools today are a lack of respect for authority. Years ago, everyone know what would happen if they disobeyed a teacher. Today, teachers must contend with students who are often bored, rarely prepared and frequently they defy the teacher. Some respect and discipline is needed to create a learning environment.

   Another problem with the schools is poorly prepare teachers. Students graduating from college without being able to read or write well. During the 1960s was the decline of strict academic standards. Students failed to learn what they should of learned. The decline may be ending, new tests and requirements are in place. For example, the college of arts and sciences at Northeastern State University changed their requirements because entering students were so poorly prepared. Some of them unable to identify Sophocles or locate spain on a map.

   Kozol's book interested me in the larger issues of literacy—it is more than learning the ABCs. Literacy is when you can read and write well enough to survive in a complex technology and making informed opinions about government policies. Teachers can help to create a literate America. After reading about the problems of illiteracy facing this country, I want to become one,

19

PUTTING IT ALL TOGETHER

PRACTICE TOPICS

You will not know in advance the topic on which you will be asked to write an essay for the examination. However, the topic is likely to involve your education, education in general, or your choice of a career.

The best way to prepare for the writing subtest is to practice the skills presented in this book and to write whole essays under conditions similar to those found in examinations. Below are several topics you may use for practice.

Practice Prompt 1

The Academic Standards Committee of your college is considering changes in the current grading system and they have asked you to write a statement about the impact of the letter grade system (ABCDF) on learning. You may want to consider how the letter grade system affects certain types of students, how it is viewed by students, teachers, or prospective employers, whether there is a practical alternative, or whether modifications should be made. Write a statement of your opinion of the letter grade system and the reasons for your opinion.

Practice Prompt 2

A screening committee is reviewing your application for a teaching position and has asked you to submit a statement of your strengths and weaknesses for the position. Imagine a specific teaching position for which you might apply and write a statement about how well you qualify for that particular job. You might want to consider how your educational background, work experiences, internships, or special interests make you a suitable candidate. You might also want to consider whether there is anything about the position, the type of students you might face, the location, or the responsibilities that might be a challenge to you. Describe the teaching position for which you are applying and explain why you would be a good candidate for the position.

Practice Prompt 3

The committee considering your application to enter a teacher training program wants to learn about your awareness of students' non-academic needs. They have pointed out that a teacher must often do more than teach subject matter. Consider the psychological, physical, social, and economic problems that affect a student's ability to learn. Describe your understanding of the ways in which the role of a teacher goes beyond teaching academic subjects.

Practice Prompt 4

Your college is hosting a conference for state high school teachers to address the problem of the inadequate preparation of the average student for college work. The conference is focusing on the average student because college teachers are concerned about the many students entering freshman courses who are unable to meet the demands of college. You might want to describe how serious the problem is, whose problem it is, and to what extent high schools should consider changing what they are doing. Use your experience, observations, and knowledge to write a statement which gives your perspective on the gap between the academic requirements in high school and those in college.

POST-TEST

Writing Subtest Directions

This part of the examination consists of one writing exercise. You should allow approximately 60 minutes to complete this assignment. You may NOT use a dictionary during the subtest. Make sure you have time to plan, write, review, and revise what you have written.

Before you begin to write, read the topic carefully and take some time to think about how you will organize what you plan to say. Your writing exercise will be evaluated on the basis of how effectively it communicates a whole message to the intended audience for the stated purpose. Your writing exercise will be judged on the success of its total impression by a panel of language arts experts. When evaluating your ability to communicate a whole message effectively, the scorers will also consider your ability to:

1. state and stay on the topic;
2. address all specified parts of the writing assignment;
3. present your ideas in an organized fashion;
4. include sufficient detail and elaboration to statements;
5. choose effective words;
6. employ correct grammar and usage; and
7. use correct mechanics (spelling, capitalization, paragraph form).

PROMPT

The screening committee considering your application for a teaching position is concerned about teacher stress and burn-out. They would like to learn about your awareness of this problem and your susceptibility to it. You might want to discuss how you have handled stressful situations in the past and any techniques that you use to cope with stress. Describe in writing how you would confront the problem of stress and burn-out in the teaching profession.

NOTES/OUTLINE

21

KEY (CORRECT ANSWERS)

In some cases where there is no one right answer, possible answers are given. If your answer is significantly different, discuss it with a teacher or tutor.

EXERCISE B

1. I must describe an activity and tell the committee why it is important to me.

2. I must explain to the superintendent why I want to teach and how an experience or subject helped me make this decision.

3. I have to select three courses or activities and justify why they would be worthwhile.

4. I have to write a letter to the director of admissions at the college of my choice and explain why I want to go there.

5. I have to describe to the committee a significant book and concentrate on what I got out of it.

EXERCISE C

Answers will vary.

EXERCISE D

Answers will vary.

EXERCISE E

1. Answers will vary.

2. A. An ideal wheel:

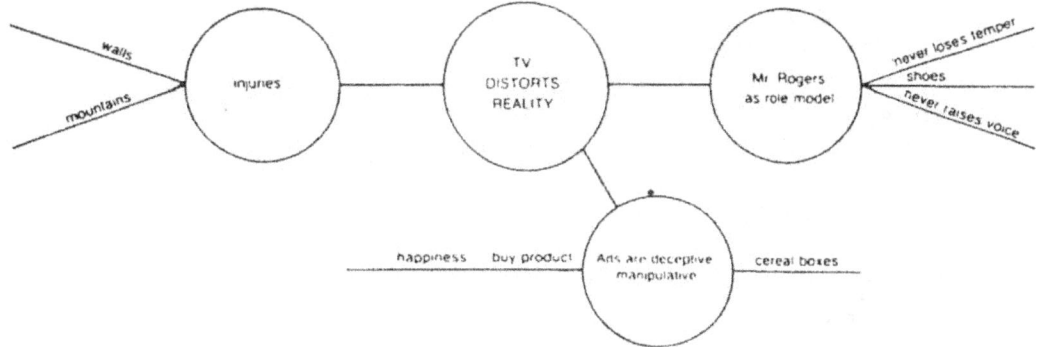

323

B. A flow chart:

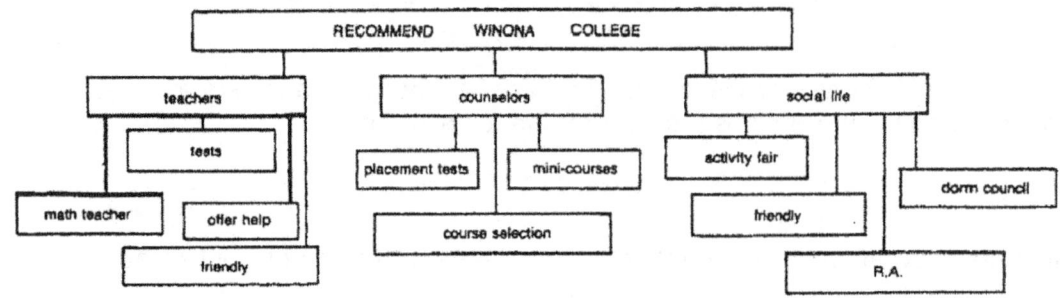

C. Using an outline:

Thesis: My job as a clerk has taught me about the reality of work and how to get along with supervisors.

I. I don't have time for special activities.
   A. School
   B. Need job
   C. Friends

II. Work is not like school because if you don't work, you don't get paid.

III. Boss is not always fair.
   A. No respect for clerks
   B. Gets impatient
   C. Got annoyed about lines

IV. I'm trying to get on top of the situation rather than just reacting.
   A. Boss is part of pecking order
   B. Make small talk
   C. Anticipate orders

V. I am still frustrated.
   A. No recognition
   B. No incentive
   C. Easily replaced

D. Using a list:
Death of a Salesman – connections between the play and my life

1. Different readings – different reactions

2. Describe characters
Willy: salesman
Linda: wife
Biff: good looking, football hero breaks with Willy, drifts around
Happy: ordinary, shadowed by Biff

3. Identified with Happy
   My older brother
   Wanted parents' attention
   School troubles
   Realized I was hurting myself
   Attention hurt Biff

4. Sympathy for Willy
   No respect from boss
   My job as a clerk, dime a dozen
   Want more than a paycheck

5. TV version – admiration for Linda
   Held family together
   Loyal to Willy
   Want someone like her

E. Another list:
   Choices: integrate courses and experiences

   1. Reading Methods Required – would choose it
      What I'll learn; assessment, skills

   2. Activity – literacy volunteer
      Why don't people learn
      How to teach skills
      Effect on a person's life
      Failure of system

   3. Course or individual study in writing
      Keep journal
      Make connections
      Write feature stories for newspaper

EXERCISE F

1. Answers will vary.

2. A. One benefit of teaching is personal satisfaction.
   B. Mr. McGrath ran a tightly structured class.
   C. Many teachers work harder than people realize.

EXERCISE G

1. Example: furthermore, for example, also, like, but
   A. but
   B. then, after, finally
   C. in addition, also, another

2. Answers will vary.

EXERCISE H

1. Answers will vary.

2. A. I will enjoy the diversity of students and the freedom to organize my own classes.

   B. The failure of people to understand the need to provide bilingual education to the increasing numbers of non-native English speaking students will be our biggest problem.

   C. Finally, failure to tackle the various forms of illiteracy will cause a decline in our economic productivity.

EXERCISE I

1. accept
2. expect
3. except
4. advice
5. advise
6. effect
7. affect
8. It's
9. its
10. there
11. they're
12. their
13. among
14. between
15. too
16. two
17. to
18. badly
19. bad
20. adapt
21. adopt
22. site
23. cite
24. complement
225. compliment

EXERCISE J

The extent of illiteracy in this country is documented in *Illiterate America*, a book by Jonathan Kozol. When I read this book and realized the extent of illiteracy, I was shocked. Kozol claims that 25 million people cannot read warning labels or a simple news story; another 35 million do not read well enough to survive in the Modern Age, because they are unable to follow printed instructions. Someone who can't read and has to support himself or her or a family is at a real disadvantage.

The problem of illiteracy will be difficult to solve. Its causes go deep into our society. Schools have failed to halt the problem and may be contributing to it. My parents say that the problem with schools today is a lack of respect for authority. Years ago, students knew what would happen if they disobeyed a teacher. Today, teachers must contend with students who are often bored, rarely prepared, and frequently defiant of the teacher. Respect and discipline are needed to create a learning environment.

Another problem with the schools is poorly prepared teachers. Students graduate from college without being able to read or write well. During the 1960s strict academic standards declined. Students failed to learn what they should have learned. The decline may be ending because new tests and requirements are in place. For example, the College of Arts and Sciences at Northeastern State University changed its requirements because entering students were so poorly prepared. Some of them were unable to identify Sophocles or locate Spain on a map.

Kozol's book interested me in the larger issues of literacy. Literacy means more than learning the ABCs. It means reading and writing well enough to survive in a complex society and making informed opinions about government policies. Teachers can help to create a literate America. After reading about the problems of illiteracy facing this country, I want to become a teacher.

www.ingramcontent.com/pod-product-compliance
Lightning Source LLC
Chambersburg PA
CBHW082026300426
44117CB00015B/2371